The Gates Foundation's Rise to Power

D1121293

The Bill and Melinda Gates Foundation has established itself as one of the most powerful private forces in global politics, shaping the trajectories of international policy-making. Driven by fierce confidence and immense expectations about its ability to change the world through its normative and material power, the foundation advances an agenda of social and economic change through technological innovation. And it does so while forming part of a movement that refocuses efforts towards private influence on, and delivery of, societal progress.

The Gates Foundation's Rise to Power is an urgent exploration of one of the world's most influential but also notoriously sealed organizations. As the first book to take us inside the walls of the foundation, it tells a story of dramatic organizational change, of diverging interests and influences, and of choices with consequences beyond the expected. Based on extensive fieldwork inside and around the foundation, the book explores how the foundation has established itself as a major political power, how it exercises this power, but also how it has been deeply shaped by the strong norms, ideas, organizations, and expectations from the field of global development. The book will be of interest to scholars and students of global development, international relations, philanthropy and organizational theory.

Adam Moe Fejerskov is Researcher at the Danish Institute for International Studies (DIIS). He holds a PhD in international studies from Roskilde University. His research lies at the intersection of global development and international relations, with a focus on norm dynamics, rising state and non-state powers, as well as organizational and sociological theory.

Routledge Studies in Development and Society

The Gates Foundation's Rise to Power

Private Authority in Global Politics

Adam Moe Fejerskov

LONDON AND NEW YORK

First published 2018
by Routledge
2 Park Square, Milton Park, Abingdon, Oxon OX14 4RN

and by Routledge
52 Vanderbilt Avenue, New York, NY 10017

First issued in paperback 2020

Routledge is an imprint of the Taylor & Francis Group, an informa business

© 2018 Adam Moe Fejerskov

British Library Cataloguing-in-Publication Data
A catalogue record for this book is available from the British Library

Library of Congress Cataloging-in-Publication Data
Names: Fejerskov, Adam Moe, author.
Title: The Gates Foundation's rise to power : private authority in global
    politics / Adam Moe Fejerskov.
Description: Abingdon, Oxon ; New York, NY : Routledge, 2018. |
    Series: Routledge studies in development and society ; 43 | Includes
    bibliographical references and index.
Identifiers: LCCN 2017060138 (print) | LCCN 2018015982 (ebook) | ISBN
    9781315142067 (eBook) | ISBN 9781138306851 (hardback)
Subjects: LCSH: Bill & Melinda Gates Foundation—History. | Charities—
    United States—History.
Classification: LCC HV97.B5 (ebook) | LCC HV97.B5 F45 2018 (print) |
    DDC 361.7/6320973—dc23
LC record available at https://lccn.loc.gov/2017060138

ISBN 13: 978-0-367-66675-0 (pbk)
ISBN 13: 978-1-138-30685-1 (hbk)

Typeset in Times New Roman
by Swales & Willis Ltd, Exeter, Devon, UK

To Janni for distracting me towards more important things in life than academia, and to our little boy who will one day open this book and come to find that his dad is kind of a nerd.

Contents

Figures

Tables

Preface

My story with the Bill and Melinda Gates Foundation began in 2013 when I became part of a large collaborative research project that studied how seven different organizations work with, and engage in, norms of gender equality and women's empowerment. My initial interest in the foundation was from a perspective of understanding its work on gender, but it soon expanded into trying to comprehend this intriguing organization more broadly. It was with this dual aim in mind that I approached foundation employees, grantees and partners, conducting more than 100 interviews over the course of three years, from 2014 to 2016. I spent nearly a year in the US (and the greatest part of that in Seattle, WA, home to the foundation), but also followed the foundation's work around the world, visiting grantees as they came together in Istanbul, Turkey, and observing it's work in India, both in the capital of New Delhi but also out in the fields on the outskirts of Bhubaneswar, in the state of Odisha. I am deeply thankful to all the current and former programme officers, advisors, fellows, directors, and grantees of the Gates Foundation without whose invaluable contributions this book would not have been possible. All of you know who you are. The same goes for the many other organizations and individuals who have provided inputs to the book. In particular, I owe my deepest gratitude to Lars Engberg-Pedersen and Peter Kragelund for steering me through three years of research on the Gates Foundation with vital encouragement and advice. Had it not been for Lars' untiring support and collegiality through the years, I would not be where I am today, if at all in academia.

Many of the issues explored in the book revolve around intraorganizational processes and struggles, between individuals, units and departments. As such the endeavour has been sensitive, and all interviewees have been aware (and some worried) about the potential danger of exposing colleagues. To me, however, there is no objective of exposure or comparable drama in the book, with many of the sensitive organizational spectacles or developments likely being experienced in everyday organizational life across the world. Still, to gain as truthful an insight into the foundation's work as possible, I protect my interviewees by securing their anonymity. Several names do appear throughout this book, but they belong to people who are to be seen as public figures, or who have allowed me to use their names. Throughout my interviewing, the intention has been to allow informants to elaborate at great length about the issues and processes discussed, allowing for as high a degree of information as possible, and many of the interviews were followed up by repeated talks in order to explore new aspects of the issues discussed. In particular, it was an explicit aim for me to combine formal meetings inside the foundation's walls with more informal conversations and meetings, where employees felt safe discussing sensitive issues, away from 'work'. That conversations could take place outside of work was even more eagerly suggested by my interviewees than by me, with many people insecure about discussing intimate work relations in their shared offices or in common rooms.

No matter the unique insights I have gained into the foundation's work, the study undertaken to prepare a book like this will likely always be faced by certain challenges just as there are natural limits to the book's exploration. It first and foremost concerns itself with the international ambitions and work of the foundation, and does not engage deeply in its efforts in US education. That is so despite the foundation's obvious influence there, with Gates having been referred to as 'the real Secretary of Education' in the US. Furthermore, it attempts to cover a broad scope of issues as they pertain to the foundation's work, and thus cannot make up for singular in-depth case studies of only one side of the foundation's influence, such as in global health, though it certainly contributes with in-depth knowledge to such. Even for a field like global health, the foundation's involvement is so expansive and vast that it is difficult to comprehend, let alone collect material on, all the subfields it remains engaged in, from vaccination coverage to low cost nucleic acid detection technologies. Furthermore, data poses a general challenge to the study of private foundations. Very little comparative data is available on the scale, reach and engagement of these actors in global development. The Gates Foundation is consistent in preparing annual reports and financial statements, but these are at a fairly superficial level, and have deteriorated over the last decade, from dozens of pages covering internal reform and organization to now only consisting of core financial statements of a few pages, as well as Bill and Melinda Gates' annual letter that targets an issue of importance to them.

Another challenge, and perhaps the one mostly intriguing colleagues and people hearing about this work, regards access (*how did you get in?*). Rather than a single door to be opened, I tend to think of access as a long hallway with a multitude of doors. Some of these are open; some are closed; some open only periodically in response to a variety of actions or talk, and may close soon after. Entering through a door is only the beginning, and one may quickly realize that not much lies beyond it. Neither is there ever a stable outside and inside, in which the researcher may reside calmly. The objective then becomes to convince the person on the other side of the door to open it, underlining the strong relational element to access. Just as in the world outside of research, such relationships need to be nurtured and upheld in order to maintain their usefulness. I usually respond to questions of access by saying that my somewhat delimited focus on gender-work meant that individuals were less suspicious of my motivations and undertaking. Like all of the foundation's areas of intervention though, it naturally has many sensitive elements to it, not least because of its status in the foundation as an emerging area in which experience and knowledge was in the process of being built up, creating some degree of uncertainty.

After all, and at all times, empirical research will be at the mercy of the real world, shaped by the people we engage with. As social scientists, we have long left the laboratory's stable conceptions and artificial usage of reality, and replaced it with complexity and unpredictability, the true 'natural' condition of reality. While complicating the design and practice of research, the inspiring and stimulating challenges this poses remain one of the core reasons why many do qualitative research. Nonetheless, it also often creates a significant discrepancy between what is hoped for and what is achieved, and especially so when it comes to the collection of empirical data, something we should be honest and open about. For research traditions that further stringent objectivism and a positivist-reductionist attitude to such processes, this human face of transparency of the researcher is often left behind in a double-sided misconstrued perception that ignoring such concerns is both scientifically possible and commendable. In this line of thought, research is a logical and linear exercise of designing, planning and executing. This has not been so, and I am grateful for the way people have opened their hearts, minds, and networks for me to exploit. In the end, research is to be found somewhere between hopefulness and the unpredictability of reality, and that is not an entirely bad thing.

1 Introduction

On the West Coast of the United States, way up north in the state of Washington, lies the 'Emerald City', Seattle. Nicknamed after the capital of L. Frank Baum's *The Wonderful Wizard of Oz*, Seattle is perhaps better known as one of the liberal strongholds of the US, for its almost 70 per cent white population, and, most of all, it is known for its rain. In reality though, the city only ranks 44th nationwide in annual rainfall. Of all the city's landmarks the most famous is the Space Needle, a 180-metre-tall observation tower that attracted great attention as the tallest building west of the Mississippi River when it was built in 1962 for the Seattle World Fair. Today, this attention has largely shifted to its most novel neighbouring building. In June of 2012, the Bill and Melinda Gates Foundation moved into its new $500 million, six-story, 7000 m^2, and 12-acre campus headquarters. The campus houses the majority of the foundation's more than 1,400 employees. Visitors without business in the foundation can appreciate the new headquarters from a viewpoint overlooking the campus. Or they can venture into the foundation's 1000 m^2 visitor centre, a presentation of its self-proclaimed history and results to the public. Here, they can try their luck at developing a vaccine for malaria by positioning a set of different levers in the right combination, or watch a movie in the cinema on the foundation's partnership with one of the world's largest football clubs, F.C. Barcelona, and its star player Lionel Messi.

Venturing into the foundation's campus, its large reception feels somewhere between the most sterile upscale hotel you have never been to, and a waiting room for meticulously well-dressed adults anticipating an oral test with strict examiners. People sit together in small groups or walk around impatiently while talking on the phone. Some with Washington, DC, and some with China. They talk about planned pitches of ideas and projects, budgets, or results and evaluation frameworks. It is fairly easy to see that people are here for the business of funding. From the reception, one moves down and into the centre of the campus, a courtyard of concrete. In what appears as a pedantically controlled area, trees grow in small squares in the concrete, containing and controlling the wildness and anarchy of nature. Three trees are bigger than the rest and are meant to symbolize three different individuals, each of whom played an import role in establishing the foundation: Bill Gates Sr, his late wife, Mary Gates, and the American epidemiologist William Foege, who has been an inspiration to Bill Gates since the foundation started its work.

Rising on either side of the courtyard are two massive building structures, almost entirely clad in glass, that hold the offices of the foundation's different divisions and departments, and with room for constructing a third building in case the foundation should come to need it. When the campus was inaugurated on a Thursday night in late May of 2012, Melinda Gates took the stage and explained to guests at the reception about the deliberate conspicuousness of the headquarters: 'We wanted to make a statement'.

Contrast these images of relative grandeur to the humble beginnings of the foundation. The Gates Foundation started in the basement of Bill Gates Sr's house in the mid-1990s, from where he would screen incoming requests for charity and pass the most interesting ones on to his son for further inspection and an eventual decision on whether to provide support or not. As the foundation outgrew the basement, it rented scattered and anonymous offices around Seattle, some famously above a pizza parlour. For years, it characterized itself as a small family-foundation, and was lauded by *The New York Times* for its lean bureaucracy and limited head count,[1] though its endowment grew exponentially to heights above the vast majority of American private foundations. Today, the Gates Foundation's rise to global prominence is known to most. Or, more precisely, its present-day position as one of the most influential non-state actors in contemporary international political life, both financially and politically, is renowned. More powerful and vastly greater in size than any other foundation in modern history, the Gates Foundation is not simply following a trend of growing influence for foundations, it literally embodies that trend. At present, the foundation is a titanic influence in numerous areas of global development, health and governance, ever-present in international political discussions in fora such as the UN, OECD, the World Health Organization or the World Economic Forum. Its endowment of approximately \$40 billion is larger than the Gross Domestic Product of more than 50 per cent of the world's countries, and its annual grant-making of approximately \$4 billion dwarfs the majority of OECD-DAC donors' development aid. Wielding a diverse repertoire of political influence through its grant-making, investment of its endowment, advocacy and powerful networks, the foundation always seems to have the right tool for the occasion. Yet, despite the familiarity of most with different sides of the financial, normative, and political weight and influence of this comparatively novel foundation, knowledge of its actual rise, the process of becoming what we consider it today, is superficial at best. The majority of the intellectual attention given to it has been to its role in global health[2] or in US-domestic education,[3] or to its specific interventions, including the founding of Gavi,[4] and the Alliance for a Green Revolution in Africa or AGRA.[5] Insights into the internal workings of the foundation have only occasionally been provided by local media from the Pacific Northwest,[6] specialist philanthropic and other media.[7]

This book represents the first attempt to genuinely open up the closed book that is the Gates Foundation. Based on fieldwork inside and around the foundation, it provides a glimpse behind the curtains into the processes the foundation has gone through as it has increasingly entered into and sought to establish itself on the international political scene. Specifically, it is a story of the Gates Foundation – how the foundation and its employees think, act, plan, exercise power and work to influence the environments surrounding it. About how, below its public face of fierce and uncompromising ambition, deep inside the organizational machinery of the foundation, we find anything but a unification of thought in which there is no contestation over discourses, practices, ambitions, or priorities. Instead, we find individuals and groups of people, sometimes with vastly different backgrounds, from public policy makers to medical doctors, and with different mind-sets and missions, who contest over ideas, meanings and resources, each one engaged in internal organizational struggles. Only by lifting the lid and not assuming the foundation to be driven by a single mind of monstrosity, as a streamlined machine, can we properly understand this immensely powerful yet also complex organization. This is not a defence of the Gates Foundation but an argued necessity if we are to genuinely scrutinize the foundation and its influence on issues that have ramifications for millions of people, particularly in the Global South. As we shall see, the story of the Gates Foundation is a story of dramatic organizational change, of diverging interests and influences, struggles over the legitimacy of ideas and practices, and of choices with path-dependent consequences beyond the expected.

Yet, the book is not only a narrow organizational tale of the Gates Foundation and the changes it has been through since its genesis. The findings and arguments made fundamentally speak to and inform at least three major discussions in contemporary international studies. The first concerns the rise of new actors and powers, whether state or non-state, or what I refer to here as the contemporary meeting between forces of heterogeneity and homogeneity in global development. That is, the exploration of what happens as new actors enter into a field that is increasingly being homogenized through global normative frameworks such as the Sustainable Development Goals. By uncovering the multifaceted organizational trajectory of the Gates Foundation over time, we come to learn some of the conceivably common processes that rising powers and emerging actors go through as they enter into and engage with spheres of international political life that are governed by norms, rules, and standards, and are being confronted with established and expected forms of behaviour and thought. Much work in this vein has been focused on how rising powers change global development, and while the Gates Foundation certainly challenges established or traditional practices and discourses, it has also been greatly shaped by these over time. The book accordingly shows the ways in which the foundation has slowly but gradually socialized to dominant modes of thought, practice and operation, and today in many stances resembles the established organizations it somewhat attempts to distance itself from. Second, the book speaks to debates about non-state and private actorness by showing how the Gates Foundation exercises a hybrid form of authority that extends far beyond any characterization as only 'private'. By negotiating and shifting its organizational identity from situation to situation, the foundation is able to draw on diverse tools of influence that sees it sometimes use those traditionally associated with private foundations, sometimes those associated with NGOs, and in other instances those of a multinational corporation and even of states. This fluidity of authority means it not only crosses different categories of non-state actors, but also increasingly transcends the public–private or state/non-state divide. Third, the book provides what we can call an organizational sociology of global development, drawing on sociological institutionalist perspectives to enrich the study of organizations in global development. It forms a suggestive framework or theoretical vocabulary fit to study the present analytical challenges of what is sometimes referred to as *big-d* development, that is the global institutional endeavour of development cooperation in the messy interplay between states, organizations and individuals. Exploring and explaining contemporary disruption and change in global development requires an ever-growing conceptual toolbox, and this book provides one way forward in understanding these currents.

Re-emergence of private foundations in global politics

Since the Bill and Melinda Gates Foundation opened its doors in 1999, it has distributed more than $42 billion to national and international issues, with grant-making amounting to $4.6 billion in 2016[8] and a current massive endowment of $40 billion. From an initial focus on education in the US, as well as international spending on vaccine development and delivery, the last ten years have seen the foundation venturing into the field of 'global development', where some of its main areas of intervention include agriculture, water and sanitation, and financial services for the poor. Since becoming a formal programme area in the foundation, this has seen massive scaling up over the last ten years, from $50 million in 2005 to $1.5 billion in 2015,[9] but so too has the entirety of the organization. Over the last decade, the annual administrative expenses of the foundation have increased tenfold to more than $550 million, and the number of employees has risen to more than 1,400 today. The astounding reach and size of the Gates Foundation is underlined by how the foundation accounts for more than half of all global philanthropic giving to development today.[10]

The rise of the Gates Foundation is often used as an illustration of the (re)emergence of private foundations in global politics, though its magnitude means it has no equal in the foundation world. Attention to private foundations in global development has greatly increased over the last decade, mainly with a view to their potential dual contribution of providing additional resources and bringing new approaches to the scene, and this can be rudely reduced to commonly fall into two categories. One side holds that institutional logics transferred from the business world by these organizations render them more successful, innovative and effective than traditional donor organizations.[11] The other believes that the transfer of entrepreneurial business skills into the world of relief and global development is not necessarily unproblematic.[12] Particular elements from these logics grounded in business and entrepreneurial lines of thought are believed to diffuse to other actors in the field, entailing a privatization of global development. This privatization can essentially be divided into three elements: (1) increased multiplicity and prominence of private actors and innovative forms of providing aid from individuals; (2) growth in private aid flows to developing countries including absolute and relative financial power of private actors in development; and (3) a shift in the practices and discourses of global development towards 'Ideas emanating out of business schools'[13] or what has been referred to as the 'California consensus'[14] in which managerialist logics such as the necessity of innovation, efficiency and evaluation, results-orientation, quantitative impact measurement, etc., are transferred to practices and discourses in global development.

Scholarly interest in private foundations within international studies was instigated in the early 1970s by Peter Bell's observation that the Ford Foundation resembled many of the features of a transnational actor, and that foundations as a group of actors were interesting to study 'Not only because of the direct outcome of their grants but also because of their direct and indirect influence on other actors in world politics'.[15] Despite Bell's work, interest waned over the next decade and more, as state-centric concerns of regimes, hegemonic stability, etc., came to dominate international relations theorization. When academic interest in foundations rematerialized in the 1980s, it transcended historical, sociological and public health research traditions more than it spoke to international relations specifically. Here, the role of American foundations in forwarding pro-US values, their elite-project nature,[16] and their perceived aim of co-optation of counter-hegemonic actors became objects of interest for scholars working from a Gramscian or critical perspective.[17] This Gramscian tradition continues to influence the contemporary critical vein working on private foundations.[18] Somewhat challenging these critical perspectives, others have argued for the importance of studying private foundations in their own right, i.e. decoupled from discussions over whether they are agents of capitalism.[19] This book is situated between these two perspectives, arguing that private foundations are indeed interesting to study as a specific actor-type, and merit attention due to many empirical and theoretical concerns beyond their perceived function as agents of capitalism. Private foundations are too significant and complex a set of actors to be black-boxed, not to mention that they are, in fact, organizations consisting of often conflicting ideas, interests and values. Not presupposing the interests and ideologies of private foundations does not imply that we should not approach them critically, it merely means wide generalizations or oversimplifications of the nature and missions of these do not do justice to their uneven and diverse dispositions. Private foundations are as fragmented an actor-type as any other, and their individual differences imply there is a need to study them as exactly that – individual actors. Doing so does not dilute any critical perspective; on the contrary, it sharpens these because of the increased analytical accuracy to which grounded empirical explorations open the way.

Rising powers: disruption and stability in contemporary global development

The story of how the Bill and Melinda Gates Foundation has entered into global development and evolved as an organization is a tangible illustration of how this field is caught at the intersection of two concurrent processes of heterogeneity and homogenization. Embodied in the first is an expanding plethora of organizations and actors with a multiplicity of approaches to aid provision and development work. Development assistance grew out of the Marshall Plan in the 1950s as Europe began promoting economic development in poorer regions and countries, many of whom were former colonies. What began as sporadic work by countries such as the United Kingdom, France, Sweden, and Denmark soon turned into structured aid agencies, policies and formalized partnerships. For the first few decades, Western countries provided the main share of global Official Development Assistance in hierarchized relationships under stable perceptions of, and clear lines between, benefactors and recipients. With the turn of the millennium however, improved macroeconomic conditions in several middle-income countries began making fluid these otherwise stable perceptions of core circumstances of development assistance. It paved the way for a hitherto unseen active and assertive foreign policy from rising powers of striving towards economic and political influence. Complementing this, the last few years has seen a growing involvement of private actors (the theme around which this book naturally revolves), from foundations to corporations and social enterprises, not least through the gradual realization that development aid can do very little on its own to spur economic and social development.

Most of these actors apply limits to their genuine newness, having earlier engaged in collaborative efforts resembling, in part, global development relationships. Yet their engagements today are substantially amplified. Most of the re-emerging non-DAC donors have been involved in forms of charity to neighbouring countries for hundreds of years, but not in the formally institutionalized sense we see today, with emerging national institutions set up to handle such collaborations, nor with the current scope that sees relations easily reaching around the planet. Private involvement too is not a novel matter. International foundation giving was initiated more than a hundred years ago, embodied mainly in the early 'big three' foundations, Carnegie, Ford and Rockefeller (with Ford as the somewhat latecomer), distributing wealth accumulated during the 19th century's rapid industrialization in the United States. Private corporations too have been involved in global development efforts for as long as there has been anything referred to as such, with the genuine difference today probably being the responsibility and anticipations we attribute to them in financing development by spurring economic growth in the developing world. What has changed then is not so much the involvement of these actors per se, but rather the size and scope of their engagement, as well as their gradual involvement in more formalized and institutionalized forms of cooperation.

With such increasing heterogeneity of actors predictably comes a set of perceived new or alternative practices of discourse, more or less through a desire for these new actors to separate themselves from established organizations. The both practical and ideational challenge from the Global South to established or hegemonic ways of development work mainly revolves around notions of increasing South–South Cooperation (SSC). Largely articulated around principles of solidarity, (political) non-interference and equality between partners, SSC in its own perception challenges the unequal power relations of traditionally dominant North–South relations, and has grown in both prominence and in volume over the past years. Partnerships across Southern partners does not necessarily imply equal power relations, however, and the group of Southern countries is as internally heterogeneous as the North–South divide itself; China and South Sudan share very few interests aside from broader ambitions of economic growth and prosperity. We definitely see new power constellations then, but the sometimes assumed equality of these and the inherent purpose of the partnerships to depoliticize conflicts of interests between states should be thoroughly questioned, something occasionally not being done across an often overly optimistic SSC discourse.

From the outset of increased SSC, traditional donors have responded to these changes from the Global South by taking on new discursive regimes or ways of legitimizing development and specific organizational and political changes. These legitimizing discourses especially revolve around *mutual* interests but also geo-economic ones coupled with an emerging re-nationalization among particularly Western OECD countries that sees aid increasingly re-tied to national concerns and interests. This is definitely spurred on by increasing challenges from the economically and politically rising South and perhaps reflect how Western states are becoming more comfortable about articulating their geo-political self-interests because of the equally strong idea of mutual interests in the SSC discourse. But it does not represent an unprecedented series of arguments to legitimize or guide aid spending. Domestic and self-centred concerns were for many years dominating during the 1970s and 1980s, as tied aid ensuring a return of the spending to the aid provider was the preferred form of development cooperation. For many European countries, current developments and crises (whether they regard volatility of global finance, growing inequality, increasing migration flows, or climate change), coupled with a swift breaking down of the boundaries between domestic and foreign policy and developments, have entailed increasing tendencies of neo-isolationism and re-nationalization in a naïve belief that the reach and spread of these crises can be stalled by way of seclusion, border control and the pursuit of narrow interests. Taken together, we see new discourses, modes of practice and patterns of interaction (be they in coordination or competition) emerge. Each of the new actors carry with them particular organizational cultures, contexts, histories and assumptions shaping their internal modes of operation and relations to other actors in the field. Together they have contributed to a definite, albeit importantly fragmented, challenge to established development orthodoxies and hegemonies, many of which have been reinforced by Western countries through time.

Against this backdrop of increased heterogeneity, disruption and flux in global development, however, a second simultaneous process of increasing homogenization can be seen as running counter to it, a process that attempts further stability and conformity in the present chaos. Homogenization in this regard denotes mounting attempts to govern and streamline the way 'development' is understood and practiced, furthering a standardization or institutionalization of global development. That is, since the late 1990s global development has witnessed significant trends towards establishing common frameworks for 'good development', including standardized rules and alignment principles. Such norm- and principle-setting is manifested in, for example, the Paris Declaration on Aid Effectiveness, the Millennium Development Goals (MDGs), and the Sustainable Development Goals (SDGs) in the contexts of the OECD and the UN. Together, these agreements establish sets of norms that all actors involved in global development are expected to adopt and adhere to, in order to be considered legitimate. Though emerging actors enter global development with a diverse set of ideas and modes of operation, they are not faced with unrestricted room for manoeuvring in which there are no expectations about adherence to certain norms and principles – quite the opposite. This is not to say that contemporary development remains a world culture that easily isomorphs or homogenizes organizations along similar trajectories of path dependency. To be sure, struggles for not just interpretive or ideological, but structural power intensify today and the field has evolved towards a multipolar picture of overlapping spaces and centres of influence and authority, as the distinction between beneficiary and donor, and legitimate and disparaged actors and organizations, becomes gradually more blurred and fluid. However, we are able to identify streams of action and discourse that hold and further an inherent desire to govern organizational action in the field, culminating in both formal and informal rules and principles to which organizations are expected to adhere in order to be considered legitimate.

The locus of this book, accomplished by investigating the evolution of the Gates Foundation, is to explore what occurs when these simultaneous processes of heterogeneity and homogenization meet, i.e., what happens as a new actor enters into the increasingly normatively regulated field of global development? Predominantly, work exploring this concern has focused on the consequences for global development itself, centring attention on implications for the legitimacy of established ideas, practices and actors of development.[20] To truly understand this concern, however, we must appreciate how change is multidirectional, and that, just as the field of global development experiences substantial changes resulting from the entrance of new actors, so these new actors likewise go through significant processes of change as they are faced with established organizations, expectations, ideas and practices of the field. This book thus explores and explains the ideational and material-organizational consequences for an actor as it increasingly enters into international political life and interacts with a new field.

Private authority in global politics

The story of the Gates Foundation is at its core one of rising private authority in global politics. Founded by one of the forefront capitalist proponents of our time, built on the fortunes of Microsoft, and shaped for almost its entire lifetime by a leadership that finds its roots deep in the US private sector. The last 50 years' academic attention and inattention to private and non-state actors in international studies is a history well known and told. Work on transnational actors (still a preferred term for some) largely emerged in the 1970s as a reference to 'Regular interactions across national boundaries when at least one actor is a non-state agent'.[21] Keohane and Nye's special issue from which this quote is taken constitutes early 1970s' work on transnationalism that challenged state-dominated views on world politics, though primarily by focusing on MNCs and not the breadth of non-state actors studied today. Non-state actors were and are still typically understood across fluid dimensions of internal structure (formal organizations or more or less loosely connected networks) and constitutive purposes (primarily driven by self-interest or by a notion of the 'common good').[22] The attention to non-state or transnational perspectives somewhat faded away through the 1980s, yet, as we approached the 1990s, fundamental changes to state sovereignty and governance beyond the state again redirected attention towards international relations as multi-layered and -dimensional, and this time with renewed strength that could take head-on (neo)realist state-centric theorization. New heterogeneous constellations of actors challenged Westphalian conceptions of power and influence, but also accountability as private authorities rose to influence with little democratic backing, an issue that naturally applies greatly to the Gates Foundation as we will see throughout this book. The late 1990s and early 2000s then saw a (re) surge in recognition of the influence of non-state actors besides IOs and corporations, in particular global civil society and transnational NGOs, networks and other organizational forms.[23] Still, the focus was often on how these actor-types influence international and national policy-making, thus continually seeing them as a peripheral or exogenous source of impact on something else.[24]

Today, the interest is not in whether private actors are important or if they are at all able to influence nation states and international politics, but rather how they do so and through what means, often through a recognition that they do not stand outside an interstate system and exercise influence but make up a core component of contemporary global governance. Despite this, the broad non-state actor-group is still often thought to occupy spaces left open by nation states, working to influence international politics through means that are removed from a state's way of acting. Thus, they are seen as having distinct ways of approaching influence that includes symbolic actions, agenda-setting, pressure on states or efforts to secure the institutionalization of certain norms, but often working through different means and channels than states.[25] As Lindblom puts it 'NGOs and civil society in general are crucial in the raising and expressing of political opinion, in disseminating information and as watchdogs and counterweights to states'.[26] Even in cases where they act as co-producers of global governance, they are thought to bring a set of alternative logics and tools to the table to those of states. Nonetheless, private actors do not only assume spaces of influence that states fail or choose not to occupy (i.e., that the emergence of global governance seemingly provides more 'governable room'). Private and non-state actors increasingly challenge and take over forms of influence that we traditionally affiliate with state action. Whether we see this process as one of a weakening or retreat of the state or a gradual nuancing of public–private influence naturally depends on our ideality of the nature of states.[27] The argument made in this book is one in which the relation between public and private authority is not an either-or form that only sees actor types governing separated aspects of global politics. On the contrary, the complexity of global governance is such that most arrangements are shaped and governed by hybrid constellations of actors, rules and norms that will see private actors working inside public institutions and public within private. The boundaries between public and private authority are fluid then and we often see private actors assume or provide functions that we would consider public, naturally enforced by our own preconceptions of which is what. When the Gates Foundation supports the World Health Organization and the provision of support to national public health systems or (more often) the delivery of vaccines, would we only consider the nature of such work private? Probably not.

The authority of the Gates Foundation is not only private in form, then, it is fundamentally hybrid. The foundation is so melded in international state affairs, whether in international organizations or in pushing for certain international agreements, that it breaks with traditional foundation behaviour. It moves far beyond NGOs and tools of influence associated with these by aggressively funding core activities in international organizations like the WHO or by seconding employees to these, to say nothing of its multi-billion commercial investments in pharmaceuticals, the entertainment industry or in extractive industries. In essence, the fluidity of its actorness means it is able to readily shift between different organizational identities, which makes it sometimes appear as a private foundation, sometimes as a multinational company and sometimes almost as a public or state actor. The last point is important as it implies an argument that the foundation not only cuts across different conceptions of non-state actors, but that it also increasingly appears to transcend the private–public divide. That is, the Gates Foundation seems to be increasingly adopting state-like behaviour in its attempts to climb the final steps on the ladder that is global political influence.

An organizational sociology of contemporary global development

The book explores contemporary processes in global development by centring attention on a single organization, and by being theoretically embedded in the sociology of institutions and organizations. At the heart of its undertaking is an aspiration to explore and explain the dynamics of change and stability as we find them in social and organizational life, and as a core feature of research on global development. The locus of work in this vein has always been about exploring and explaining the changing of societies, people's lives, or ideas and practices, organizations and institutions. Change is essentially the crux of not just institutional and organizational life but life itself, occurring in all social systems and processes, all the time, everywhere. It is rarely radical and revolutionary in form, far more often assuming a continuous or incremental nature that sees gradual change over the course of longer periods of time, and intimately associated with logics of reproduction and inertia that sees social interaction, organizations, or people steadily change to become something else or to remain what they are. While we have witnessed significant changes to conceptions of legitimate action, global governance structures, and logics of global development through time, such regimes have changed incrementally over the course of years with gradual weakening of exist- ing norms and emergence of new ones. Or perhaps with a decoupling that sees changes in discourses and practices essentially facilitate the continuous hegem- ony of certain structures or relationships. There is profound discrepancy between doing things differently and doing different things, then, and instead of expe- riencing short-term radical change, the field of global development has almost continuously been in a state of reluctant fluctuation.

The relationship between sociology and research on global development is a peculiar one. Much work on development issues is sociological in nature, but seldom do we see explicit references to sociological perspectives, and very lit- tle is done to collapse such perspectives into more abstract theoretical notions. The notion of a 'sociology of development' emerged in the 1950s and 1960s and was tightly coupled to ideas of economic growth, modes of production, and Rostowian ideas about underdeveloped economies as aeroplanes waiting to 'take off'. From a functional–structural point of departure, the social structures of developing societies were considered a hindrance to modernization, and the answer remained to change or replace these to increasingly resemble developed countries (i.e., what would be known as modernization theory). This work was critiqued and almost downright dismissed in 1970s, not least by the Marxist perspectives furthered by Andre Gunder Frank[28] and many others that centred attention on the socio-cultural praxis of economics. Drawing attention to power, inequality and to some extent gender, theories of underdevelopment inverted the view of the Global North as having inherent adaptive advantages for diffusion to the Global South, and held responsible imperialism and exploitation for the persis- tent poverty in developing countries.[29] Drawing on Wallerstein's world-systems approach, the economic growth and prosperity in the North was explained by a relative decline of other regions, emphasizing the co-constitution of development and underdevelopment. After the 'impasse' of the 1980s, post-structural Marxist and 'post-development' theories[30] began growing in prominence, alongside more actor-focused studies that appreciated the agency of individuals, contrary to the determinist–structuralist perspectives of the 1970s.[31]

Much time has passed since these conceptualizations of development had their heyday, and today the 'sociology of development' literature is largely split along at least two lines of thought and theorization. In the first line, it is largely still taken to reflect the exceedingly broad interface of economy and society in the developing world, albeit a much more nuanced and multiparadigmatic one than in the mid- and late-20th century, with a focus on what drives and shapes (what is popularly referred to as *small-d*) development. This is not least the case in Anglo- American traditions of 'sociology of development'.[32] The second line we might refer to as a sociology of global development (thus concerning itself more with issues of *big-d* development). Here, economics have largely fallen out of the equa- tion, while anthropological and (particularly micro-) sociological perspectives have prevailed. This line concerns itself with the sociology of practicing forms of development or planned interventions in developing countries, and often the projects or programmes of foreign development agencies or the relationships between these and recipient institutions and communities.[33] It has substituted macro-structuralist perspectives and their perspective that social change predominantly occurs from external sources of power, with a much more micro-sociological appreciation of the agency of individuals to incite endogenous forms of change through their everyday lives. At the centre of this work is often how we find 'Little link at times between the theory of rationally planned development and the implementation of development policies',[34] mainly because the world of development projects and policy remains socially managed, and policy in itself is seen as an end rather than a cause, intrinsically unable to discipline or control. From this follows an argument for focusing attention on the everyday organizational life of development workers in which these engage in negotiations of meaning, identity, representation and interpretation.

This book stands on the shoulders of these wider conceptions of a sociology of development, though particularly the second line of work, and rather than studying how development is best achieved and what drives it at national or local levels, it concerns itself with the endeavours of organizations and individuals engaged in the field of global development. To a large extend then, it is an organizational sociology of global development. Organizational sociology because it primarily studies the practices and discourses of development-related work as it takes place within organizational environments (though it is naturally up for discussion whether some of the work that the Gates Foundation engages in actually has anything to do with even the widest conceptions of development). But also to indicate an appreciation of the importance of institutions, valuing how the work of actors engaged in global development does not enjoy isolated actorness nor that only exogenous shocks around them may incite change. That is, all actors engaged in development-targeted or related work have differing degrees of agency, potentially allowing them to reproduce, translate or defy policies, practices or norms as they experience them from their organizations, colleagues or partners. Moreover, the organizational environments studied are fundamentally based within the aid industry, thus not targeting the many different forms of local or indigenous development processes that some parts of the sociology of development literature have focused on. It thus primarily remains interested in different inter- and intra-organizational processes of stability and change, from organizational perceptions of and attitudes towards norms dominant in the field to the institutional work of individuals to reproduce or challenge ideas, policies or practices of development.

Labelling this study as organizational in form means situating it in a field that concerns itself with the nature of organizing, from the most tangible forms of organizational life to abstract forms of human organizing. The field of organization studies brings together scholars from across diverse disciplines of economics, psychology, political science, sociology, development studies and many more, and should not be considered a unified body of thought as much as an exceedingly broad analytical and multiparadigmatic umbrella. It may be seen to historically reflect origins that include some of the earliest systematic human writing, for example John Locke, Thomas Aquinas, or Jean-Jacques Rousseau, but is most commonly thought to start from central contributors of the last half of the nineteenth century, including Karl Marx, Max Weber and Émile Durkheim.[35] Today, the boundaries of organization studies remain highly fluid, as it in essence represents a large quasi-discipline for exploring forms of organizing and continues to span disciplines, which is of little surprise given that the forces shaping social organization and human action are indeed economic, political, cultural, psychological and beyond. The past decades have seen us cast away earlier assumptions about the inherently rational and ethical qualities of modern organization, and replace them with the complexity and uncertainty of organizational life. Organizations may be seen as attempts at ordering, structuring and controlling the chaotic world, achieving a more stable and predictable form, and may be created because of the values and legitimacy they embody as much as for the efficiency they produce. On the other hand, and despite intentions of stability and order, organizations are at their core often about unpredictability, flux, and uncertainty. No matter how hard organizations may try to eliminate irrational or unpredictable forms of pathology, it is more or less unavoidable. This inherent duality or meeting of order and disorder make for an exceedingly interesting dynamic.

More so than just any approach to the study of organizational life, this book is deeply embedded in the sociology of institutions and organizations, or what we would refer to as organizational institutionalism today. The strong connection between organizational institutionalism and the book's research question lies in the core interest of both in understanding the nature of organizational and institutional change. The issue of what happens as new actors enter into an established field is a cornerstone of organizational institutionalism, from initial theorizations of isomorphism and organizational similarity[36] to newer research traditions on institutional work[37] or institutional logics.[38] Institutional perspectives on organizations and forms of organizing arguably remain the 'Intellectual technology par excellence of post-1980s organization theories',[39] not least because of DiMaggio and Powell's[40] relatively simple yet convincing arguments about isomorphism and how that which is held in high regard, culturally, becomes a normalizing modality to which other organizations aspire. They of course kick-started what would become known as new institutionalism, though it had already been informally commenced by Meyer, Rowan and Zucker[41] some years prior. A widely used distinction within this new institutionalism came from political science, in which Hall and Taylor identified three schools of thought: historical, rational choice, and sociological institutionalism.[42] Today, the accuracy of these distinctions is questioned,[43] and the application of institutional perspectives drawn from sociology to address questions of organizations and forms of organizing is widely known as organizational institutionalism. From Weber and Marx, intellectual work on the relationship between institutions and organizations was invigorated by the post-Second World War organizational sociology of, amongst others, Selznick[44] and Stinchcombe.[45] This and similar work was fundamentally political in nature, focusing on group conflicts and organizational strategy, as well as the issue of bringing about consensus between the formal and informal forces of organizational structure and culture. Sources of constraint from institutionalization were mainly seen as a result of political trade-offs and alliances, directing attention to the 'Shadowland of informal interaction'[46] within organizations.

Towards the end of the 1970s, as mentioned, organizational institutionalism made an important turn when the first arguments of a 'new' institutionalism were set forth. This new direction opposed perceptions of organizations as instruments to secure efficiency, the contingency approach (the then dominant approach to explain organizational structure and design), as well as the neglect of political, cultural and social factors that had somewhat come to characterize the work of the two prior decades through a rationalist and technocratic focus on organizations. It argued that organizational structure not only reflects technical demands and resource dependencies, but is also shaped by institutional forces and knowledge legitimated through, for example, professions. Organizations in consequence came to be understood as deeply embedded in social and political contexts, with practices reflecting rules, meaning systems, and beliefs from a broader environment, not least leading to a focus on isomorphism among organizations. This stream of research has continued to grow both in size and in explanatory strength. From it, however, another has emerged, criticizing the isomorphic-centred studies for employing an over-socialized view of action and not properly addressing institutional change.[47] Shifting focus from examining how institutions diffuse within a field, to the micro-foundations of institutional processes, this direction is preoccupied with exploring how organizational actors remake existing or create new practices, shaping actions and belief systems, and producing changes at field level. Studies complementing this stream of research have since explored agency within notions of institutional entrepreneurship,[48] institutional work[49] and institutional logics.[50] This (re)turn to the micro-foundations of institutional and organizational life has challenged the conceptions of 'old' and 'new' institutionalisms, or at least the devaluation of the former as sometimes expressed. It is a fundamental return to the political nature of organization, focusing on conflicts (of interests, of cultures, of material/immaterial resources and capital) within and among organizations, a political nature that was basically lost as attention turned to structural isomorphism in the 1980s. With an increasing reconciliation of old and new institutional perspectives also comes a much more delicate and sensitive balancing of endogenous and exogenous explanations of institutional and organizational change. It is *inter alia* increasingly recognized how institutional isomorphism (or organizational responses to institutional pressures from entering into a new field) is a much more complex process combining inter- and intra-organizational elements, than earlier theorized.

These recalibrations not only imply a change of perspective theoretically; they have significant methodological implications. Refocusing attention away from how institutions diffuse among organizations, towards the micro-foundations of institutional processes means substituting multivariate and quantitative methodological paradigms for much greater proximity to organizations themselves and their empirical realities, and the employment of qualitative and micro-sociological approaches. This naturally creates dialogical tensions between situational specificity and theorization, i.e., the more one wants to explore the situational uniqueness of the case at hand, the more theoretically open-ended it will be and, on the other hand, the more one attempts to situate the case within the developed theories about such phenomena, the less unique the case may become. The ideal endeavour, as I attempt to pursue in this book, is to balance these two concerns by alternating between empirical specificity and theoretical conceptualization and generalization.

After all this then, what does an organizational institutionalist approach imply for the rest of the book, theoretically and analytically? Approaching the case of the Gates Foundation's rise to influence in global development armed with the full history of organizational institutionalism provides me with at least five fundamental considerations that shape the analysis. First, it allows me to treat *organizations as autonomous yet embedded*. The autonomy and agency of organizations is a foundational reality. Yet organizations are not detached rational responses to issues in society, but rather social entities embedded in complex environments. It is a basic argument then that 'Organizations operate according to a logic of appropriateness rather than a logic of instrumentality'.[51] They are indeed shaped by, and may in turn shape, the different contexts they are embedded in, such as organizational fields. Organizational institutionalism thus has an important capacity to stimulate contextualization, seeking to understand the phenomena we study as socially constructed within their broader contexts.

Second, contemporary organizational institutionalism provides a *nuanced view on institutional and organizational change*. While the new institutionalism was mostly interested in stability and homogeneity, contemporary organizational institutionalism is much more focused on drivers of change, and approaches these by equally considering factors external and internal to organizations. Increasingly acknowledging such nuances of exogenous and endogenous institutional and organizational change, overcoming the strict boundaries earlier placed between the two, is a key concern of contemporary work in this tradition. Agency and structure/institution do not just matter sequentially then, but are constantly caught in a process of negotiation. This of course also provides us with a potential issue, as the inherent duality of institutions then means that they both arise from and constrain social action. I will return to this discussion frequently, as it also implies a paradox of embedded agency, i.e., how actors can work to change institutions of global development if they are simultaneously shaped by them.

Third, it emphasizes the *dynamism of organizational life*. Organizations rarely stand still, despite the language of stasis sometimes evoked in discussions about them.[52] Seldom, if ever, is organizational life a matter of long periods of stability followed by short disruptions and subsequent stability in a new form. Organizations require active maintenance, recalibration and renegotiation to remain what they are (or to change), in interaction with the contexts in which they are embedded. This emphasizes the importance of the micro-foundations of institutional work and practice, with, e.g., actors setting in motion path-altering dynamics by introducing new or different elements, that over time may result in redirection of an organization's purposes or goals and thus fundamental change. This is an exceedingly important perspective for a diachronic study like this, in which the history of the Gates Foundation is explored to study forms and sources of change.

Fourth, it allows me to consider *individuals as embedded in institutional and social structures constraining but also enabling action*. That is, the choices and actions of actors are constrained and enabled by institutional logics, contexts or environments. Agency cannot be equated with interests, as the social identifications or networks of individuals will guide or shape their actions.[53] These elements form an assumption of bounded individual intentionality. Taking this assumption one step further, individuals should be acknowledged as embedded in not only one social or institutional context, but in *multiple contexts* – as part of an organization, a team at a workplace, a professional field, age group or gender. Assuming individuals and organizations to be embedded in multiple social structures and institutional logics renders them never completely free (undersocialization), nor completely determined (oversocialization), this allows them to socially construct and transform institutions. As such, actors do not operate in a vacuum but are influenced by their institutional, organizational or social contexts (constraining and encouraging certain patterns of action) that are conversely reproduced or transformed by the practices of individuals. The macro-level becomes an abstraction reflecting the consequences of micro-action, while action and interaction at the micro-level is in turn simultaneously constrained and enabled by institutions.

Fifth and lastly, organizational institutionalism has a strength *of interfacing with numerous other theories or contexts*. The core ideas of this literature have an inherent productive usage across research fields that share an interest in organizations, social action or sense making, furthering a great sense of pluralism. The book accordingly also forms a suggestive framework or theoretical vocabulary fit to study the organizational and institutional challenges of contemporary global development. The interdisciplinary nature of how global development is studied means those of us engaged in it are required to continuously look for novel inspiration as we attempt to strengthen its analytical capacity and extend its theoretical foundations. There is a constant need to uphold theoretical pluralism, drawing on different research traditions and insights while combining constructs and concepts as a form of metaphorical bricolage, to better understand the empirical phenomena at hand. Upholding paradigmatic boundaries will only result in intellectual stagnation and increasing inability to explain the rapidly changing nature of global development that is already questioning the foundation of what development remains, as well as how and by whom it is pursued and practiced. Exploring and theoretically explaining contemporary disruption and change in global development requires an ever-growing conceptual tool box, and this book proposes one way forward in trying to comprehend these currents. The aim of the next chapter is specifically to construe an analytical framework for how to study the processes of change occurring in organizations as these enter into global development.

Themes and organization

At the centre of the book is the Bill and Melinda Gates Foundation, sometimes treated with micro-sociological details allowed by empirical proximity and sometimes at a level of abstraction that draws conceptual and theoretical lines of thought to broader discussions on the complex and interweaving processes taking place over time as a new actor enters into international political life. The chapters that follow together provide empirically grounded and theoretically informed explorations of the intra- and inter-organizational processes that have come to shape the evolution of this particular organization. Through them we begin to comprehend how and why the foundation thinks and acts as it does, but also gain insight into the complexity, contestation and struggles taking place as it continuously reconsiders its work, tries to apprehend the social, economic and cultural ramifications of its multi-billion grant-making, and balances its ambitions and scope with internal and external expectations, critique and pressures. In the end, it is obviously impossible to do justice to this almost mythical beast and turn every stone in the organizational history of the foundation, and the content of the chapters thus reflect a compromise of what forms the core of my interest in the foundation, limits of access to material, and conceptions of what would be most appealing to those eventually reading this book. Nonetheless, it is my hope that it altogether forms, if anything, the individual beginning of a collective pursuit to increasingly try and understand what transpires inside the foundation (and others like it). A requirement, I believe, necessary for those wanting to also launch profound critiques. With those words, the themes and organization of the book are presented next.

The two chapters that follow this introduction both stand out in that they do not directly concern the Gates Foundation. Instead, they set the stage, analytically and contextually. Chapter 2 opens up the rest of the book by attempting to construe an analytical framework for how to study the processes of change occurring in organizations as these enter into global development. It does so from a sociological perspective that appreciates the dynamics and power of ideas, norms, and practices, and not least introduces a great sense of agency to processes of organizational change in global development. Not in a deterministic way that mainly sees the intentional strategies of actors, but one that also appreciates the contingency of social interaction, a contingency that is nonetheless felt and shaped by actors. The first part of the chapter treats some of the key concepts that come into play as an actor increasingly interacts with and involves itself in the field of global development. Here, the framework appreciates the complex balance between exogenous and endogenous sources of change in organizations that renders intra-organizational concerns of staff, culture and alterations of ideas and practices as important as shifts in the organization's external relationships and environments. From here, two specific processes of change are conceptualized and theorized. The first is how ideas move and find their way into an organization. As emerging actors enter into global development they are increasingly exposed to sets of ideas, some of which may find their way into these organizations and entail fundamental change. The construed framework argues that ideas or norms are reinterpreted, appropriated or domesticated to fit the new situation, entailing a transformation of both ideational and material elements, rather than just a transfer of fixed structures across boundaries. The second is how these ideas, as they are being institutionalized, move between different layers of the organization, not least towards and back from sites of implementation. This is an attempt to conceptualize development projects as systems of continuous meaning negotiation and translation that are shaped by the individuals that inhabit and practice them as much as by the organizations that govern them, through funding or implementation. Key components of the framework are continuously used throughout the book, serving as tangible illustrations of how it works in analytical practice and might be extended to other similar academic endeavours.

From attempts to build an analytical approach to study the entrance of new actors into international life, Chapter 3 takes us closer to the empirical context of the Gates Foundation. It initially deals with current thinking and research on the entrance of new actors into global development, tracing and discussing main streams of work as they have materialized over the past years. Private foundations are then situated as a central piece of the puzzle in this work. Born out of the American industrialization, foundations became a powerful force in society in the early 20th century as the first golden age of philanthropy swept across the US in particular, with the 'big three' – Carnegie, Ford and Rockefeller – at the centre. Wealth creation along the same heights can be said to have characterized the past decades, and it is the fortunes amassed during this time, particularly from companies emanating out of Silicon Valley, that we can currently observe being distributed by newer charities. While there are many obvious overlaps, there are significant disparities between the old and newer foundations that see the latter motivated and driven by a different set of ideas and logics. In particular, what is perceived as a more systematic and strategic approach to philanthropy in contemporary grant-making has led some to argue that we are witnessing a new group of philanthrocapitalists, successfully applying a business approach to tackling global problems.[54] The chapter discusses both traditional and modern approaches to philanthropy, and whether there is any difference between the two, before moving on to try and trace central lines of work on the (re)emergence of private foundations in areas of global development.

Next, we finally enter Seattle and the Bill and Melinda Gates Foundation. Chapter 4 is the first attempt to synthesize and tell a (hi)story of the Gates Foundation's development since its inception. In spite of the foundation's reach into most corners of global development and international relations, we have yet to see the different snippets of its history come together in a single narrative. Here, then, I track the evolution of the foundation from the basement of Bill Gates Sr's house to the opening of the new $500 million headquarters in 2012, and beyond, focusing on the dynamics and organizational consequences of a perpetual scaling up of its grant-making, including a ten-fold growth in administrative expenses across a ten-year period from 2002 ($45 million) to 2012 ($450 million). Over the last 15 years the foundation has grown from a lean family-run foundation with few ambitions beyond the Pacific Northwest of the US to a beasty bureaucracy aspiring to take centre-stage on issues of global development, health, education and gender equality. From a view to its past, the final parts of the chapter provide a discussion of the foundation as it stands today, including programmes and priorities.

When new actors enter into global development, they are not faced with ideational vacuums but rather internationally established or dominant ideas and norms that help dictate and shape legitimate courses of action. Chapter 5 tells the story of how a set of strong ideas from global development have gradually made their way into the Gates Foundation and caused changes to the way it thinks and works, confronting and contesting core foundational logics of the organization along the way, but also being manipulated itself. In the fall of 2014, Melinda Gates was the author of an article in which she made it clear that the Gates Foundation cannot achieve its goals unless it can 'Systematically address gender inequalities and meet the specific needs of women and girls'[55] wherever it works, and that it intends to systematically increase its focus on women's specific needs and preferences. This chapter focuses on everyday practices of bureaucratic life in the Gates Foundation to explore how ideas and practices on gender equality and women's empowerment made their way into the foundation, otherwise known as a beacon of the natural sciences and with an inherent aversion towards politically contentious issues. It explores how such processes of institutionalizing and translating ideas into the internal machinery of an organization are about sense making, consensus production, and negotiation and contestation over frames or systems of interpretation. Emphasizing the importance of not conceiving development organizations as coherent systems of thought, it paints a picture of these as political arenas in which the institutionalization of ideas and practices is shaped by struggles over interpretation, power, and material as well as immaterial resources, all facilitating or resisting organizational change. What happens as ideas find their way into organizations and are institutionalized is not the production of grand narratives or scripted translations, but rather messy processes of agency, contingency and unintended consequences. A second part of the chapter extends this last point of contestation over meaning by exploring how logics of gender equality and women's empowerment have clashed with another core logic of the foundation, that of impact-effectiveness. This perspective illuminates how logics that in their ideal-type share very few fundamental traits may be near impossible to blend without losing significant core characteristics of one or the other. In the Gates Foundation, this means that work on gender equality and women's empowerment cannot simultaneously be structural and functional, political and technical, context-sensitive and scalable. Key choices are made as these logics meet, in this case resulting in the strong logic of impact-effectiveness stripping the foundation's approach to gender equality of its gender-transformative potential.

Chapters 6 and 7 together help us lift our gaze from the internal workings of the Gates Foundation towards its work in and approach to the Global South. The first of these, Chapter 6, targets a central point of emphasis that structures much of the way the foundation thinks, acts and approaches issues of global development – the strong belief in social and economic progress through technological innovation. Here, I reflect on the renascent role of technology in global development as we see it advocated from the Gates Foundation in order to understand how their experimentalist aspirations aim to influence and structure human life and relations in the

Global South. Contrary to earlier approaches to technology in global development, contemporary technology aspirations, particularly from private foundations, centres on 'live' experimentation and innovation in developing countries. Drawing on critical intellectual thought on the political and social ramifications of technological innovation and experimentation, the chapter explores questions such as technologies of development for whom and for what? And with what consequences? I argue here that this newfound focus on technology in global development may challenge the essence of democracy, reduce participation, and have undesirable consequences for populations in the Global South, leading us to not assume a straight line between the philanthrocapitalist approaches to technological experimentation and equitable or democratic societal progress.

Chapter 7 moves us from Seattle to the fields of India. When an organization enters the field of global development, it obviously engages in projects that are to be planned, designed and executed or implemented (or rather, it engages in development projects and thus increasingly becomes part of the field). For many organizations, including the Gates Foundation, this means tasking other organizations with responsibility to facilitate implementation. This opens up significant room for interpretation and struggle over the meanings and functions of the project, between different organizational layers, as it travels to and from contexts. By following how a specific Gates Foundation-funded project on women's ownership of land is framed and practiced at different organizational levels, from the foundation itself to the INGO that implements the project on the ground in the Indian state of Odisha, this chapter explores how the same project can radically change form as its functions and objectives are reinterpreted differently at each level. Beyond incoherence or weakness of project design and execution, such reinterpretations are attempts to localize ideas and practices that have not just ideational but also material consequences on the ground. The chapter thus shows how resistance can be productive, but also the infertility of applying the same yardstick to all of the foundation's work and assume it to successfully spread an ideology of neoliberalism wherever it moves and works. The foundation might have an ambition of furthering certain circumscribed values and objectives, but leaving implementation to other organizations means that the goals and ambitions of any project or programme will go through massive translation and renegotiation as it moves through the organizational system. We thus have to appreciate development cooperation and work as open and loosely coupled systems, where policy and implementation may be far from each other, where political decisions may be resisted, and where change can not only come from the core but also from what is sometimes seen as the periphery.

As the last before the conclusion, Chapter 8 explores the wide repertoire of tools of influence available to the Gates Foundation. The foundation not only forms a private force of authority in global development, but a hybrid one, at all times allowing it to draw upon different characteristics of actorness as it sees fit. As a chameleon changes colour to respond to different occasions and situations, the foundation is able to readily project shifting organizational identities, sometimes appearing as an NGO, sometimes as a multinational company, and sometimes even as a state actor. From the case of attaining official relations with the WHO, despite existing criteria that private actors are not allowed such privileges, the chapter tells a story of how, as the foundation has ascended to power, it has moved from a state of resistance or isolation to one of deep interaction, strongly relating to and enacting norms, practices and organizational forms towards which it earlier stood in opposition. This has not least been coupled with a growing self-realization of how it may utilize its hybrid organizational nature to influence political processes or impact its areas of engagement. The chapter accordingly explores how the Gates Foundation strategically practices a hybrid authority, allowing it to alternately expand and compress its organizational identity, sometimes assuming multiple organizational forms and at other times (particularly when faced with questions of legitimacy) reducing itself back to its initial shape as a private foundation, with limited accountability obligations. It asks what the consequences of this shape-shifting ability are for its capacity to influence political processes and for our understanding of contemporary actorness in international studies. Because exactly what kind of actor is the Gates Foundation becoming, and does it matter if we cannot exactly pinpoint this?

Finally, the last chapter concludes the book, though perhaps by way of providing more questions than answers for the future study of the Gates Foundation. Entering into and becoming part of the field of global development, I argue, is a process that occurs over time, as a layering of different sediments of organizational and institutional history. Organizations may (as this book certainly argues the Gates Foundation has) evolve from being loosely to more tightly coupled to the field's ideas, practices, or logics. Entering into new areas of intervention has a fundamental impact on the organization, beyond what may be immediately identifiable. All emerging actors continuously relate to and are confronted with new ideas, practices, norms, and specific sets of principles, all of which map out forms of legitimate action and discourse to which they, to some degree, are expected to adhere. These actors may certainly bring with them a challenge to such established orthodoxies, but they are as likely to experience substantial changes themselves. A rudimentary closing argument of the book thus remains the importance of attentiveness to the multidirectionality of change in the study of new actors' entrance into global development. This concern extends beyond the field of global development far into the heart of international relations or global governance, where the entrance or rise of emerging powers is equally pertinent. Animated by the conviction that the study of emerging actors entering into international political life obliges us to not make widespread generalizations on what drives and shapes the work of these, I further an argument of the necessity to look below what is often presented as exteriors of monstrosity. Only by diving beneath the surface of formal organizational discourse and action can we gain insight into the stories of (dis)continuous organizational change, diverging interests and influences, necessary to understand the organization itself. The book finally ends with a set of critical perspectives on the nature and influence of private foundations in global development today, leading to the argument that their greatest purpose and aim perhaps ought to be eliminating the very reason they exist – the perverse discrepancy between those who have and those who do not.

Notes

1 Strouse, J. 2000. 'Bill Gates's money'. *The New York Times*, 16 April.
2 Moran, M. 2014. *Private Foundations and Development Partnerships: American Philanthropy and Global Development Agendas*. London and New York, NY: Routledge; McCoy, D., Chand, S. and Sridhar, D. 2009. 'Global health funding: how much, where it comes from and where it goes', *Health Policy* 24: 407–417.
3 See Tompkins-Stange, M. 2016. *Policy Patrons: Philanthropy, Education Reform, and the Politics of Influence*. Cambridge, MA: Harvard Education Press.
4 Muraskin, W. 2004. 'The Global Alliance for Vaccines and Immunization: is it a new model for effective public–private cooperation in international public health?', *American Journal of Public Health* 94(11): 1922–1925; Nossal, G. 2003. 'Gates, GAVI, the Glorious Global Funds and more', *Immunology and Cell Biology* 80: 20–22.
5 Holt-Gimenez, E., Altieri, M. and Rosset, P. 2006. *Ten Reasons Why the Rockefeller and the Bill and Melinda Gates Foundations' Alliance for Another Green Revolution Will Not Solve the Problems of Poverty and Hunger in Sub-Saharan Africa*, Food First Policy Brief No. 12. Oakland, CA: Food First; Holt-Gimenez, E. 2008. 'Out of AGRA: the Green Revolution returns to Africa', *Development* 51(4): 464–471; Moran, M. 2011. 'Private foundations and global health partnerships: philanthropists and "partnership brokerage"', in *Partnerships and Foundations in Global Health Governance*, edited by S. Rushton and D. Williams, Basingstoke: Palgrave Macmillan, 123–142; Moran, 2014; Herdt, R. W. 2012. 'People, institutions, and technology: a personal view of the role of foundations in international agricultural research and development 1960–2010', *Food Policy* 37(2): 179–190.
6 Including veteran Gates Foundation reporter Tom Paulson, who has reported on the foundation since its inception (first at the now bygone *Seattle Post Intelligencer*, and since then through humanosphere.org), current and former *Seattle Times* journalists Sandi Doughton and Kristi Heim, as well as others.
7 Including *Alliance Magazine*, who ran a special issue 'Inside the Gates Foundation' in 2011, and regular contributions by the *Chronicle of Philanthropy*. But also including *The Wall Street Journal*, *Fortune Magazine*, *Time Magazine*, *The New York Times*, *The Economist*, and the *Guardian*. *The LA Times*, furthermore, had a reporter working full-time on the foundation for three months in 2007, resulting in a series of articles critical of its investment practices. There have, however, also been a few stimulating contributions in the form of Moran, 2014; McGoey, L. 2015. *No Such Thing as a Free Gift: The Gates Foundation and the Price of Philanthropy*. London and New York, NY: Verso; and Tompkins-Stange, 2016.
8 Comparably, this figure is far greater than for any other foundation, with, e.g., the Ford Foundation (the second largest foundation in the US) awarding grants worth approximately $500 million in 2014 (latest available figures).
9 Part of the reason for this scaling up is also that several departments handling delivery in the Global Health division have moved to Global Development. This is further explicated in Chapter 4.
10 OECD. 2017. *Global Private Philanthropy for Development*. Paris: Organisation for Economic Co-operation and Development.
11 Bishop, M. and Green, M. 2010. *Philanthrocapitalism: How Giving can Save the World*. London: A. & C. Black; Hudson Institute 2011. *The Index of Global Philanthropy and Remittances 2011*. Washington, DC: Hudson Institute; Adelman, C. 2009. 'Global philanthropy and remittances: reinventing foreign aid', *The Brown Journal of World Affairs* 15(2): 23–33.
12 McGoey, 2015; Edwards, M. 2009. *Just Another Emperor? The Myths and Realities of Philanthrocapitalism*. London: The Young Foundation and Demos; Desai, R. and Kharas, H. 2008. 'The California consensus: can private aid end global poverty?', *Survival* 50(4): 155–168.

13 Moran, 2014.
14 Desai and Kharas, 2008.
15 Bell, P. D. 1971. 'The Ford Foundation as a transnational actor', *International Organization* 25(3): 465–478.
16 Fisher, D. 1983. 'The role of philanthropy foundations in the reproduction and production of hegemony Rockefeller Foundation and the social sciences', *Sociology* XVII (2): 206–233.
17 Berman, E. H. 1983. *The Influence of the Carnegie, Ford and Rockefeller Foundations on American Foreign Policy: the Ideology of Philanthropy*. Albany, NY: SUNY Press.
18 Roelofs, J. 2003. *Foundations and Public Policy: The Mask of Pluralism*. Albany, NY: SUNY Press; Parmar, I. 2012. *Foundations of the American Century*. New York, NY: Columbia University Press; McGoey, 2015.
19 Anheier, H. K. and Toepler, S. (eds) 1999. *Private Funds, Public Purpose, Philanthropic Foundations in International Perspective*. New York, NY: Kluwer.
20 See Gore, C. 2013. 'Introduction – the new development cooperation landscape: actors, approaches, architecture', *Journal of International Development* 25(6): 769–786; Zimmermann, F. and Smith, K. 2011. 'More actors, more money, more ideas for development cooperation', *Journal of International Development* 23(5): 722–738.
21 Nye, J. and Keohane, R. 1971. 'Transnational relations and world politics: an introduction', *International Organization* 25(3): 329–349.
22 Risse, T. 2013. 'Transnational actors and world politics', in *Handbook of International Relations*, edited by W. Carlsnaes, T. Risse and B. Simmons, London: Sage, 426–453.
23 Risse-Kappen, T. 1996. *Bringing Transnational Relations Back In*. Cambridge: Cambridge University Press; Prakash, A. and Hart, J. 1999. 'Globalization and governance: an introduction', in *Globalization and Governance*, edited by A. Prakash and J. Hart, London and New York, NY: Routledge, 1–25; Reinalda, B., Arts, B. and Noortmann, M. 2001. 'Non-state actors in international relations: do they matter?', in *Non-State Actors in International Relations*, edited by B. Arts, M. Noortmann and B. Reinalda, Farnham: Ashgate, 1–11; Hall, R. and Biersteker, T. 2002. 'The emergence of private authority in the international system', in *The Emergence of Private Authority in Global Governance*, edited by R. Hall and T. Biersteker, Cambridge: Cambridge University Press, 3–23; Cutler, A., Haufler, V. and Porter, T. 1999. 'Private authority and international affairs', in *Private Authority and International Affairs*, edited by A. Cutler, V. Haufler and T. Porter, Albany, NY: State University of New York Press, 3–31.
24 Risse, 2013; Hale, T. and Held, D. 2011. 'Editors' introduction: mapping changes in transnational governance', in *Handbook of Transnational Governance*, edited by T. Hale and D. Held, Cambridge: Polity Press, 1–37.
25 See Joachim, J. 2009. 'Non-governmental organizations and decision making in the United Nations', in *The Ashgate Research Companion to Non-State Actors*, edited by B. Reinalda, Farnham: Ashgate, 291–303.
26 Lindblom, A. 2011. 'Non-governmental organizations and non-state actors in international law', in *The Ashgate Research Companion to Non-State Actors*, edited by B. Reinalda, Farnham: Ashgate, 147–160.
27 Strange, S. 1996. *The Retreat of the State*. Cambridge: Cambridge University Press.
28 Frank, A. G. 1969. *Capitalism and Under-Development in Latin America*. London: Monthly Review Press.
29 Hooks, G. 2016. *The Sociology of Development Handbook*. Berkeley, CA: University of California Press.
30 Ferguson, J. 1990. *The Anti-Politics Machine*. Minneapolis, MN: University of Minnesota Press; Escobar, A. 1995. *Encountering Development: The Making and Unmaking of the Third World*. Princeton, NJ: Princeton University Press.
31 Long, N. and A. Long (eds) 1992. *Battlefields of Knowledge: The Interlocking of Theory and Practice in Social Research and Development*. London: Routledge; Long, N. 2001. *Sociology of Development: Actor Perspectives*. London and New York, NY: Routledge.

32 See Cohn, S. and Hooks, G. (eds) 2016. *The Sociology of Development Handbook*. Berkeley, CA: University of California Press.
33 Long, 2001; Mosse, D. and Lewis, D. 2006. 'Theoretical approaches to brokerage and translation in development', in *Development Brokers and Translators: The Ethnography of Aid and Agencies*, edited by D. Lewis and D. Mosse, Boulder, CO: Kumarian Press, Inc., 1–27; Bierschenk, T. and Olivier de Sardan, J. P. 2014. 'Studying the dynamics of African bureaucracies: an introduction to states at work', in *States at Work: Dynamics of African Bureaucracies*, edited by T. Bierschenk and J. P. Olivier de Sardan, Leiden: Koninklijke Brill, 1–33; or Rottenburg, R. 2009. *Far-Fetched Facts. A Parable of Development Aid*. Cambridge, MA: MIT Press.
34 Hobart, M. 1993. *An Anthropological Critique of Development*. Abingdon: Routledge.
35 See Augier, M., March, J. G. and Sullivan, B. N. 2005. 'Notes on evolution of a research community: organization studies in Anglophone North America, 1945–2000', *Organization Science* 16(1): 85–95.
36 DiMaggio, P. and Powell, W. 1983. 'The iron cage revisited: institutional isomorphism and collective rationality in organizational fields', *American Sociological Review* 48(2): 147–160; Meyer, J. and Rowan, B. 1977. 'Institutionalized organizations: formal structure as myth and ceremony', *American Journal of Sociology* 83(2): 340–363.
37 Lawrence, T. B. and Suddaby, R. 2006. 'Institutions and institutional work', in *The Sage Handbook of Organizational Studies*, edited by S. Clegg, C. Hardy, T. Lawrence, and W. North, London: Sage, 215–254; Lawrence, T. B., Leca, B. and Zilber, T. B. 2013. 'Institutional work: current research, new directions, and overlooked issues', *Organization Studies* 34: 1023–1033.
38 Thornton, P. H., Ocasio, W. and Lounsbury, M. 2012. *The Institutional Logics Perspective: A New Approach to Culture, Structure, and Process*. New York, NY: Oxford University Press.
39 Clegg, S. 2009. 'Editor's introduction: directions in organization studies', in *Sage Directions in Organization Studies*, edited by S. Clegg, London: Sage, XXI–3.
40 DiMaggio and Powell, 1983.
41 Meyer and Rowan, 1977; Zucker, L. G. 1977. 'The role of institutionalization in cultural persistence', *American Sociological Review* 42(5): 726–743.
42 Hall, P. and Taylor, R. 1996. 'Political science and the three new institutionalisms', *Political Studies* 44: 936–957.
43 Greenwood, R., Oliver, C., Sahlin-Andersson, K. and Suddaby, R. 2008. 'Introduction', in *The Sage Handbook of Organizational Institutionalism*, edited by R. Greenwood, C. Oliver, K. Sahlin-Andersson and R. Suddaby, Thousand Oaks: CA: Sage, 1–47.
44 Selznick, P. 1949. *TVA and the Grass Roots*. Berkeley, CA: University of California Press.
45 Stinchcombe, A. 1968. *Constructing Social Theories*. New York, NY: Harcourt, Brace & World.
46 Selznick, P. 1957. *Leadership in Administration: A Sociological Interpretation*. Berkeley, CA: University of California Press.
47 DiMaggio, P. 1988. 'Interest and agency in institutional theory', in *Institutional Patterns and Organizations: Culture and Environment*, edited by L. G. Zucker, Cambridge, MA: Ballinger, 3–22; Campbell, J. L. 2005. 'Where do we stand? Common mechanisms in organizations and social movements research', in *Social Movements and Organization Theory*, edited by G. F. Davis, D. McAdam, W. R. Scott and M. N. Zald, Cambridge: Cambridge University Press, 41–68; Hallett, T. and Ventresca, M. 2006. 'Inhabited institutions: social interactions and organizational forms in Gouldner's "patterns of industrial bureaucracy"', *American Journal of Sociology* 94: 52–94; Hirsch, P. and Lounsbury, M. 1997. 'Ending the family quarrel: toward a reconciliation of "old" and "new" institutionalisms', *American Behavioral Scientist*, 40: 406–418.

48 DiMaggio, 1988; Boxenbaum, E. 2009. 'How actors change institutions: toward a theory of institutional entrepreneurship', *Academy of Management Annals* 3(1): 65– 107.
49 Lawrence, T., Suddaby, R. and Leca, B. 2011. 'Institutional work: refocusing institutional studies of organization', *Journal of Management Inquiry* 20(1): 52–58.
50 Thornton, et al. 2012.
51 March, J. G. and Olsen, J. P. 1989. *Rediscovering Institutions*. New York, NY: Free Press.
52 Streeck, W. and Thelen, K. 2005. 'Introduction: institutional change in advanced political economies', in *Beyond Continuity: Institutional Change in Advanced Political Economies*, edited by W. Streeck and K. Thelen, Oxford: Oxford University Press, 1–39.
53 Thornton, et al. 2012; Granovetter, M. 1985. 'Economic action and social structure: the problem of embeddedness', *American Journal of Sociology*, 91(3): 481–510.
54 Bishop and Green, 2010.
55 Gates, M. 2014. 'Putting women and girls at the center of development', *Science*, 345(6202): 1273–1275.

2 Organizational change and new actors in global politics

The complexity of contemporary changes in global development means these are not easily captured or comprehended. To study new actors or rising powers is not only to understand how these influence development itself or other actors in it. Equally important, yet frequently evaded, is to understand the consequences for new actors as these enter into international political life and become engaged in fields such as global development. In fact, these two perspectives are difficult to separate as the consequences of entering into a new field and exercising influence starts processes that may eventually lead to change in the actor itself. The Gates Foundation is a prime example of the changes actors go through as they become increasingly engaged with global development, as we will see throughout this book. The conceptual or theoretical argument of the book is that to properly understand the increasing meeting between what I call forces of heterogeneity (new actors, modes of operation and ideas in development) and homogenization (attempts to govern and set forth principles about development) in global development we have to be more attentive to theories of organizational and institutional change. This chapter serves that end by introducing core perspectives from contemporary sociological, institutional and organizational thought to show how these may be used to study change in global development in general and in new actors in particular, thus also laying out an analytical framework for the book's discussions. It thus briefly turns our attention away from the Gates Foundation and towards broader conceptual debates about change in global development. As the crux of organizational life, change occurs in all social systems and processes, all the time, everywhere, but, for the most part, such change is not radical or revolutionary. Rather, it is incremental in nature, occurring in the almost mundane day-to-day work of actors. This entails a coexistence of stasis and change in organizations that creates a key theoretical tension. To explain organizational change is to explain how these form, persist, transform or wither away, requiring us to employ multiple levels of analysis, from the microfoundations of individual life inside organizations to the macrostructures of fields shaping institutional creation and disruption. The book's theoretical endeavour is not a radical rethinking of the analysis of global development but rather forms the addition of a set of helpful conceptual and theoretical vocabularies for analytically exploring some of the core concerns preoccupying contemporary studies of this field.

With a particular interest in the power of ideas and norms to foster change in organizations, this chapter fundamentally concerns three arguments made over the course of three sizable sections. The first is an argument for increasing attention towards institutional and organizational change by appreciating the conception of global development as a field in which we have to comprehend the central drivers of change, from both inside actors engaged in development and different forms of institutional pressures from the surrounding environment. The second and third sections further a similar argument but across different metaphorical latitudes, namely that the key driver of change for organizations involved in contemporary global development remains the movement of ideas and practices. The first section conceptualizes how ideas move horizontally (if we are to simplify the organizational landscape) across different organizations, eventually making their way into and entailing changes inside the organizational machinery of development organizations. The third and last section then attempts to conceptualize the "vertical" movement of ideas inside the systems that comprise any development project or programme, as ideas move back and forth from sites of implementation.

Global development as an organizational field

Much of the literature surrounding new actors or rising powers intrinsically treats global development as what we can call a field or even an organizational field, paying attention to how these actors bring with them new ideas or resources, eventually leading them to become sources of authority that produce change amongst other actors. Yet rarely if ever is this notion of field explicated, and this is where we will start then. The notion of field provides us with a conceptual and theoretical vocabulary appropriate for explaining and exploring empirical phenomena during unsettling times, such as those witnessed in contemporary global development. It directs our attention to how actors collectively constituting a field engage in, or resist, forms of principle and norm setting, as well as the changing ideas and practices at field-level, potentially affecting what is considered legitimate and illegitimate. It also underlines that consequences from the entrance of new actors into international political life may as well be forms of stability and increased homogenization as they may be forms of radical change, and that these actors are as likely to go through processes of substantial change themselves, as they are to incite change. Furthermore, with the current observable phenomena in global development, we have been handed an ideal context to not just apply notions of organizational fields, but to also build on them by empirically exploring what occurs as these new actors enter into established fields in which norm and principle setting is prevalent, building theory that is grounded in reality.

The notion of organizational field has long been used as a favoured level of analysis in the stream of literature in organizational theory arguing that the greatest factor in catalyzing organizational or institutional change is pressure from the environment. That is, field-level structures and interaction between peer organizations gathering around a constitutive object. In its primeval state in social science, a field defines a 'Structured social space with its own rules and actors, schemes of domination, legitimate opinions, and identifies a number of nodes, points of observation or positions, and their mutual relations in the analysis'.[1] In organizational theory, fields are commonly perceived of as spheres of activity constituted by organizations that share cognitive and normative frameworks, and 'A similar conception of legitimate action'.[2] Opposite earlier-used concepts in institutional theory, such as organizational environment, field offers a less deterministic account implying that fields are made; they are never given.[3] Others have in turn highlighted other individual features of an organizational field, such as the conflictive interplay between actors shaping and determining power relations and the opportunity to shape institutional rule-making in the centre of the field, or have maintained that fields form around issues (rejecting the idea of markets and technologies as the only possible constitutive objects), and that evolving power relations thus entail contestation over issue interpretation, i.e., institutional war rather than isomorphic dialogue.

Fields may be seen as characterized by at least three features: a constitutional object binding the different organizations together, power relations shaping interaction between the different organizations in the field, and emerging rules and principles that organizations are expected to adhere to in order to be considered legitimate.[4] Reconceptualising Giddens'[5] structuration to account for the connectedness and structural equivalence of a field, DiMaggio and Powell[6] likewise underline four constituting points determining a growing maturity of the field: increases in interaction between organizations; the emergence of inter-organizational structures of domination and patterns of coalition; increases in the information load for the organizations; and a rising mutual awareness among organizations that they are involved in a common enterprise. As such, organizations constituting a field interact are aware of each other's existence, consider each other as more or less peer units, though with different power relations and degrees of authority, and are interdependent. An ensuing question becomes how fields subsist, i.e., their potential variation and transformation over time. Do fields such as that of global development experience a linear evolvement towards a predetermined end-state of stability from formation, or should they be assumed dynamic in nature, with high degrees of fluidity and volatility entailing potential infinite motion of change? If global development has taught us one thing about fields, it is surely that of constant change, with development itself having been in a state of almost permanent flux since the 1960s, characterized by ongoing struggles for not just interpretive or ideological but also structural power. When conceptualizing fields then, we should substitute statist perceptions with dynamism, giving attention to the ever-changing nature of fields. The principles and rules governing or shaping organizational action may change because internal or external factors or circumstances are transformed (such as the entrance of new actors into global development), and power relations and hierarchies of authority guiding interaction between organizations in the field change because of shifts in resources, capacity, mandate or legitimacy of actors.

In organizational theory, dominant lines of thought suggest that a process of homogenization (isomorphism) is sparked among organizations gradually constituting a field.[7] This will in turn render these more similar over time through a mix of three homogenizing mechanisms relating to external pressure (coercive isomorphism), imitation of legitimate or successful organizational models (mimetic isomorphism) and normative pressure (normative isomorphism).[8] Importantly, organizations do not become homogenized because of an external technical environment, but 'Through adaptation to a socially constructed environment'.[9] Coercive isomorphism occurs when organizations are pressured to conform to certain principles or rules established in the field, and ranges from the obvious homogenization by regulation through authorized bodies to the more subtle effect of preferences for organizational forms.[10] Mimetic isomorphism relates to imitations of a specific organizational model because of the particular perceived legitimacy or success attained through adoption of a set model. As a form of voluntary imitation, organizations may adopt different organizational models because these are seen as improvements to their own (attraction). Attraction in this sense is linked to socialization processes through professional training and networks. Through training, and influenced by associated environments, individuals adopt cognitive and normative frames shaping their perception of appropriate organizational practices. Professional networks and staff migration across organizations help diffuse institutional logics across time and space. Similar to attraction but also differing, change may also be a product of disorientation (caused by uncertainty) as much as of the socialization and influence of an individual's cognitive frames and the diffusion of institutional models through professional networks and staff migration. Normative isomorphism is induced by professionalization as groups of professionals develop specific roles within the field, developing a 'Cognitive base and legitimation for their occupational autonomy'.[11]

Central to these thoughts of isomorphism or homogenization is the notion of 'rationalized myths' taking the form of meta-level solutions to perceived problems of what constitutes 'proper' organizations and organizing.[12] Once such myths emerge, they may become institutionalized as universal truths, which organizations then in turn adopt, leading to isomorphism. In global development, we know these truths in the form of buzzwords and fashionable concepts such as participatory, rights-based, or even disruption. When faced with myths and pressured to adopt them by the environment, organizations may be confronted with the problem that the myth may not be an efficient solution, or an unfit one for its organizational characteristics, and that competing rationalized myths may exist simultaneously.[13] To account for solutions to these problems, Meyer and Rowan[14] suggested that organizations decouple practices from formal structures, and thus sometimes only superficially adhere to this incoming myth (being loosely coupled systems in the words of Scott[15]). By decoupling practices from action, they can appear legitimate in the eyes of peer organizations while maintaining stability of practices.

The agency of change

A conceptual weakness of perceiving global development as a field is that by emphasizing the dominant impact of institutions on organizational forms and practices, the agency of organizational actors may become a secondary concern, and change only understood as reactions to institutional pressures from the field. Fortunately, there is ample room for us to confront any lack of appreciation of agency and the work of organizational actors by turning attention on the micro-foundations of organizational and institutional life in global development. Instead of relying on metaphysical pathos, we may choose to see organizations and institutions as objects of ongoing skirmishes between actors.[16] Institutional entre-preneurship is one such concept from organizational theory that aims to refocus our attention towards actors working to influence their contexts.[17] These 'entre-preneurs' are considered change agents who leverage resources to transform organizations and institutions or create new ones, initiating divergent changes and actively participating in implementing these.[18] This form of agency has been explored by relating it to either the properties of the actors or their specific posi-tions in a given field.[19] The first stream directs attention to the special abilities, characteristics and qualities of such actors, allowing them to ignite institutional change by promoting alternative 'templates' or logics to the existing ones. These entrepreneurs are thus described as an 'Analytically distinct social type who has the capacity to take a reflective position towards institutionalized practices and can envision alternative modes of getting things done'.[20] The second stream is more interested in how a number of different subject or social positions[21] are cre-ated, from which actors may catalyse change. The connection to organizational fields then becomes that these are understood as loaded with positions granting actors access to resources and power, which in turn provides them with the capacity to ignite change.

A weakness of the idea of institutional entrepreneurship remains that it tends to overemphasize the hyper-muscular and rational dimensions of such actors, to the point of almost detaching these from organizational and institu-tional influences. Merging different perspectives on the importance of agency and the micro-foundations of institutional life, and thus also building on insti-tutional entrepreneurship, institutional work has been introduced as a broader concept, aiming to understand the 'Broad patterns of intent and capacity to create, maintain and alter institutions'.[22] In the recursive relationship between institutions and action, institutional work is primarily concerned with how action and actors affect institutions. This work draws on insights from the practice turn in social theory,[23] inspired by the sociology of practice,[24] which engages in the situated actions of the everyday lives of individuals and groups, and attempts to explain the relationship between such action and the cultures or structures within which it is based. Here as well, the concept of 'field' plays a central part: 'Practice approaches promulgate a distinct social ontology: the social is a field of embodied, materially interwoven practices centrally organized around shared practical understandings'.[25] Through its attention to practice and action then, institutional work is more concerned with the processual aspects of how actors engage in creating, maintaining or disrupting institutions than in the accom-plishment of eventually having done so. This opens up room for unintended consequences and contingency to enter into and underline the non-linearity of processes of institutional and organizational change, emphasizing the 'Muddles, misunderstanding, false starts and loose ends'[26] that characterize these. An important part of studying organizational change in global development then, is to explore how institutions shape patterns of action and organization, yet are also created, maintained or disrupted by human action, leading us to understand the vital role of actors in driving and shaping institutional and organizational change. At the field level, it may help explain large-scale historical events by linking the actions of individuals to collectives through social mechanisms, making us aware that change to development organizations, or to forms of norm and principle setting in the field for that matter, are not only results of exogenous pressure or shocks forcing mechanical organizational response. All development organizations, whether NGOs, public aid agencies or private foundations, are comprised of people who have the ability to directly and indirectly influence key processes, with consequences for both the organization itself and for the field.

The power of ideas to incite change

In the field of global development, few influences are as powerful in driving change as that of ideas. Ideas justify actions and interventions by lending legitimacy,[27] direct policy agendas, distribute resources, and incite change wherever they move.[28] In the context of this book and its exploration of the Gates Foundation, we are both interested in what happens as ideas move across organizations and entail change by doing so, and in how ideas change as they move inside the organization itself. The first (forming the second set of arguments in this chapter) helps us to explain the consequences as a new actor enters into global development and is faced with norms, rules, and principles there. The second perspective (forming the third set of arguments) is more interested in the relationship between policy and practice as ideas move between different organizational levels. The last decade has seen significant attempts to untangle this question, mainly through arguments that devaluate understandings of 'gaps' between policy and practice as merely technical in nature, stressing the importance of how meaning, ideas and practices are transformed between different organizational levels, as individuals make sense of them in the context of their own position, values and interests. To understand change inside the Gates Foundation, but also its ability to exercise influence and power through outward ideational efforts, we need to comprehend both of these perspectives. Before we move on to them, however, a short discussion of the nature of movement of ideas is necessary, starting from the most widely used concept to explain this – diffusion.

Conceptually, diffusion is an explanatory principle for insurmountable processes, from the socially meaningless and unintentional to the meaningful intentionality of deliberate action: from the transmission of physical illness from one human being to the next, to the sophisticated diffusion of social practices between institutions within a shared social space. The extensive literature on diffusion has explored different forms of sociological and economic mechanisms guiding the spread and adoption of practices and ideas, emphasizing respectively technical and cultural imperatives for adoption. In the first perspective, adopters are perceived as rational actors making efficiency-enhancing decisions on the basis of presumed economic benefits. The second perspective adopts a sociological perspective stressing pressure for social conformity (homogenization) as the key mechanism for diffusion. To a great extent, this is the stream of research evolving from DiMaggio and Powell's emphasis on organizational imitation as a way for an organization to appear legitimate. One part of this perspective accentuates that rational behaviour and adoption of diffusion practices may actually guide organizational adoption, but only to a certain point in time at which efficiency concerns become largely irrelevant. At this point then, social mechanisms such as the group pressure of imitation come into play. The other part holds that legitimacy concerns (adhering to the normative expectations of other actors) at all times incite actors to adopt diffusion practices, and that these are rarely increasing technical efficiency, often having the contrary effect. Some argue diffusion is especially likely to occur in the wake of crisis or failure, others that it is basically a spatial process, meaning that the probability of diffusion is dependent upon geographical proximity.[29] Research into this concept is traditionally built around assumptions of modernity, studying the spread of innovations: drinking water, new drugs, agricultural technologies, etc. This has led some scholars to assume that processes are more likely to be adopted (via diffusion) if they are considered modern by potential adopters.[30] What affects the diffusion of social material in this line of thought then is that 'Perceptions of similarity provide a rationale for diffusion'.[31] This may be done in order to catch up with perceived leading institutions but also functions as a release from the responsibility of individual choice (following fashions). We know this well from global development, where the adoption of fashionable concepts and practices denotes conformity more than innovation.

Traditionally, diffusion studies have explored how ideas or practices find their way into organizations by employing an input/output research strategy in which attention is mainly given to the sources of inspiration for change, and the subsequent identification of what has changed. This assumes a binary acceptance/rejection dichotomy by holding that new ideas and practices are either adopted or not adopted in the organization.[32] Such approaches largely see the movement of new ideas and practices as a mechanical process of information transfer from one context to the next. This may be true for some ideas or practices, but it often risks neglecting the very important issue of how these are remade and contextualized as they make their way through organizations, becoming institutionalized. The adoption of new ideas of practices in development organizations certainly requires adaptation and interpretive efforts far beyond a simplistic process of 'acceptance', and in order to make diffused practices meaningful in the specific organizational or social context, these need to be reconfigured and domesticated. This is not to say that diffusion studies have not contributed greatly to our understanding of how ideas and practices travel between organizations and contexts, but rather that the dominant approaches in such research cannot account fully for the immensely dynamic processes that take place as this occurs. Only very few practices or ideas will diffuse in a fixed state without significant processes of localization and contextualization.

Instead of diffusion then, or rather standing on the shoulders of diffusion, the concept of translation has often been turned to. Translation fundamentally draws on Latour's[33] and Callon and Latour's[34] work. For Latour,[35] the issues of implicitly or explicitly basing social research on the natural science metaphor of diffusion are that, (1) it presumes the existence of an original energy emanating out of an unknown source and pushing the idea or practice along; (2) the metaphor of diffusion implies inertia, i.e., resistance to change; and (3) the medium being diffused may eventually cease to do so. While this is certainly a somewhat simplified reading of diffusion research, there is some truth to such a critique of the realist–objectivist ontology that has characterized and still characterizes some diffusion studies. In suggesting translation as an alternative metaphor, Latour thus aimed to identify the movement of ideas as a social interpretation process in which actors are involved in a continuous process of producing and constructing society. Translation in essence implies that 'Setting something in new context means constructing it anew',[36] recognizing how ideas and practices are reformulated and transformed as they make their way through organizations, becoming institutionalized. That is, as practices and ideas flow from one context to another, those implementing them will do so in different ways and to greater or lesser extents, depending on their context. As opposed to the transfer of fixed structures of meaning and practices across boundaries, as sometimes described by studies employing a static view on adoption, translation involves the transformation of ideational and material elements. Such an approach further underlines how organizations are inherently political arenas in which struggles over power, information and resources greatly shape processes of institutionalization and translation. In the diffusion literature it is often assumed that there is a threshold for an idea to overcome before it spreads widely. The translation concept follows a similar logic by arguing that the force of the idea is not inherent in the idea but gained through the attention it gets from different actors. The difference here, then, is that while diffusion focuses on the dissemination of the idea to other organizations, translation underlines that the impetus for imitation must come from the imitators themselves,[37] i.e., that actors ready and concerned with adopting and localizing the idea are the ones facilitating the movement, not the idea itself or its point of departure or sender (if we can ever talk of one such). The movement of ideas then is not so much about spreading as about receiving or taking them in.

These processes speak widely to other disciplines and fields of study as well. Attention to the movement of ideas and norms across contexts is widespread in international relations, where such processes are often examined in the multidirectional relations between international organizations, as legitimizers of norms, and local adopters in the process of localization these norms go through as they reach domestic contexts, or emerge from them in the first place.[38] As norms are localized, they are essentially reconfigured to fit with the context they enter into, not least by careful work of norm entrepreneurs.[39] These perspectives are somewhat mirrored in elements of anthropology, and in particular Levitt and

Engle-Merry's[40] concept of vernacularization that attends to how norms and ideas are reconfigured in different local contexts. By approaching the process from a perspective of cultural circulation and translation, they suggest conceiving of diffusion as a cultural act in itself, not a separate process that somehow transports culture or ideas. Vernacularization, literally to translate into local language, thus implies processes of local appropriation and adoption in which ideas take on some of the ideological and social attributes of the local context while maintaining some original formulation, changing the composition of ideational and practical elements. The act of vernacularization varies according to a number of factors: 'Where its communicators are located in the social and power hierarchy and their institutional positions, the characteristics of the channels and technology through which ideas and practices flow, the nature of the ideas and the idea packages in which they are embedded, and the topography of the terrain in which these transfers take place'.[41] Finally, in studies of policies and their travels, the notion of transfer is increasingly questioned for its overly rational understanding of how policy is learned and moves across space and time.[42] Unlike international relations and anthropology's adoption of 'local' concepts such as norm localization and vernacularization, the policy transfer literature draws directly and explicitly on the Latourian notion of translation as organizational institutionalism.[43] In this line of thought, policies are seen as manifestations of different ideas and practices that are not infused with fixed, definitive meanings, and are always up for interpretation, negotiation and configuration. Like social facts, policies thus become meaningless outside those situations in which they are manifested. Though somewhat disparate, these different perspectives underpin the work of translation in organizational institutionalism and indicate a break with linear or reductionist perspectives that treat ideas and practices as static entities spreading by osmosis and resulting in adoption or rejection, and that are inattentive to how these transform as they move and are constructed anew in novel contexts.

The uptake of ideas in development organizations

From these broad considerations on the movement of ideas and practices, we are subsequently interested in how ideas moving across the field of global development make their way to, are localized, and entail change in organizations, forming the second set of arguments in this chapter. I analytically divide such processes into three different yet interwoven stages, and later in the book we will see how these tangibly came into play in the Gates Foundation. The first of the three processes, *emergence*, concerns the question of how ideas emerge and come to the attention inside organizations in a very first phase. When ideas move between organizations, they largely do so in the hands or heads of people. People, who bring with them new ideas, may come from the outside and enter into the organization. Individuals who have been, or who are, embedded in different organizational structures are often seen as more likely to not take the prevailing institutional arrangements for granted when they enter into a new organization, increasing the probability of them importing practices from one organizational context to another, or of questioning the organizational status quo.[44] This is an important point in relation to a field like global development where professionals often shop between organizations and are exposed to different organizational cultures and normative frameworks. But these actors may just as well already be embedded in the organization, and do not necessarily have to physically travel from one organization to another. In such instances, ideas will often emerge on the basis of inspiration from the organization's environment (perhaps as a fashionable idea from partners or peer organizations) and as they over time accumulate sufficient attention from individuals they may come to the foreground of discussions in the organization. The types of actors who have the capacity or competence to initiate or shape the movement of ideas between organizations may be referred to, as I described earlier, as institutional entrepreneurs, or perhaps as norm-entrepreneurs as they are commonly known in international relations theory.[45] In both these conceptions of this actor type, their ability to incite change is understood as either coming from their inherent properties (i.e., their characteristics or qualities), or from specific positions that they may hold in their organizations or in the field that grant them access to different forms of power.[46] Emergence, then, in terms of how ideas find their way into organizations in the hands of people, is equally conceivable from individuals from other institutional environments as in situations where an idea at a certain point in time accumulates sufficient attention from a single or a group of individuals, already inside the organization in question. This is essentially the very first step of new ideas entering into organizations, and from here continues the process of making the idea in question workable in the new organizational context, as it is struggled and negotiated over by different actors that may support or resist it.

As ideas begin finding their way into organizations, a second process of *internal negotiation and consensus production* commences, during which proponents of the to-be institutionalized idea must create a coherent vision for change that appeals to, and can win over, those actors needed to implement it.[47] To do so they need to understand and create resonance with the existing organizational context to justify divergence from existing practices or ideas.[48] If an idea is presented as fundamentally breaking with dominant ideas and practices already established in the organization, its likelihood of institutionalization is assumedly not very high. It needs to mobilize allies and cultivate alliances, while being simultaneously faced with 'institutional defenders'[49] who prefer and perhaps benefit from a situation of status quo, and may therefore resist institutionalization of this new idea. To do so they may create stories, define heroes and villains, and construct imageries that lends coherence to plots, and attains them the intellectual attention of key actors in the organization (especially important for actors who do not possess formal authority). A central means for constructing such a coherent vision for change is the use of framing. Framing is used to construct meaning and guide action, and by, e.g., framing new ideas within the realm of already dominant ones in the organization, actors can attempt to make these acceptable by instilling resonance in other organizational actors.[50] These forms of internal negotiation and consensus production are greatly shaped by factors such as organizational structures and cultures that set out different institutional ground rules for actors. By determining the organizational positions of all individuals, organizational structures are key in defining actors' access and possession of formal or informal authority, with which they can influence the potential institutionalization of the new idea, or oppose it. Likewise, different organizational cultures may over time evolve and develop more or less coherent meanings, beliefs and rituals for different groups of individuals.[51]

As a third process, but in practice occurring simultaneously with the processes of internal negotiation and consensus production, the process of ideas entering into organizations goes through what we can call *external negotiation and appropriation*. All organizations are embedded in different normative environments or organizational fields that may espouse different values and encourage particular forms of actions and goals.[52] External stakeholders may also hold more formal kinds of authority and exert power directly or coercively through control over resources, decision-making competencies or the like. Moreover, an organization is often part of not just one but numerous fields to which it needs to relate, and where other organizations may hold some power over it. The Bill and Melinda Gates Foundation, as an example, relates to the field of global development and the norms, values and organizations dominant here. Yet it is simultaneously a private foundation embedded in this particular environment, meaning it needs to relate to dominant normative frameworks here as well. When an idea has reached a level of somewhat institutionalization then, perhaps as a new policy issue slowly becoming a priority, it begins to be reflected in the organization's relations to partners, grantees or peer organizations. What happens subsequently are processes in which these respond to the approach or translation of the idea, on the basis of their own perception of it. They may react encouragingly, but they may also disagree with the particular approach. If the last outcome is the case for actors that have some form of power to influence the organization, then a process of negotiating the approach, or perhaps outright appropriating to the reaction of the environment, begins. In a field such as that of global development many different ideas or regimes of ideas are at play, each with their own form of legitimacy and distinct forms of organizing principles and vocabularies for actors. These continually relate to one another but may also contend because of radically different forms making it impossible to co-exist or blend. During such instances of rivalling ideas inside organizations, actors may work through covert operations to gradually but slowly bring their supported idea to dominance. By focusing on ideas and ideational change, we can come to understand what drives certain discourses and practices in global development, and what happens when these meet or contend.

How ideas change as they move inside development organizations

Having explained how new ideas come to the attention of organizations and go through processes of institutionalization, often entailing significant changes, we move to the third and last set of arguments, specifically focused on why and how ideas and practices change as they move across different organizational layers. This is crucially important for organizations such as private foundations that do not implement projects or programmes themselves in the developing world, but have to rely on partners to do so, leaving open ample room for reinterpretation and negotiation of ideas throughout the chain or system of planning and implementation. This question has been explored extensively in global development over the last decades, as well as across different research traditions. Though disparate, they collectively challenge linear or reductionist perspectives that treat ideas and practices as static entities spreading as osmosis and resulting in adoption/non-adoption, inattentive to how these transform as they move. In this context, we see how ideas cannot move by themselves; it is people who move, not ideas in some static form disconnected from individuals. To fully comprehend how ideas and practices associated with specific development projects are reinterpreted and renegotiated, we have to appreciate translation as micro-sociological processes of agency, the influence from organizational context, history and culture, and finally how we can understand development projects as systems of continuous meaning negotiation and reinterpretation.

Translation as micro-sociological processes of agency

How then are ideas and practices manifested in development projects translated and transformed as they move within organizations and between different organizational layers? Such translation processes are largely understood as micro-sociological ones greatly shaped by agency and facilitated by human intervention, as continuously highlighted up until this point.[53] What can actors do then to reinterpret and transform development projects? Through forms of strategic intervention, they may work to undermine existing ideas and practices, and introduce new ones that need to become legitimate in the eyes of other actors, or they may work to create hybrid forms in which new and old are morphed together,[54] basically using forms of 'social construction power'.[55] To achieve this, they may mobilize resources and framing to make new practices or rules acceptable and to instil resonance in other actors.[56] From this they may establish new inter-actor relations and alliances (entailing various forms of collaborative relations) to facilitate collective adoption and legitimization of new ideas and practices.[57] Within the study development organizations and projects, agency-driven ideas have been elaborated in the anthropology of development streams of work,[58] through a focus on translation and brokering (brokering in itself of course has a prominent history in political anthropology[59]). The fundamental purpose of this work is to establish the world of development projects and policy as socially managed, the relationship between policy and practice as multidirectional in which a significant part of the latter is devoted to reproducing and stabilizing models of the former, and policy in itself as an end rather than a cause, unable to discipline or control. This does not render policy irrelevant, quite the contrary, it just means that policy is not implemented in a straightforward sense, as practices too are shaped by the logic and demands of institutional relations. From this follows an argument for focusing attention on the real-life situations of development workers in which these engage in negotiations of meaning, identity, representation and interpretation. The aid worker as a broker, translator, and not just policy implementer but policy maker, has a similar history in public administration and implementation research. Lipsky's[60] street-level bureaucracy is well known to most, and his explanations of how these cope, use discretion or their adaptive capacity[61] to not just respond to policies and strategic directions in headquarters, but to actively adjust them, producing informal practices and discourses, is quite similar to the inherent mechanisms of translation in development. When actors exercise discretion, they basically engage in processes of interpreting the context and their own position, acting accordingly in a competent way. What actors may do between different levels of development projects then is to resist dominating interpretations from other actors and construct alternating and contending interpretations (i.e., translations). It is not so much a direct form of power (A getting B to do something whether through persuasion or coercion) as it is an indirect form that does not necessarily entail direct or symbolic confrontations with actors further up in the system (not least because these development projects are generally loosely coupled systems[62]).

Organizational context, history and culture

The translation and reinterpretation of development projects, we can conclude from the above, occurs as micro-sociological processes in which actors, or groups of actors, interpret or engage in struggles over interpretation, thus transforming or adapting ideas and practices. Such processes are obviously not only determined by individuals and can be influenced by a magnitude of more structural conditions and factors. The actor-focus should not become a straightjacket at the expense of broader structural factors, both facilitative and constraining, that development organizations like all organizations are subjected to, including organizational context, history and culture. Contextuality is decisive in shaping and facilitating different forms of translation. Ideas do not move through unmarked, smooth terrain but are constantly shaped by different geographies of history and culture. Here, contextuality refers as much to proximity to implementation on the ground as it refers to the field in which the organization or the actor is embedded. The first basically means that the closer we get to implementation on the ground, the more actors have to not just relate to forms of policies or programme documents, but to the social, political and historical context within which they are to act. This does not mean that organizational levels far from implementation are not faced with influence from such structures, but action here remains more decontextualized from the empirical reality. Related to this, the second refers to what we may also call the normative environment, i.e., actors sharing different organizational or social spheres with the organization in question that may espouse different values and influences to the organization and actors within it through normative measures. It may be actors that are part of a similar organizational field, but also others capable of applying normative pressure, such as the media or academic environments. Such actors encourage particular forms of action, logics, and goals, and accordingly may favour particular kinds of translation to others, exerting indirect power (through knowledge, legitimacy or prestige). Nevertheless, it may also be more direct stakeholders that have some kind of formal authority and may be able to exert power directly (coercive pressure) through control over resources, decision-making competencies or the like. Just as organizations are embedded in specific political, social and historical contexts, so too do they individually form a specific context. As ideas or practices find their way into organizations, they never enter into vacuums or empty halls. Instead, they meet ideas, practices and rules embedded in the institutional and organizational history. Some of those ideas and logics prevalent during organizational genesis, or on which the organization is built, as an example, may have fairly significant path dependency implications, years on. The Gates Foundation, *inter alia*, is largely build on a foundation of dominant notions of societal progress through technology, innovation and measurability, and an inherent scepticism towards all things political, which greatly shapes how it relates to new ideas and practices.

Development projects as systems of continuous meaning negotiation and reinterpretation

Lastly, the actual field of global development has certain consequences for the way we should consider how ideas move and change between the different organizational layers, requiring some elaboration. The perhaps most distinctive feature of many development organizations is the fragmented or decentralized structure of separated head office and local implementing bodies, whether directly (as in a public aid agency's embassy) or indirectly (as in an independent implementing agency) associated with the organization, creating not just physical but political, cognitive, and cultural space between the two. One piece of work that has dealt with this decentralization of development management is Engberg-Pedersen's study of the Danish development agency Danida.[63] He highlights the apparent twofold purpose of decentralization: making donor support more relevant and flexible with respect to the recipient country's preferences and as a tool to 'Assemble the troops on the donor side'. The distance between agencies basically means that 'Decentralization is likely to strengthen the separation of policies from aid-management practices',[64] because head offices and embassies or implementing agencies face different realities. Taking decentralization one step further, we may even understand development management as forms of multi-level governance. As Chapter 7 in particular will show, the organizational context of development carries quite some resemblance to forms of multi-level governance as we know it elaborated in public administration, because of its 'multiscalarity' (understood as 'A property of trans-scalar action, or action across more than one geographical scale'[65]). The notion of multi-level governance comes out of the conceptual work of EU studies, emerging from the rescaling of the territorial articulation of the nation-state. By following this work, we can come to understand the entirety of the

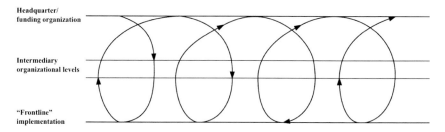

Figure 2.1 Development as systems of continuous meaning negotiation and reinterpretation.

organizational arrangement surrounding the management of development projects as systems of continuous negotiation of meaning and translation at several territorial and organizational tiers.[66]

The notion of a 'system' in this quasi-definition connotes how development projects are embedded in sets of nested organizations and organizational levels that are mutually dependent, and among whom translation and reinterpretation processes continue to shape the project. Most development projects function in a hierarchical form of governance where a donor, somewhere, has the last say on financial and formal policy matters, but this does not mean that there is no room for interpretation and ideational influence along the chain – quite the opposite. There is a natural difference in formal authority that sees more money and power concentrated in Seattle than with the local implementing agency in India, but, beyond material resources, different forms of power flow in complex ways that potentially allow for influence at all levels. What we can witness then are fluid spheres of influence, often manifested in different forms of resistance, as we will see later. This has consequences for translation processes and leads us to understand that policies or projects may be transformed between every organizational level as different actors potentially reinterpret them, and implementing agencies not only conform then, but also actively participate in interpreting and thus transforming projects and policy.

Final remarks

To understand the Gates Foundation and its rise to power is to not only account for its political, economic and normative influence today, but also to appreciate its history and development, however short that may be. It is to understand where it comes from and the changes it has been through over the last almost 20 years – changes that have significantly altered its ways of behaving and operating. In this chapter, I have woven different theoretical perspectives together on the power of ideas and normative change, influences that have greatly formed the Gates Foundation's trajectory. I have done so through arguments for an increasing focus on organizational and institutional change necessary to dismantle sweeping statements of disruption in global development from the entrance of new actors, and in particular because of a dire need to turn attention towards these new actors themselves, lifting their lids to explore and understand what makes them that which we consider them. Throughout the remaining parts of the book, these different abstract concepts and notions will be unfolded and put to use in tangible meetings between the foundation and organizations, actors, and ideas. Next, we gradually approach the Gates Foundation by moving through the contextual layers of new actors, private foundations, and the role of these in global development.

Notes

1 Byrkjeflot, H., Strandgaard-Pedersen, J. and Svejenova, S. 2013. 'From label to practice: the process of creating new Nordic cuisine', *Journal of Culinary Science and Technology* 11(1): 36–55.
2 Fligstein, N. 1990. *The Transformation of Corporate Control.* Cambridge, MA: Harvard University Press.
3 Dingwerth, K. and Pattberg, P. 2009. 'World politics and organizational fields: the case of transnational sustainability governance', *European Journal of International Relations* 15(4): 707–743.
4 Vetterlein, A. and Moschella, M. 2014. 'International organizations and organizational fields: explaining policy change in the IMF', *European Political Science Review* 6(1): 143–165.
5 Giddens, A. 1979. *Central Problems in Social Theory: Action, Structure and Contradiction in Social Analysis.* Berkeley, CA: University of California Press.
6 DiMaggio, P. J. and Powell, W. 1983. 'The iron cage revisited: institutional isomorphism and collective rationality in organizational fields', *American Sociological Review* 48(2): 147–160.
7 DiMaggio and Powell, 1983.
8 Keck, M. and Sikkink, K. 1998. *Activists beyond Borders.* Ithaca, NY: Cornell University Press; Finnemore, M. and Sikkink, K. 1998. 'International norm dynamics and political change', *International Organization* 52(4): 887–917; Risse, T., Ropp, S. and Sikkink, K. (eds) 1999. *The Power of Human Rights*, Cambridge: Cambridge University Press.
9 Boxenbaum, E. and Jonsson, S. 2008. 'Isomorphism, diffusion and decoupling', in *The SAGE Handbook of Organizational Institutionalism*, edited by D. A. Buchanan and A. Bryman, Thousand Oaks, CA: Sage, 602–620.
10 Dingwerth and Pattberg, 2009.
11 DiMaggio and Powell, 1983.
12 Meyer, J. and Rowan, B. 1977. 'Institutionalized organizations: formal structure as myth and ceremony', *American Journal of Sociology* 83(2): 340–363.
13 Boxenbaum and Jonsson, 2008.
14 Meyer and Rowan, 1977.
15 Scott, W. R. 1992. *Institutions and Organizations, 1st Edition*, Thousand Oaks, CA: Sage.
16 Streeck, W. and Thelen, K. 2005. 'Introduction: institutional change in advanced political economies', in *Beyond Continuity: Institutional Change in Advanced Political Economies*, edited by W. Streeck and K. Thelen, Oxford: Oxford University Press, 1–39.
17 DiMaggio, P. 1988. 'Interest and agency in institutional theory' in *Institutional Patterns and Organizations: Culture and Environment*, edited by L. G. Zucker, Cambridge, MA: Ballinger; Maguire, S., Hardy, C. and Lawrence, T. 2004. 'Institutional entrepreneurship in emerging fields: HIV/AIDS treatment and advocacy in Canada', *Academy of Management Journal* 47(5): 657–679.

18 Battilana, J., Leca, B. and Boxenbaum, E. 2009. 'How actors change institutions: toward a theory of institutional entrepreneurship', *Academy of Management Annals* 3(1): 65–107.

19 Hardy, C. and Maguire, S. 2008. 'Institutional entrepreneurship', in *The Sage Handbook of Organizational Institutionalism*, edited by R. Greenwood, C. Oliver, K. Sahlin-Andersson and R. Suddaby, Thousand Oaks, CA: Sage, 99–129.

20 Beckert, J. 1999. 'Agency, entrepreneurs, and institutional change. The role of strategic choice and institutionalized practices in organization', *Organization Studies* 20(5): 777–799.

21 Battilana, et al. 2009.

22 Lawrence and Suddaby, 2006.

23 Schatzki, T. R., Knorr-Cetina, K. and von Signy, E. 2001. *The Practice Turn in Contemporary Theory*. London: Routledge.

24 Giddens, A. 1979. *Central Problems in Social Theory: Action, Structure and Contradiction in Social Analysis*. Berkeley, CA: University of California Press; Bourdieu, P. 1977. *Outline of a Theory of Practice*. Cambridge: Cambridge University Press.

25 Schatzki, et al. 2001.

26 Blackler, F. and Regan, S. 2006. 'Institutional reform and the reorganization of family support services', *Organization Studies* 27(12): 1843–1861.

27 Cornwall, A. 2007. 'Buzzwords and fuzzwords: deconstructing development discourse', *Development in Practice* 17(4/5): 471–484.

28 Sehnbruch, K., Burchell, B., Agloni, N. and Piasna, A. 2013. 'Human development and decent work: why some concepts succeed and others fail to impact the development literature', *Development and Change* 46(2): 197–224.

29 Land, K. C., Deane, G. and Blau, J. R. 1991. 'Religious pluralism and church membership: a spatial diffusion model', *American Sociological Review* 56(2): 237–249.

30 Strang, D. and Meyer, J. W. 1994. 'Institutional conditions for diffusion', in *Institutional Environments and Organizations: Structural Complexity and Individualism*, edited by R. W. Scott and J. W. Meyer, Thousand Oaks, CA: Sage, 100–113.

31 Ibid.

32 Rogers, E. 1962. *Diffusion of Innovations.* New York, NY: Free Press; Ansari, S. M., Fiss, P. C. and Zajac, E. J. 2010. 'Made to fit: how practices vary as they diffuse', *Academy of Management Review* 35(1): 67–92; March, J. G. 1999. *The Pursuit of Organizational Intelligence.* Malden, MA: Blackwell.

33 Latour, B. 1986. 'The powers of association', in *Power, Action and Belief: A New Sociology of Knowledge*, edited by John Law, London: Routledge, 264–280.

34 Callon, M. and Latour, B. 1981. 'Unscrewing the big leviathan: how actors macrostructure reality and how sociologists help them to do so', in *Advances in Social Theory and Methodology: Toward an Integration of Micro- and Macro-Sociologies*, edited by K. D. Knorr-Cetina and A. V. Cicourel, Boston, MA: Routledge & Kegan Paul, 277–304.

35 Latour, 1986.

36 Czarniawska, B. and Joerges, G. 1996. 'Travels of ideas' in *Translating Organizational Change*, edited by B. Czarniawska and G. Joerges, Berlin: De Gruyter Studies in Organization, 13–49.

37 Sevon, G. 1996. 'Organizational imitation in identity transformation', in *Translating Organizational Change*, edited by B. Czarniawska and G. Joerges, Berlin: De Gruyter Studies in Organization, 49–69.

38 Nadelmann, E. A. 1990. 'Global prohibition regimes: the evolution of norms in international society', *International Organization* 44(4): 479–526; Acharya, A. 2004. 'How ideas spread: whose norms matter? Norm localization and institutional change in Asian regionalism', *International Organization* 58(2): 239–275; Checkel, J. T. 1999. 'Norms, institutions, and national identity in contemporary Europe' *International Studies Quarterly* 43(1): 83–114; Keck, M. and Sikkink, K. 1998. *Activists beyond Borders.*

Ithaca, NY: Cornell University Press; Risse, T., Ropp, S. and Sikkink, K. (eds) 1999. *The Power of Human Rights*. Cambridge: Cambridge University Press.
39 Finnemore, M. and Sikkink, K. 1998. 'International norm dynamics and political change', *International Organization* 52(4): 887–917.
40 Levitt, P. and Merry, S. 2009. 'Vernacularization on the ground: local uses of global women's rights in Peru, China, India and the United States', *Global Networks* 9(4): 441–461.
41 Ibid.
42 Dwyer, P. and Ellison, N. 2009. '"We nicked stuff from all over the place": policy transfer or muddling through?', *Policy & Politics* 37(3): 389–407.
43 Johnson, B. and Hagström, B. 2005. 'The translation perspective as an alternative to the policy diffusion paradigm: the case of the Swedish methadone maintenance treatment', *Journal of Social Policy* 34(3): 365–388; Stone, D. 2012. 'Transfer and translation of policy', *Policy Studies* 33(6), 483–499.
44 Boxenbaum, E. and Battilana, J. 2005. 'Importation as innovation: transposing managerial practices across fields', *Strategic Organization* 3(4): 355–383. Strang and Meyer, 1994.
45 Acharya, 2004.
46 Maguire, et al. 2009.
47 Brown, A. D., Colville, I. and Pye, A. 2015. 'Making sense of sensemaking in organization studies', *Organization Studies* 36(2): 265–277.
48 Czarniawska and Joerges, 1996.
49 DiMaggio, 1988.
50 Benford, R. D. and Snow, D. A. 2000. 'Framing processes and social movements: an overview and assessment', *Annual Review of Sociology* 26: 611–639.
51 Schein, E. H. 2010. *Organizational Culture and Leadership, 4th Edition*. Hoboken, NJ: John Wiley & Sons, Inc.
52 See Mosse, D. 2005. 'Global governance and the ethnography of international aid', in *The Aid Effect: Giving and Governing in International Development*, edited by D. Mosse and D. Lewis, London: Pluto Press, 1–37; Oestrich, J. 2007. *Power and Principle: Human Rights Programming in International Organizations*. Washington, DC: Georgetown University Press.
53 Czarniawska and Joerges, 1996; Latour, 1986; Boxenbaum, E. 2006. 'Lost in translation: the making of Danish diversity management', *American Behavioral Scientist* 49(7), 939–948.
54 Saka, A. 2004. 'The cross-national diffusion of work systems: translation of Japanese operations in the UK', *Organization Studies* 35(2): 209–228.
55 Barnett, M. and Finnemore, M. 2004. *Rules for the World: International Organizations in Global Politics*. Ithaca, NY: Cornell University Press.
56 Nadelmann, 1990; Strang and Meyer, 1994.
57 Mamman, A. 2002. 'The adoption and modification of management ideas in organizations: towards an analytical framework', *Strategic Change* 11(7): 379–389; Perkmann, M. and Spicer, A. 2007. 'Healing the scars of history: projects, skills and field strategies in institutional entrepreneurship', *Organization Studies* 28(7): 1101–1122.
58 Mosse, D and Lewis, D. 2006. 'Theoretical approaches to brokerage and translation in development', in *Development Brokers and Translators: The Ethnography of Aid and Agencies*, edited by D. Lewis and D. Mosse, Boulder, CO: Kumarian Press, Inc., 1–27; Bierschenk, T. and Olivier de Sardan, J. P. 2014. 'Studying the dynamics of African bureaucracies: an introduction to states at work', in *States at Work: Dynamics of African Bureaucracies*, edited by T. Bierschenk and J. P. Olivier de Sardan, Leiden: Koninklikje Brill, 1–33.
59 See Long, N. and Long, A. (eds) 1992. *Battlefields of Knowledge: The Interlocking of Theory and Practice in Social Research and Development*. London: Routledge.
60 Lipsky, M. 1980. *Street-Level Bureaucrats*. New York, NY: Russel Sage.

61 Lipsk, 1980; Brodkin, E. 2011. 'Policy work: street-level organizations under new managerialism', *Journal of Public Administration Research and Theory* 21(1): 253–277.
62 See Rottenburg, R. 2009. *Far-Fetched Facts. A Parable of Development Aid.* Cambridge, MA: MIT Press.
63 Engberg-Pedersen, L. 2014. 'Bringing aid management closer to reality: the experience of Danish bilateral development cooperation', *Development Policy Review* 32(1): 113–131.
64 Ibid.
65 Sommerville, P. (2011) 'Multiscalarity and neighbourhood governance', *Public Policy and Administration* 26(1): 81–105.
66 For the original definition of multi-level governance in EU Studies see Marks, G. 1993. 'Structural policy and multilevel governance in the EC', in *The State of the European Community*, edited by A. Cafruny and G. Rosenthal, New York, NY: Lynne Rienner, 391–410.

3 Rising powers, American capitalism and private foundations

Over the past decade, the once 'silent revolution' from rising powers with its alleged subtle changes to global development[1] has ignited into a loud disruptive force. Whether public or private in form, these actors have ascended to the forefront of discussions on the nature and future of development. And we do seemingly not have to look very far into contemporary international relations to see this reflected in the political realm as well. Consider the Sustainable Development Goals, a strong normative and political framework guiding global development work towards 2030. As the 2015 UN General Assembly looked to formally end the negotiation of the goals and ratify the new framework, Western countries were increasingly concerned with growing migration flows suddenly affecting them (albeit with just a fraction of the impact it had elsewhere in the world), and the temptations of turning their backs on global ambitions in the name of neo-isolationism and renationalization were strong. Yet, a new and ambitious framework was secured, not least because of the inclusive negotiation process that saw continued political pressure from non-state actors and states from the Global South. Compared with their side-lining during the finalization of the SDGs' predecessor, the Millennium Development Goals, the political influence of developing countries and non-state actors in the SDGs-process truly represents a recalibration of power.

Yet, not everyone was fully pleased with the shape of the Agenda 2030. In the Grand Ballroom of the Westin Seattle Hotel in early May of 2015, the Gates Foundation hosted its annual Global Partners Forum. From the stage, Mark Suzman, chief of policy and advocacy in the foundation, jokingly referred to the SDGs as 'No targets left behind', while Bill Gates himself referred to them as analogous to the Bible, adding that he would prefer to start with something simpler, 'Like the Ten Commandments'.[2] Other speakers at the meeting also poked fun at the SDGs, referring to them as a 'fantasy', a 'train wreck', or an unworkable and 'encyclopaedic' wish list. Though not exactly productive, the attitude of the foundation is fairly unsurprising, as Bill Gates has often publicly expressed his preference for the MDGs' more narrow and limited focus on core issues dear to the foundation. To the foundation, the SDGs appear far too political, complex, and unhelpful in their broad priorities, which is also why it heavily invested in promoting a much narrower, more measurable and perhaps more pragmatic agenda during the negotiation of the new goals, as opposed to the grandeur of the adopted SDGs.

The rising powers, from growing economies in Eastern Europe to American foundations, are as diverse in their dispositions, motivations and opinions as any group of actors, and approaching them as a collective force makes little sense. In this chapter, after attention to the question of (re)emerging actors in global development and the treatment of this question in academia, we will narrow the scope to the actor-group that forms the centre of attention in this book; private foundations. Driven by extreme individual wealth accumulation, private foundations have been distributing grants to and participated in international endeavours for more than a century, though with varying intensity of engagement. We end up at discussions on the nature of private foundations, including their distinct traits and the histories of difference between old and new foundations, as well as their approaches, before discussing the role of these in global development.

Rising powers and disruption in contemporary global development

The 'new actor' label has for some time now been associated with different groups of state and non-state actors. Emerging state actors in global development include new global powers,[3] industrializing countries,[4] and post-socialist states,[5] while non-state actors are often seen to encompass private foundations,[6] celebrity organizations,[7] religious organizations,[8] corporations and social enterprises, and novel forms of grass-roots or do-it-yourself development endeavours.[9] In a common narrative, these actors can be considered entrants to the field of global development, either because they have recently established cooperation programmes or because they are re-emerging as cooperation providers. Analyses highlighting the novelty of these actors tend to focus on their cooperation profiles, including descriptive overviews of priorities, resource flows, and the evolving institutional set-up for cooperation.[10] Attention is typically given to the question of whether new actors enter into global development with an interest in, and an ability to alter the field, and whether (and to what degree) they are socializing to already dominant norms and practices, thus reinforcing existing cooperation approaches. Advocates of the first line of thought typically highlight the role of these actors as potential competitors or alternatives to established cooperation providers and modes of operation.[11] It is a perspective that largely sees the architecture of global development as being in a state of flux, even to a point of systemic fracturing, initially emphasized as a silent revolution driven by the attractiveness of alternative approaches to recipient countries.[12] These shifts have given way to new paradigms aimed at re-centring power away from the North,[13] though with changes perhaps more strongly traceable in discourses than in the actual modes of cooperation employed by new actors.[14]

In particular, South–South Cooperation (SSC) has been presented as a distinctive model compared with OECD–DAC development cooperation approaches. SSC is often taken to reflect respect for principles of solidarity, (political) non-interference and equality between partners, and offered as a cooperation form that challenges the unequal power relations characterizing North–South relations.[15] In addition to such components, SSC is also often associated with particular cooperation modalities, which tend to privilege enhancing economic growth over multidimensional poverty reduction.[16] These modalities include the exchange of knowledge, technology and human resources as well as project funding directed to infrastructure or concessional lending, at times tied to the purchase of goods and services from cooperation providers.[17] Triangular cooperation is another example of a new cooperation modality associated with SSC, often perceived as a mechanism to break with the North–South aid dichotomy by emphasizing a collaborative relationship among cooperation providers with diverse experiences and competences.[18] From a critical perspective, the concept of South–South Cooperation has been portrayed as an attempt to depoliticize development, presenting a 'natural' congruity between states across the Global South that are in fact very different,[19] with the emphasis on horizontal partnerships in SSC discourse downplaying the presence of economic and power asymmetries in cooperation relationships.[20] The neglect of power relations in the conceptualization of SSC is problematic both with respect to how relations among SSC partners are characterized – China and South Sudan are clearly not equal partners – and with respect to the assumption of distinctiveness of SSC principles from OECD–DAC approaches, given that national ownership of development processes represents a cornerstone of the normative aid effectiveness framework. While SSC discourse clearly breaks with unequal power relations dominating North–South relations, whether the practiced mode of cooperation in fact does the same remains an open question.

In a related perspective questioning the taken-for-granted interest and capacity of the new actors to alter the field of development, some are asking whether the difference between new and old is actually as genuine as sometimes postulated[21] and underlining that both groups are exceptionally diverse.[22] Acknowledging that new actors carry alternative understandings of the appropriate balance between the state, market, and civil society in promoting development objectives, Banks and Hulme[23] question the transformative potential of new actors because of their neglect of civil society. Quadir[24] draws attention to the material basis for influencing the global development architecture, arguing that resources are a key determining factor and that actors must increase the scale of resources provided in order to truly alter the field. These studies point to the linkage between the presence of diverse actors and power dynamics at different levels of analysis, whether assessing the potential for collective action to change global development cooperation norms or their leverage within the countries where they disburse resources. Lastly, a third perspective falls in between the first two by seeking to move away from the descriptions of individual actors and the opposition of established and new cooperation provider groups, emphasizing instead the processes of interaction among the varied actors and their contributions to reshaping the global institutional frameworks for development cooperation. Woods[25] and Chin and Frolic[26] emphasize how emerging donors generally have little interest in collaborative or multilateral frameworks, mainly because of their limited influence on these bodies. Brautigam[27] similarly highlights China's limited and largely symbolic engagement at this level because of the inability of Chinese aid to fit with ODA definitional requirements.

Ultimately, this book emphasizes that new actors are dynamic, subject to internally- and externally-driven change, and as likely to go through changes themselves as they are to espouse changes in the field. As an extremely diverse group of state and non-state actors, they enter into global development with differing levels of ambition, authority and legitimacy, eventually also responding differently to the pressures that are unavoidable in this field, whether from other organizations, ideas, etc. From the broad sweeps of the new actors research we now move on to the specific group of actors that the Gates Foundation represents – the private foundations.

American capitalism and private foundations

The historical antecedents of philanthropy and organized giving tread a thousand-year-old path. Every major culture or religion has encouraged not just philanthropic giving, whether to those individuals less fortunate than oneself or to the institutions of society, from churches to hospitals, but also organized forms of giving that have seen vast amounts of funds change hands. Whether in China or Denmark, ancient Rome or Persia, Islam or Judaism, philanthropic endeavours have cut across motives of universal human impulses of altruism, expected responsibility to give back, and the power and influence obtained by gifting away funds and resources. Continuously through history, the accumulation of wealth and private giving in the hands of a few organizations or institutions has caused upheaval and scrutiny, from the Roman Emperor Severus' withdrawal of the right to will property to the church because its wealth had reached proportions that allowed it to self-confidently challenge the emperor and the state,[28] to the Gates Foundation's agenda-setting influence in contemporary global politics. Vast funds have for thousands of years allowed men and women to create institutions in society that can drive the form of change that the founder sees fit, not always for the benefit of the greater good of society.[29] There is, though, a significant difference between the concept of philanthropy and the private foundations dealt with here, namely that the abstract altruism affiliated with philanthropy is not nearly guaranteed in the endeavours of private foundations (this is also one of the reasons why this book refers to them as such and not as philanthropic foundations). The word philanthropy itself originates from Greek and can be translated as the 'The love of humanity'. It is probably naïve to expect all private foundations to demonstrate this.

Modern-day private foundations emerged in the late 19th century as some of the world's early billionaires increasingly searched for ways to spend their fortunes. During this golden age of American philanthropy, incredible wealth was generated as rapid industrialization swept across the country. Most famous were the three individuals Andrew Carnegie, John D. Rockefeller and Henry Ford, the frontrunners of contemporary philanthropic giving.[30] The Carnegie Corporation was founded in 1911 as the first of the 'big three' foundations, holding the fortune of Andrew Carnegie. Growing up in an impoverished Scottish family that had emigrated to the US before the Civil War, Carnegie's compelling story is one that saw him progress from a bobbin boy in a cotton factory to the owner of several companies at the age of 33. Introduced to methods of mass production of steel in 1872, Carnegie built an empire through the steel furnaces of Pittsburgh, eventually being bought out of his companies in 1900 by J. P. Morgan for $492 million (equivalent to $15 billion today). Philanthropy had always been important to Carnegie, and in 1889 he published writings on the act of private giving in the *North American Review* under the title 'The gospel of wealth'. Proclaiming the disgrace of dying rich, this work has immortalized him in philanthropic circles, almost just as much as his foundation that would form some 20 years later. Before organizing his giving, Carnegie built more than 2,000 local libraries in the US and set up many of the Carnegie institutions we know today, such as the Carnegie Endowment for International Peace. In the first decades since its formation in 1911, the Carnegie Corporation, which was given the last parts of Carnegie's fortune, largely supported other Carnegie institutions and provided aid to higher education. When Alan Pifer took over as president in 1967, the foundation recalibrated its focus towards disadvantaged groups, pursuing equal opportunity for these, particularly in education. Despite having to settle for a life as a large-but-limited foundation in the second half of the 20th century, it was one of the first to truly engage in global development, conducting ambitious international grant-making on education in East and Southern Africa from the late 1920s. Today, the Carnegie Corporation of New York is just within the top 25 of US foundations, with assets of approximately $3 billion and annual grant-making around $100 million.

Since its inception two years after the Carnegie Corporation, in 1913, the Rockefeller Foundation has been a powerful force in the advancement of science, and today its 'scientific philanthropy' is often compared with the technological mantras of the Gates Foundation, as extrapolated later in Chapter 6. The patriarch of the Rockefeller family was of course John D. Rockefeller Sr (1839–1937), a fiercely contested figure of American capitalist history whose frequently illegal and unethical business practices made him a symbol of the 'robber barons' metaphor. His oil business gained speed after the end of the Civil War, with the forming of Standard Oil, and, following a strategy of aggressive market takeover, he absorbed 22 of his 26 Cleveland competitors in less than four months (of 1872), during what would become known as the 'Cleveland Massacre'. Ultimately, the strategy of industry monopolization resulted in Standard Oil being responsible for 90 per cent of the US oil market. When Rockefeller's fortune was at its highest he was encouraged to set up a formal foundation, not least by his trusted advisor. It just so happens that this man, who would go on to define 'The principles of scientific giving', was named Gates. Not Bill, but Frederick. By way of Gates' advice, Rockefeller institutionalized his philanthropy in 1913 and made his own son president of the new foundation. There was plenty of funds to take from to form it, as, adjusted for inflation, Rockefeller's fortune amounted to almost $400 billion, unsurprisingly making him the wealthiest man in modern history. Over its lifetime, the Rockefeller Foundation has provided more than $14 billion in grants, primarily to issues of education (e.g., transforming the University of Chicago) and science (particularly the medical and natural sciences). In developing countries it is particularly known for its support to disease eradication (targeting hookworm, yellow fever and malaria), agricultural technologies and particularly funding of the Green Revolution (starting with agricultural projects in Mexico in 1941) and later AGRA (with the Gates Foundation).

As the latest bloomer of the 'big three' of modern philanthropy in the 20th century, the Ford Foundation was established in 1936, some 24 years after Carnegie's first efforts in organized philanthropy. For the first decade the foundation was mainly a vehicle to provide gifts to the Ford family's favourite charities (including the Henry Ford Hospital in Detroit and the Edison Institute) while awaiting the receipt of Henry Ford's fortune so as to avoid estate taxes. During this time the Ford Company was in significant decline, not least owing to Henry Ford who was in his 80s and on the brink of madness, said to have driven his son Edsel to death by harassment, and leaving the formal hold over the company to disconcerting individuals (in particular Harry Bennett, a notorious union-buster who was a former head of Ford's 'internal security' and famous for having lions as pets and practising his gun-aim inside his office). Over the next years, however, Edsel Ford's widow and his son Henry Ford II managed to regain control over the company and secure its turnaround. After the death of Henry Ford, and the reacquisition of the company into family hands, the foundation was quick to establish itself as a major force in US philanthropy with assets many times greater than both Rockefeller and Carnegie. By 1950, the president of MIT had been tasked with producing recommendations for the foundation's future work, and in a report advised it to tackle issues concerning 'Man's relation to man, not his relation to nature'. Instead of science and technology, the foundation centred around issues of world peace, democracy, economy, and education, characteristic of the hopeful spirit that had replaced the human terrors of the Second World War. In the McCarthy-spirited US of the 1950s, the emphasis on social issues often led to heavy accusations of the foundation being a 'communist front'.[31] From 1956–1965, Henry T. Heald steered the foundation in a more conservative direction, and also gradually away from international activities. Since then, however, though naturally with fluctuating levels of intensity, the Ford Foundation has been deeply engaged in international social and political matters, not least as they pertain to civil rights, gender equality, and education. In 2015 the foundation announced that all of its future grants would target inequality in its many forms, and it is currently the second biggest US Foundation with assets of $12 billion and annual grant-making of $500 million.

The 20th century can largely be seen as a period of the mass-institutionalization and organization of private giving, increasing not just the volume of philanthropy but also systematizing the ways in which it is provided. For many of the older foundations, their gradual evolvement over time saw them develop from traditional family-style charities to professionalized institutions, some with great distance from the founders that once provided their initial assets. This part of the history of private foundations is also one of recurrent critique and conflict, especially so in the US, where the influence of these have arguably been felt the strongest. These apprehensions have related to both democratic concerns over the extent of influence from private foundations, but also to the type of influence exercised, emanating out of both sides of the political spectrum, from the support of unfortunate scientific research directly benefiting the Third Reich to the support of strong liberal agendas of social reform. One of the strongest examples could be witnessed during the 1960s, when an anti-foundation movement formed with Texan Congressman Wright Patman at the helm. As a first witness during a 1969 House committee hearing on tax reform, Patman set forth a striking critique that 'Put most bluntly, philanthropy – one of mankind's most noble instincts – has been perverted into a vehicle for institutionalized, deliberate evasion of fiscal and moral responsibility to the nation'.[32] After the hearings, the committee posted a press release that issued a harsh judgment on foundations, and the battle shifted to the Senate. Here, the end result was the Tax Reform Act of 1969. Though entailing a new regulatory system, new regulatory sanctions, a new tax on investment income and new restrictions on the deductibility of property gifts for private foundations, the de facto influence on grant-making for foundations was limited. Today, struggles about the tax-exempt conditions of foundations occasionally makes it to the forefront of US political debate, though seldom with the negative drive manifested 50 years ago.

Private foundations today

Wealth creation at the same heights as in the late-19th-century and early-20th-century industrial expansion can be said to have characterized the last 30 years, and it is from this period in time that we can witness the amassed fortunes of today's billionaires being given away as charity to the developing world. In 1972, Waldemar A. Nielsen, in his scrutiny of American private foundations, wrote that the combined assets of the country's 25,000 foundations, amounting to approximately $20 billion, was a clear sign of megalocephaly. Dwarfing these numbers, there are around 86,000 foundations today in the US, though the combined assets of these 'only' equal $90 billion, which is less than the numbers for 1972 if calculated for inflation. A private foundation is often understood, based on Frank Emerson Andrews' definition derived from his seminal work on the societal role of these in America in the early 1950s, as a 'Non-governmental, non-profit organization having a principal fund of its own, managed by its trustees or directors, and established to maintain or aid social, educational, charitable, religious, or other activities serving the common welfare'.[33] What separates these foundations from the many other types of non-governmental organizations with a mission to do good then is not least the 'Principal fund of its own', allowing it to exercise, in theory, complete self-determination. Through continuous reinvestment of the initial endowment made by the founding individuals, the foundation is excused from external resource allocation. This provides foundations with financial independence, perhaps even making them the most independent institutions in modern society,[34] but also greatly blurs lines of accountability. They may provide grants exclusively to other organizations or handle implementation of programmes and projects themselves. This is also likely to have consequences for in-country presence, as foundations handling implementation are more likely to have local or country offices, whereas the majority of the work in grant-making foundations is done from headquarters, often in the originating country. Likewise, they may be established by a limited set of individuals or a company, which in turn is likely to determine the focus and field of the organization beyond providing the financial means.

We oftentimes hear claims of a direct line between the early philanthropic endeavours in the US and the current generation emanating out of Silicon Valley. For one, as we shall see later in this book, overlaps between the 'scientific philanthropy' of Rockefeller and the technological bias of contemporary philanthropists, and especially the Gates Foundation, are pronounced. Though articulated almost a hundred years apart, both the (early) Rockefeller Foundation and the Gates Foundation see science as the surest means of advancing society. Both foundations have invested heavily in the development of vaccines against diseases such as hookworm infection, yellow fever, or malaria, and both have (or have had for extended periods), international divisions for health, natural or medical sciences. Frederick Gates, John D. Rockefeller Sr's philanthropic advisor, framed this belief clearly:

> If science and education are the brain and nervous system of civilization, health is its heart. It is the organ that pushes the vital fluid into every part of the social organism, enabling each organ to function and measuring and limiting its effective life ... Disease is the supreme ill of life and it is the main source of almost all other human ills – poverty, crime, ignorance, vice, inefficiency, hereditary taint, and many other evils.[35]

Bill Gates has repeated this view a hundred years after Frederick Gates, explaining to a Microsoft Faculty Summit in 2013 that 'The average IQ in sub-Saharan Africa is about 82 and that's nothing to do with genetics or race or anything like that – that's disease and that's what disease does to you, and that's why these things are such an extreme poverty trap'.[36] In opposition to both Frederick and Bill Gates, many would likely hold that the opposite is just as much (if not more) true, namely that disease is a consequence of poverty, not the other way round. A related similarity pertains to the choice of issues or areas of intervention for the foundations. Though these often lay claim to their innovative nature, the overriding issues have largely remained the same across a century of foundation giving. The Gates Foundation's predominant funding of education and health, as an example, was more or less mirrored in the broader US foundation world 50 years ago, where 33 per cent was provided to education and 14 per cent to health. These are naturally wide categorizations and the approach in how to fund and tackle specific issues have certainly changed, yet this illustrates that the newer foundations often reflect the old block when it comes to selecting areas of grant-making.

An additional point of similarity is how they have all been strongly shaped by, and appeared as agents of, capitalism. All of them laid the foundations for their fortunes through innovations and different forms of industrial or techno-logical progress, but likely only cemented their positions because of aggressive business skills, from buying up all local newspapers to ensure they would only feature positive product reviews, to controlling the lives of their employees (Ford famously had a large 'social department' investigating employees to ensure no drinking, gambling or parental sloppiness), to the widespread practice of vacuum-ing up smaller businesses in the same field (particularly applicable to Carnegie and Gates).[37] This last point deserves a few more words as, for several of the magnates, old and new, it led to strong monopolistic tendencies and accusations of unfair industry domination. Rockefeller, Carnegie and Gates have all seen charges of illegal monopoly from the US state (Henry Ford, on the other hand, was often able to present himself as an antithesis and an anti-monopolist to his contemporaries). Standard Oil, Rockefeller's company, created intense contro-versy during its entire lifetime for its strong monopoly and industry control (up through the 1880s, 80–90 per cent of the world's oil was refined by Standard Oil), underselling competitors, and for innovating a new legal entity that allowed it to gather and control companies in every state of the US (cross-state operation was illegal at that time) under one roof.[38] Though many associate Bill Gates with his early days of developing software, Gates was known for the greatest part of his working life in Microsoft for his uncompromising management style and for the company's aggressive product strategies. The latter led to the 2001 *United States* vs *Microsoft Corp* antitrust case in which the company was accused of abusing monopoly power, and the 2007 *Microsoft Corp* vs *Commission* case in which the European Commission accused the company of abusing its dominant position in the market.

Despite these similarities, however, there are pronounced differences as well. Industry is perhaps the first and most striking. Whereas early philanthropists made their fortunes in the fires of the industrial revolution (John D. Rockefeller famously revolutionized the petroleum industry, Andrew Carnegie the steel industry, and Henry Ford the automobile industry), the new foundations are built on riches reaped from digital technology and innovation (with Microsoft at the centre repre-sented by Bill Gates of course, but also Facebook in the form of Mark Zuckerberg and Jeff Bezos' Amazon). A second difference relates to spatiality. While the first generation of philanthropists was largely based in the Midwest (and further east in Massachusetts), the new generation has emerged on the West Coast of the US, in Silicon Valley, in the Bay Area south of San Francisco. Despite both groups shaping the connectivity of people (from cars and railways to computers, email and Facebook), there is also a difference in spatiality that sees the newer genera-tion reaching the far corners of the globe, something the early philanthropists did not achieve. Lastly, there is an interesting difference in the type of skill or perhaps materiality that underpins the different fortunes. The new philanthropists have been characterized as nerds or hackers, famously working out of their parents' garages, with their skills being in coding or computer science. Contrasting this, the early philanthropists were deeply affiliated with manual labour, rarely conducting such themselves but widely required by their industries: from the assembly lines of mass production (Ford), and the early techniques of drilling, refining and transporting oil (Rockefeller), to the blast furnaces of steel production (Carnegie).

The new philanthrocapitalists

Modern organized philanthropy can be grouped into three distinct periods and approaches to giving and grant-making, of which we have visited the first two thus far.[39] Charity was characteristic of the late 19th century, with inadequate provision by governments and non-profits prompting foundations to provide social services. Eventually, as social security schemes were introduced, foundations began working in complementarity to forms of government support. Such an approach saw foundations generally assume roles that were equally being filled by religious and other institutions, with little sustainable impact and potential for further scaling, because of the short-term aim of providing food aid and the like. Scientific philanthropy, as a second phase, developed as increasingly professionalized and organized foundations were set up in the early 20th century. Not least because of mounting assets, many of these foundations developed considerable ambitions for what to target, and shifted focus towards addressing the causes rather than symptoms of issues such as poverty, to pursue a more lasting impact. Instead of providing services to the poor, funding research and education was perceived as a way to identify and understand, and thus provide the potential for, the eventual funding of solutions to the root causes of societal issues. In recent years, and as a third period, 'new scientific' approaches have seen the light of day, many of them overlapping across notions of strategic philanthropy, creative philanthropy, venture philanthropy, social (impact) investment and the like. Collectively, these favour the adoption of business techniques to foundation processes, aiming to shift philanthropy from altruistic charity to strategic social impact investment. This movement is not least led on by the emergence of the new generation of givers and foundations that hold Silicon Valley as their epicentre.

    For private foundations, then, the last hundred years has seen as many new developments and changes as it has seen insistence and stasis. The one continuous force running through this history seems to have been the growing encroachment of business into all sides of political and social life, and the privatization and commercialization of social action. Rather than just a new scientific philanthropy, the changes in contemporary foundations are perhaps better captured under the heading of philanthrocapitalism. In 2006, Matthew Bishop coined the term to describe what he perceived as a new generation of private foundations and individuals successfully applying a business approach to tackling global problems.[40] This new generation emphasizes efficiency and measurability, and their business-oriented approach may be considered a departure from traditional philanthropic practice.[41] This includes the deployment of diverse sets of financing tools, such as social impact bonds, equity, debt, loans, but also non-financial forms of support through networking and mentoring.[42]

At least three organizational processes of change have come to characterize contemporary foundation work as well as notions of philanthrocapitalism. The first concerns the adoption of proactive and strategic approaches. Traditional forms of grant-making have long emphasized 'responsive' and bottom-up approaches to philanthropy in which a board or group of selected individuals in the foundation would screen incoming proposals and accept those most convincing and in line with the foundation's mission.[43] At the heart of this approach is often belief in the necessity for grant proposals to emerge more naturally from the ground, to ensure ownership of projects, but also a reliance on local NGOs to know better where to intervene and how. Contrary to these forms of thinking, newer approaches to international foundation-giving have been described as high engagement and directive forms of grant-making, driven by an emphasis on direct involvement, efficiency, and effectiveness, oftentimes serving a purpose of increasing control over the manner and uses of funding.[44] Being more 'strategic' in this sense implies a top-down approach to grant-making that almost sets the foundation in the driver's seat when it comes to designing interventions, and thus in the endeavour of social problem solving. A tangible example of proactivity is the Ford Foundation's recent announcement that all its grants would now be targeted towards inequality in all its manifestations. Such a proclamation greatly narrows the scope for potential grants and clearly signifies a decision to proactively guide the future work of the foundation in a specific direction. Another tangible example of proactivity is the way in which many of the world's largest foundations today initiate first contact with and approach potential partners with project ideas, rather than waiting for them to submit proposals, often on the grounds of wanting to influence project design from its earliest stage.

The second process of change in contemporary foundations denotes intra-organizational capacity building. Traditionally, those who have been known to take decisions on grant-making are often not experts in the field within which the grant is to have an impact.[45] Instead, they have formal power to decide on grants by virtue of their organizational position. After decisions are made to fund certain proposals, responsibility for grants have traditionally been moved to programme officers whose main competence was in accounting and making sure that agreements on reporting were upheld by the grantee, i.e., that these could deliver what they in fact had promised. Increasing focus on more strategic or proactive modes of grant-making, on the other hand, requires quite an amount of expertise on the side of the foundation, relating this factor to the first. Engagement in not just identification of relevant partners and issues of intervention, but also in designing, monitoring and evaluating impact all the way from beginning to end requires an immense amount of expertise. Increasingly, then, some of the largest foundations have been hiring employees with specific issue-based expertise, not least in the field of development, from agriculture to microfinance to water management.[46] Issue-specific expertise thus moves from the grantees and partners inside the foundations themselves, underlining the point of how these new approaches to philanthropy blur the lines of knowledge and skill between funder and implementer.

The third point of change is an increasing focus on global grant-making. Perhaps most important because it captures the essence of why foundations are an important issue for the study of global development. Foundation and philanthropic giving to international causes has significantly increased over the last years. Foundations have traditionally focused their efforts on the near proximity of their founders or their headquarters, and targeted local libraries, schools or hospitals. While not fundamentally substituting this pattern of philanthropy, a growing amount of funds from private foundations and other philanthropy are used in relation to the developing world, either by directly investing there or by indirectly investing in organizations whose main work is there.[47] The increase in foundation spending on development-related issues alone is one of the primary reasons why we are witnessing such attention to private foundations in development. Not least because with mounting levels of funding follows political influence on global decision-making processes governing development work, but also because expectations from the development milieu increases as the material and immaterial influence of foundations does. It is obviously difficult to conclude that all foundations are going through such processes of change in recent years, and generalizing on account of several hundred thousand foundations around the world is not exactly wise. Yet these fairly transformational processes are not only experienced by the world's largest foundations, whether the Gates or Ford Foundation. In a historically development-aid-committed country such as Denmark, for example, many of the smaller foundations go through similar processes of active strategizing and professionalization, with ambitions to increasingly take the driver's seat in the implementation of their grant-making,[48] as they target it outwards to all corners of the world.

Private foundations in global development

In global development, private foundations have attracted increased attention over the last decade for their potential dual contribution of providing additional resources and bringing new approaches to the field.[49] The involvement of private foundations in global development is far from novel, however. The Rockefeller Foundation was active in the diffusion of Western medicine and health technologies to the Global South (and particularly China) from the 1920s onwards, but also in establishing the international health architecture, including the WHO's predecessor, the League of Nations Health Organization,[50] and later became involved in agricultural productivity and genetically modified crops in Asia and in Latin America, leading to the so-called 'Green Revolution'. In fact, the Rockefeller Foundation is sometimes described as having been the world's largest development actor until the 1940s, spending more funds internationally on development than any state.[51] The Carnegie Foundation likewise was active in educational programmes in Africa from the 1920s, while the Ford Foundation became a great supporter of civil society and democracy promotion in the second part of the 20th century.

After diminishing relative grant-making to and influence in global development since the Second World War, not least with the introduction of the large state aid programmes and the multilateral institutions, private foundations have once again today come to the forefront of global development. Though now with ambitions and resources far beyond those of earlier times. The Gates Foundation significantly embodies this movement, sufficiently rich and powerful to leave all other founda- tions in the dust, but other foundations have also stepped up their international involvement. As described, the growing attention to foundations in global devel- opment is equally driven by a massive scaling up of funds from these provided to international purposes, and a growing fatigue both from traditional development donors and towards these very same organizations from other actors. The first is difficult to account for in detail, as data on international foundation giving is poor at best. Few countries collect reliable data, and we are left to either rely on the OECD-DAC's surveys, with the newest concluding that, on average, $7.6 billion was provided in philanthropic giving to development from 2013–2015,[52] or on the Hudson Institute's significantly more optimistic estimation that around $64 billion was provided in global philanthropy in 2014.[53] The fairly modest but likely realistic estimation of the OECD-DAC means that the Gates Foundation is seen to account for 52 per cent of all global philanthropic spending to development, its grant-making 15 times larger than the second greatest benefactor, the Children's Investment Fund Foundation from the UK.

Thematically, global health remains the primary sector targeted by private foundations in development, estimated at $9.2 billion from 2013–2015, and far beyond the $2.9 billion granted to reproductive health and population, which forms the second-largest sector. Global health remains a foundation focus par excellence across the last 100 years, but if the Gates Foundation is taken out of the equation, education interestingly becomes the most favoured sector among foundations today, underscoring the special affinity from the foundation towards issues of global health, but perhaps also signals that they are crowding out or discouraging other foundations from contributing to this sector. Geographically, India is the greatest beneficiary of private grant-making to development, followed by Nigeria and Mexico, and in total two thirds of the philanthropic spending is provided to middle-income countries, a number that follows closely trends of ODA spending, in which aid to the Least Developed Countries has accounted for around one-third over the last years.[54] Just as the spending level of private foundations to LDCs follows that of traditional OECD-DAC donors (and even geographical prevalence – India remains the second largest recipient of gross ODA), so too do their main modes of operation when it comes to implementing or realizing development projects. The vast majority of grants to development from private foundations is channelled through third parties at around 81 per cent of their total spending. Almost two thirds of it is channelled and implemented through NGOs, research institutions, universities, PPPs or private enterprises, and the vast majority of that in the form of earmarked contributions allocated for a specific purpose or a specific country. The last third is predominantly provided to multilateral organizations (equalling around 20 per cent of all spending through third parties, not far from the 25 per cent that OECD-DAC donors channel through multilaterals as well), and a very small share of funds related to specific activities is implemented directly by foundations.

Proponents of private foundations often maintain that the institutional log-ics transferred from the business world by these organizations render them more successful in tackling issues in global development, and that these founda-tions are more innovative, effective and results-oriented than traditional donor organizations.[55] Likewise, in the mainstream literature on private foundations, new fortunes and philanthropic initiatives from emerging industries are praised as solutions to transnational problems.[56] Rising optimism among this group has given way to the perception that private actors and emerging private–public part-nerships are supplanting existing donor–recipient relations, and even prompting more sustainable forms of development.[57] Private aid, in this line of thought, is framed as a contrast to the unsuccessful top-down and centrally planned public aid programmes, able to deliver effective results by seeking out what Easterly,[58] in his searchers vs planners discussion, refers to as 'Opportunistic innovations'. This is a widespread conception among foundations and their strongest propo-nents, namely that they are significantly better placed than public aid agencies to task risks and fund innovations. They are certainly better placed with little accountability towards a tax-paying public (i.e., financial independence), but this innate ability and will to take risks has often been questioned. For one, the geo-graphical preference of foundations for projects in middle-income countries and thereby limited focus on the fragile LDCs certainly conflicts with a risk-bearing approach. Grant-making to middle-income countries is far more safe and effi-cient, both in terms of finances and impact, whereas engagement in LDCs will always be characterized by unsteady political, economic and social factors. On the one hand, the Gates Foundation is famous for its Grand Challenges in which smaller amounts are provided to high-risk projects on a competitive basis, yet on the other the vast majority of its largest grants are made to fairly conventional and low-risk engagements such as vaccine delivery, scholarships, and core fund-ing for different agencies and organizations. Though generalizing, it seems fair to make the conclusion that foundations certainly value high-risk investments above that of traditional donors, but also that it represents a small part of their overall endeavour, not least because project failure does not go well with another core ambition of foundations – impact effectiveness. This discussion also begs the question of whether risk-taking is in fact automatically productive or a posi-tive endeavour, something that will be further scrutinized in Chapter 6 where the Gates Foundation's experimental practices are discussed.

At the same time, there are others who question the involvement of private foundations in development, asking firstly whether there is altogether something genuinely new about these actors and their modes of operating in development, and, secondly, if they are at all able to deliver the results their proponents claim. These perspectives often hold that private actors may well be more effective in providing quick results in developing countries, but that some notes of caution are needed. Not least because the history of philanthropy is replete with scandals about misused funds.[59] Over the last 100 years, foundations have been used as often for shielding riches and fortunes from tax authorities, ensuring tax-exempt inheritance or straightforward salary disbursements to family members or friends, as they have for the greater good of the otherwise tax-paying public. And they have been used for dubious political purposes, whether in smearing presidential candidates through public campaigns, lobbying against socially progressive legislation, or even in counteracting the civil rights movement and the anti-apartheid movement in the second part of the 20th century. It is important to remember that foundations often appear as vehicles for those who provide the funds, and not all human beings aid purposes other than their own. Foundations, of course, do not work in a vacuum but rather in deeply social and political contexts, in which they influence the work of many organizations and the lives of millions of people. This only further emphasizes issues of accountability and transparency, a pertinent question as many private actors feel little need to be answerable to public scrutiny. This is also why some have long considered them to be 'The least accountable major institutions in America'.[60] They face limited pressure from accountability-influencing forces of government, and have historically functioned within an insulated culture that accepts and perhaps even encourages inappropriate levels of secrecy and independence.

In the US, private foundations are registered with the Internal Revenue Service as so-called 501(3)c organizations, and are thus obliged to publish their annual tax declarations but not much more, though most foundations provide some insight into their operations through annual reports. On their websites, some inform about grants in more or less systematic ways, from keeping a database of information on individual grants, to only telling success stories from selected grants. Most US foundations provide basic information about individual grants to the US Foundation Center's database, but such insight often only includes the size of the grant, the name of the grantee, and a few words on the focus of the grant. The Gates Foundation itself, as an example, has taken an unfortunate turn when it comes to something like annual reporting, even despite joining the International Aid Transparency Initiative (IATI) in late 2013 and some initial work on a plan on how to increase transparency. The 2000 annual report was 64 pages long and featured insights from leadership on intraorganizational processes, on ongoing programmatic and strategy work, and a comprehensive view on finances. The 2012 annual report, by comparison, was seven pages long and only featured a short introduction by then Chief Financial Officer Richard Henriques. From that point in time the annual reports would go on to only feature financial statements, while a new annual letter has been introduced in which the co-chairs, Bill and Melinda Gates, take up and elaborate upon an issue of importance to them. In fact, the latest available annual report only comprises a short letter from the CEO and a small set of figures, all of it directly on the foundation's webpage. Figure 3.1 below shows the gradual shrinking of the annual reporting exercise in quantitative terms for the Gates Foundation.

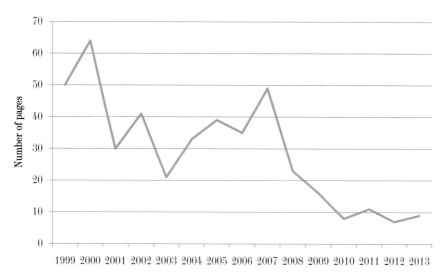

Figure 3.1 Size of annual reports from the Gates Foundation in pages, 1999–2013.
(Source: Gates Foundation reports, 1999–2013.)

The foundation would perhaps argue that most of this information is found on the website, but neither organizational restructuring and ongoing strategy nor programmatic work are featured online except for in exceptionally abstract forms. The only systematic annual update the public has access to thus remains the 990-PF tax return forms that the foundation is obliged by law to provide to the Internal Revenue Service, and the audited financial statements from KPMG, both requiring quite some accounting skills to fully comprehend. In spite of these developments, the Gates Foundation's IATI rating has developed from 'very poor' in the 2013 transparency index, to 'fair' in 2016. In 2012 and 2013 the Gates Foundation produced a series of podcasts with the intriguing name 'Inside the Gates Foundation', covering a series of issues pertaining to their internal workings and being a foundation-grantee, but these have since been removed and are no longer available.

The autonomous nature of many private foundations further entails a very limited interest in engagement in coordination, alignment or harmonization efforts with other donors. It is not exactly a productive behaviour for poverty-reducing efforts, as demonstrated by our knowledge of how duplication and fragmentation may arise, making it difficult to ensure effective and sustainable change in developing country contexts. Some foundations may be working as somewhat niche-fillers or from a perception that they occupy areas of intervention isolated from others, but the reality remains that no issues or sectors, no matter how narrow, can be pursued separately and without contact with others. In particular, many foundations working in development (including the Gates Foundation, as we shall see), often characterize their work as 'neutral' or 'apolitical' in arguments for why they do not need to be accounted for as or enter into harmonization and coordination efforts with other donors. Some established donors have earlier aired their concern over private foundations' influence on the implementation of the Paris Agenda,[61] which, despite seemingly suffering a slow and quiet death by way of donor-indifference, continues to comprise core values that deserve to be maintained. The risks of either influencing negatively (and perhaps even unknowingly) the work of others or of creating parallel implementation structures and thus further incoherencies at best, and counterproductive efforts at worst, remains pertinent.

Critics of the growing influence of private foundations in development further-more maintain that the transfer of entrepreneurial or business skills into the world of relief and development cooperation is not necessarily unproblematic. In particu-lar, many have portrayed the supposed superiority of business and managerialist approaches inherent in the commercial rhetoric of economism as conflicting with mainstream international development discourses.[62] Ramdas[63] has moved these arguments further to contend that social transformation is impossible to ensure by the foundations as long as they support economic models that enable inequality. The shift towards business approaches in global development efforts by private foundations also seems to have entailed changes in foundation–grantee relations. Jenkins[64] argues that traditional foundation–grantee relations were characterized by 'A coequal partnership', in which foundations attempted to contribute to societal change by supporting actors and institutions capable of inducing long-term systemic change. In contrast, the managerialist or business approaches of the new foundations imply much more paternalistic relations in which grantees are disempowered by foundation-centred problem-solving models or self-interests. Related to this, some hold that short-term projects and quick fixes driven by the zeal of the trustees will often be favoured over long-term impact for foundations.[65] This is surely the case for many foundations, but it is certainly not a critique we cannot also direct at traditional donor agencies who have furthered their own interests through bilateral agreements and projects ever since the genesis of development cooperation. Ultimately, whether we consider the ideology of business as inherently efficient, and the world a system where levers and handles can be pulled to change different parts and achieve an expected outcome, or social transformation a job that should not be left to market forces, private foundations are inescapable as politically and financially powerful actors in international political life. And of all the private foundations engaged in global development efforts, one has clearly risen to a position of power beyond all the others: the Bill and Melinda Gates Foundation. Next, we finally move our attention towards Seattle, home to history's most powerful private foundation.

Notes

1 Woods, N. 2008. 'Whose aid? Whose influence? China, emerging donors and the silent revolution in development assistance', *International Affairs* 84(6): 1205–1221.
2 Paulson, T. 2015. 'Gates Foundation rallies the troops to attack UN development goals', *Humanosphere* 6 May 2015; Paulson, T. 2015. 'Gates Foundation says it does support the U.N. development agenda', *Humanosphere* 11 May 2015.

3 Chaturvedi, S., Fues, T. and Sidiropoulos, E. 2012. *Development Cooperation and Emerging Powers: New Partners Or Old Patterns?* London: Zed Books; Mawdsley, E. 2010. 'Non-DAC donors and the changing landscape of foreign aid: the (in)significance of India's development cooperation with Kenya', *Journal of Eastern African Studies* 4(2): 361–379; Mawdsley, E. 2012. 'The changing geographies of foreign aid and development cooperation: contributions from gift theory', *Transactions of the Institute of British Geographers* 37(2): 256–272; Quadir, F. 2013. 'Rising donors and the new narrative of "South–South" cooperation: what prospects for changing the landscape of development assistance programmes?', *Third World Quarterly* 34(2): 321–338; Reilly, J. 2012. A norm-taker or a norm-maker? Chinese aid in Southeast Asia', *Journal of Contemporary China* 21(73): 71–91; Sidiropoulos, E., Pineda, J., Chaturverdi, S. and Fues, T. 2015. *Institutional Architecture & Development: Responses from Emerging Powers*. Johannesburg: South African Institute of International Affairs; Tan-Mullins, M., Mohan, G. and Power, M. 2010. 'Redefining "aid" in the China–Africa context', *Development and Change* 41(5): 857–881.

4 Tok, E., Calleja, R. and El-Ghaish, H. 2014. 'Arab development aid and the new dynamics of multilateralism: towards better governance?' *European Scientific Journal* Special Edition 1: 591–605; Momani, B. and Ennis, C. A. 2013. 'Between caution and controversy: lessons from the Gulf Arab States as (re-)emerging donors', *Cambridge Review of International Affairs* 25(4): 605–627.

5 Szent-Iványi, B. 2012. 'Aid allocation of the emerging Central and Eastern European donors', *Journal of International Relations and Development* 15(1): 16–89; Lightfoot, S. 2010. 'The Europeanisation of international development policies: the case of Central and Eastern European States', *Europe-Asia Studies* 6(2): 329–350.

6 McGoey, L. 2015. *No Such Thing as a Free Gift: The Gates Foundation and the Price of Philanthropy*. London: Verso; Moran, M. 2014. *Private Foundations and Development Partnerships: American Philanthropy and Global Development Agendas*. London and New York: Routledge.

7 Richey, L. A. and Ponte, S. 2008. 'Better (Red)™ than Dead? Celebrities, consumption and international aid', *Third World Quarterly* 29(4): 711–729.

8 Petersen, M. J. 2015. *For Humanity or For the Umma? Aid and Islam in International Muslim NGOs*. London: Hurst & Co; Petersen, M. J. and Jones, B. 2011. 'Instrumental, narrow, normative? Reviewing recent literature on religion and development', *Third World Quarterly* 32(7): 1291–1306.

9 Elbers, W. J. and Schulpen, L. W. M. 2015. 'Reinventing international development NGOs: the case of ICCO', *European Journal of Development Research* 27: 1–18.

10 Walz, J. and Ramachandran, V. 2010. 'Brave new world: a literature review of emerging donors and the changing nature of foreign assistance', Center for Global Development Working Paper No. 273; Udvari, B. 2014. 'Impacts of aid for trade on trade with the EU: the role of old and new member states', *Journal of Global Policy and Governance* 3: 77–93; Kragelund, P. 2011. 'Back to BASICs? The rejuvenation of non-traditional donors' development cooperation with Africa', *Development and Change* 42(2): 585–607; Sidiropoulos, et al. 2015.

11 Gore, C. 2013. 'The new development cooperation landscape: actors, approaches, architecture', *Journal of International Development* 25(6): 769–786.

12 Woods, 2008.

13 Sato, J., Shiga, H., Kobayashi, T. and Kondoh, H. 2011. '"Emerging donors" from a recipient perspective: an institutional analysis of foreign aid in Cambodia', *World Development* 39(12): 2091–2104; Zimmermann, F. and Smith, K. 2011. 'More actors, more money, more ideas for international development co-operation', *Journal of International Development* 23(5): 722–738.

14 Chin, G. and Quadir, F. 2012. 'Introduction: rising states, rising donors and the global aid regime', *Cambridge Review of International Affairs*, 25(4), 493–506; Walz and Ramachandran, 2010.

15 Modi, 2011.

16 Mawdsley, 2012.

17 Manning, R. 2006. 'Will "emerging donors" change the face of international co-operation?' *Development Policy Review* 24(4): 371–385.

18 Farais, D. 2015. 'Triangular cooperation and the global governance of development assistance: Canada and Brazil as "co-donors"', *Canadian Foreign Policy Journal* 21(1): 1–14.

19 McEwan, C. and Mawdsley, E. 2012. 'Trilateral development cooperation: power and politics in emerging aid relationships', *Development and Change* 43(6): 1185–1209.

20 De la Fontaine, D. and Seifert, J. 2010. 'The role of South–South cooperation in present Brazilian foreign policy: actors, interests and functions', *Stockholm Papers in Latin American Studies*: Stockholm.

21 Richey, L. A. and Ponte, S. 2014. 'New actors and alliances in development', *Third World Quarterly* 35(1): 1–21.

22 Mawdsley, 2010.

23 Banks, N. and Hulme, D. 2014. 'New development alternatives or business as usual with a new face? The transformative potential of new actors and alliances in development', *Third World Quarterly* 35(1): 181–195.

24 Quadir, 2013.

25 Woods, 2008.

26 Chin, G. and Frolic, B. 2008. 'Emerging donors in international development assistance: the China case', *Research Report*, International Development Research Centre, Ottawa.

27 Brautigam, D. 2011. *The Dragon's Gift: The Real Story of China in Africa*. Oxford: Oxford University Press

28 Nielsen, W. 1972. *The Big Foundations*. New York, NY: Columbia University Press.

29 See Arnove, R. 1982. 'Introduction' in *Philanthropy and Cultural Imperialism*, edited by R. Arnove, Bloomington, IN: Indiana University Press, 1–23.

30 See Parmar, I. 2012. *Foundations of the American Century*. New York, NY: Columbia University Press; Zunz, O. 2012. *Philanthropy in America*. Princeton, NJ: Princeton University Press; Dowie, M. 2001. *American Foundations: An Investigative History*. Cambridge, MA: The MIT Press.

31 Nielsen, W. 1972. *The Big Foundations*. New York, NY: Columbia University Press.

32 Nielsen, 1972.

33 Andrews, F. E. 1956. *Philanthropic Foundations*. New York, NY: Russel Sage Foundation.

34 Anheier, H. K. and Daly, S. 2007. *Politics of Foundations: A Comparative Analysis*. London: Routledge.

35 Nielsen, 1972.

36 Farber, D. 2013. 'Bill Gates on education, patents, Microsoft Bob, and disease', *Cnet*, 15 July.

37 See Fleishman, J. 2009. *The Foundation: A Great American Secret*. New York, NY: PublicAffairs™.

38 Parmar, I. 2012. *Foundations of the American Century*. New York, NY: Columbia University Press.

39 Anheier, H. K. and Leat, D. 2006. *Creative Philanthropy: Towards a New Philanthropy for the Twenty-First Century.* Abingdon: Routledge.

40 Bishop, M. 2006. 'The birth of philanthrocapitalism', *The Economist*, 23 February.

41 Lundsgaarde, E., Funk, E., Kopyra, A., Richter, J. and Steinfeldt, H. 2012. *Private Foundations and Development Cooperation: Insights From Tanzania*. Bonn: German Development Institute.

42 Moran, M. and Stone, D. 2016. 'The new philanthropy: private power in international development policy?' in *The Palgrave Handbook of International Development*, edited by J. Grugel and D. Hammett, Basingstoke: Palgrave Macmillan.

43 See Fleishman, 2009.
44 Jenkins, G. 2011. 'Who's afraid of philanthrocapitalism?' *Case Western Reserve Law Review*, 61(3): 753–821; Bishop, M. and Green, M. 2010. *Philanthrocapitalism: How Giving can Save the World*. London: A. & C. Black.
45 Fleishman, 2009.
46 see Fejerskov, 2015.
47 Hudson Institute. 2011. *The Index of Global Philanthropy and Remittances 2011*. Washington, DC: Hudson Institute; Organisation for Economic Co-operation and Development (OECD). 2017. *Global Private Philanthropy for Development*. Paris: Organisation for Economic Co-operation and Development – The Development Assistance Committee, June.
48 See Fejerskov, A. and Rasmussen, C. 2016. 'Going global? Micro-philanthrocapitalism and Danish private foundations in international development cooperation', *Development in Practice* 26(7): 840–852.
49 Nelson J. 2008. 'Effecting change through accountable channels', in *Global Development 2.0: Can Philanthropists, The Public, and The Poor Make Poverty History?*, edited by L. Brainard and D. Chollet, Washington, DC: Brookings Institution Press, 149–187.
50 See Moran and Stone, 2016.
51 Williams, O. D. and Rushton, S. 2014. 'Private actors in global health governance' in *Partnerships and Foundations in Global Health Governance*, edited by S. Rushton and O. D. Williams, Basingstoke: Palgrave Macmillan, 1–25.
52 OECD, 2017.
53 Hudson Institute. 2016. *The Index of Global Philanthropy and Remittances 2016*. Washington, DC: Hudson Institute.
54 OECD, 2017.
55 Hudson Institute. 2011.
56 Bishop and Green, 2010.
57 Adelman, C. 2009. 'Global philanthropy and remittances: reinventing foreign aid', *The Brown Journal of World Affairs* 15(2): 23–33.
58 Easterly, W. 2006. *The White Man's Burden: Why the West's Efforts to Aid the Rest Have Done so Much Ill and so Little Good*. London: Penguin Books.
59 Desai, R. and Kharas, H. 2008. 'The California consensus: can private aid end global poverty?', *Survival* 50(4): 155–168.
60 Fleishman, 2009.
61 House of Commons. 2012. *Private Foundations. Thirteenth Report of Session 2010–2012*. London: International Development Committee, House of Commons.
62 Edwards, M. 2009. *Just Another Emperor? The Myths and Realities of Philanthrocapitalism*. London: The Young Foundation and Demos.
63 Ramdas, K. 2011. 'Philanthrocapitalism: reflections on politics and policymaking', *Society* 48(5): 393–396.
64 Jenkins, 2011.
65 Edwards, 2009.

4 Enter Seattle

The '800-pound gorilla of philanthropy', a 'Benevolent dictator for global health', and 'Fortress Bill'; the Bill and Melinda Gates Foundation has known many names in its relatively short lifetime. Fuelled by immense ambition and confidence about the potential impact of its effectively more than $40 billion endowment, the world's largest private foundation has embarked on a self-titled expedition to help 'All people live healthy, productive lives'.[1] When employees of the Gates Foundation travel throughout the developed and the developing world, all of them start presentations about their workplace with a particular story. Sometime in the mid-1990s, Bill and Melinda read an article about a simple disease killing hundreds of thousands of children every year from diarrhoea.[2] Eager to find out more, they began to read about the disease called rotavirus. Unable to grasp that it was in fact a preventable disease, whose main lethality came from the great health disparities between rich and poor, they were eager to do something about it, and sent the article with a note to Gates' father, spelling out, 'Dad, maybe we can do something about this'. Such a story is compelling; it speaks of an undoubted empathy for the world's poorest, and the humility of engaging in not just a complex and tremendous task, but one in a field largely unknown to you. And it is probably somewhat true, but of course the story of Gates' call to philanthropy did not start that day.

In 1987 a company called Microsoft went public on the stock exchange, making the Harvard dropout and software developer Bill Gates the youngest billionaire in history at the age of 31. In the following years, he and his friend Paul Allen would build a software empire. Notorious for its aggressive marketing, penetrative expansion into most corners of the world and its hostile work environment, but also as a pioneer in bringing a technological revolution to the world, Microsoft is unfamiliar to few. As Gates' fortune blossomed in the late 1980s and early 1990s, his hesitancy towards charity entailed accusations of miserliness.[3] To counter this the William H. Gates Foundation was initiated in 1994, with an initial endowment of about $106 million, as the first organized endeavour into philanthropy for the Gates family. It was formed with the purpose of providing grants for health, population and education projects worldwide, as well as in the Pacific Northwest of the US where the Gates family resided. Perhaps not unrelated, Bill had married Melinda a little earlier in 1994. At a bridal lunch before the wedding, Gates' mother, Mary Gates, read a letter to Melinda in effect saying,

'From those to whom much is given, much is expected'.[4] Sadly, Gates' mother died the following June after fighting breast cancer. Both Mary and Melinda are said to have played significant roles in directing the attention of Gates away from Microsoft and towards the world.[5] Gates Sr, Bill's father, also had a pivotal role to play in the commencement of the foundation. In the early 1990s charity requests would end up coming to his office and he 'Told Trey (family nickname for Bill) that we needed to set up a real foundation'.[6] Accordingly, the William H. Gates Foundation was started and initially run by Gates' father, a Seattle lawyer, from the basement of his house. A system was created in which Gates Sr would screen requests for charity and send the appropriate ones to his son. Bill would then approve the ones he found promising, usually all of his father's picks (around 25 every three months), and Gates Sr would make Bill's investment manager write out the cheques. The system seemed to function well and was kept several years into the foundation's life. Though Gates was urged to replace his father with a professional (Gates Sr had no experience in running a foundation though he was familiar with charity and civic activities), Gates Sr was in charge of the foundation until Patty Stonesifer took over in 1999, at which point the endowments had grown to $5.2 billion. Stonesifer was a former Microsoft senior vice president and a close friend of Gates who started working in Microsoft as early as 1988. With Stonesifer in place, the foundation began a process of professionalization that would add a more structured and organized approach to its grant making, not least through the extensive making and following of internal guidelines and policies. Over the first years, the Gates family added around $2 billion to the foundation's assets. Grants were given to projects benefitting the Pacific Northwest, but a growing attention to education and global health arose in the foundation.

With a $200 million cash contribution (matched by Microsoft with a $200 million software pledge) meant to support all US public libraries in providing free internet access, the Gates Library Foundation was launched in 1997 as a separate charitable programme. It was managed by soon-to-be CEO of all of Gates' charities, Patty Stonesifer, from her office in Redmond, famously above a pizza parlour. Expanding on the work of Microsoft's community affairs initiative, Libraries Online, the foundation aimed at providing low-income communities with the hardware and software necessary to gain internet access (aiming to close the so-called 'digital divide', the gap between those who have access to the power of technology and the internet and those who do not).[7] Patty Stonesifer was named president and chairperson of a board that also included Bill and Melinda Gates, and Vartan Gregorian, president of the Carnegie Foundation. As opposed to the William H. Gates Foundation, the Learning Foundation was an operating entity, meaning it ran most of its own programmes without passing on implementation to partners. Over the next three years the foundation would install 22,000 computers in 4,500 libraries in the US, and 4,000 computers in 1,400 libraries in Canada. All of them with Microsoft software, to the great attention of critics who claimed that Gates was only attempting to expand the market for his own company.[8] By then, it was expected that the US library programme would be finalized in 2005, with the further aim of expanding the scope to libraries elsewhere in the world.

Despite his firm belief in technology as a driver for social change, Gates was early on introduced to the limits of pursuing technology improvements in isolation. In a *New York Times Magazine* article, Gates recounted a trip to South Africa in the mid-1990s where inhabitants of the Johannesburg township Soweto had eagerly shown him its only computer that happened to be connected to its only electrical outlet. Gates told the magazine 'I looked around and thought, hmm, computers may not be the highest priority in this particular place'.[9] A few years after its inception then, the William H. Gates Foundation began searching out other potential areas for impact. It found one such in the area of global health. During the mid-1990s, annual support for vaccine research was limited at around $60 million despite more than 200 million people being affected by malaria every year. Pharmaceutical companies had little interest in leading research on products that were not likely to be profitable, as most customers would be found in the world's poorest countries with limited if any purchasing power. Eyeing an underfunded area of importance to global health, the William H. Gates Foundation began providing grants aimed at vaccine development and some other forms of improvement to healthcare in developing countries. In 1997 commitments and grants from the foundation to global health totalled around $10 million, and in 1998 it significantly increased giving to this area, providing $50 million to malaria research (making it the single largest supporter in the world at the time) and $100 million to the Bill and Melinda Gates Children's Vaccine Program at Seattle-based organization PATH (Program for Appropriate Technology in Health).

When the February edition of *Fortune* magazine was released in 1999, the world learned that Gates had donated $3.3 billion to the foundation, designated for health and education projects around the world. Formally provided a few days earlier on 29 January, it formed the world's largest-ever individual donation at the time, surpassing CNN founder Ted Turner's 10-year donation to the UN of $1 billion. The gift was made in the form of about 20 million shares of Microsoft stock, which closed at $172 per share that day and was immediately converted to cash. Already at this early time, Bill Gates had given away more money than any other living 'philanthropist', with the then President of the US Foundation Center, Sara Engelhardt, proclaiming that the addition of assets from a living philanthropist was very unusual and that 'Not since the time of Andrew Carnegie and John D. Rockefeller in the early part of this century has that happened'.[10] Interestingly, the gift was not announced publicly, just as neither of the Gates were available for comments, a very different low-key approach when compared with their giving-style of today. It was not entirely surprising at that specific point in time though, seeing as the public announcement of a $100 million grant to Seattle-based PATH a few months earlier had created public uproar since Microsoft was fighting government antitrust charges in the Federal District Court in Washington, DC. Of the $3.3 billion, $2.23 billion went into the William H. Gates Foundation and $1.11 billion was given to the Gates Library Foundation, which then changed its name to the Gates Learning Foundation. The donations put the William H. Gates Foundation in the US top ten foundations in assets (with $4.2 billion) and the Gates Learning Foundation in the top 30 (with $1.3 billion). In 1998 both foundations made combined grants of more than $150 million. Only a few months later, Gates topped the donation by giving $5 billion to the William H. Gates Foundation, raising its assets to $10 billion. At the time, Bill Gates' holdings were worth more than $82 billion, but he was simultaneously battling a headwind as Microsoft was embroiled in a court case over its alleged attempts to monopolize parts of the software industry.

Becoming the Bill and Melinda Gates Foundation

By 1999 Gates' charity activities were spread out across two different founda-tions: The William H. Gates Foundation and the Gates Learning Foundation, both of which were run by a fairly limited staff. In August 1999 these were joined into one foundation, the Bill and Melinda Gates Foundation (or the Gates Foundation for short). Having moved into a new building in Seattle, the Gates quickly began increasing the endowments of the foundation to around $17.1 billion. Four priori-ties dominated giving by the Gates Foundation in 1999, several of which would go on to dominate future strategies to this day: 1) extending the availability of existing vaccines to the world's poorest children; 2) researching and develop-ing new vaccines to prevent malaria, tuberculosis and HIV/AIDS; 3) addressing women's reproductive health needs; and 4) closing the digital divide, i.e., provid-ing access to computers for the poor (with a particular domestic focus). During this time, the foundation received more than 30,000 requests for grants each year, and for the year 1999 provided around $2 billion in grants. In mid-September of 1999, the foundation announced its largest grant, which is still one of the largest grants today, the Gates Millennium Scholarship programme amounting to $1.37 billion over 20 years and provided to outstanding African-American, Latino, Native American and Asian students by the United Negro College Fund. Undergraduates can in theory pursue any available degree, but financing for mas-ter's and doctoral degrees is mostly reserved for science, math, engineering, and computer technology, maintaining a 'science' focus.

Over the following years, annual grant-making would amount to $1.5 billion (2000), $1 billion (2001), $1.1 billion (2002), $1.1 billion (2003), and $1.2 billion (2004). Keeping a low profile was a guiding principle for the foundation during these years, but as it increasingly gained domestic and international trac-tion as one of the world's largest private foundations, this began to change. 'In the beginning we let other voices be heard' Stonesifer explained in 2004, but 'Now we intend to share our point of view'.[11] The Gates family had now also become 'More comfortable using their status as celebrities to call attention to the foundation's work' and people in the US non-profit world were beginning to describe the foundation as the first superpower of philanthropy, comparing it with the US government in terms of international political traction. In the fall of 2001 an East Coast office was opened as the first outside Seattle, led by David Lane, a former White House National Economic Council head. The purpose of opening up an office in Washington DC was naturally to approach US policy making, but the mind-set was still somewhat humble in the beginning. The foundation was just starting to realize the potential of advocacy, and it was a deliberate choice to refer to the office as the 'East Coast' one, and not the DC office, particularly as the Bush administration was in charge and the liberals of Seattle were not interested in becoming too affiliated with the federal policies being promoted. Still, becoming increasingly aware of its role vis-à-vis other organizations, the foundation was now gradually ready to get more vocal about how its philanthropic efforts, in order to achieve lasting large-scale change, had to incorporate strategies to encourage effective public investment and leverage private sector potential, pursuing catalytic investments that augmented rather than supplanted government funding. And with the Obama administration coming to power in 2008, there would be plenty of opportunity to shape policy-making only a few years later.

In 2005 the foundation debuted what would be a recurring event – its Grand Challenges. These are essentially competitions in which organizations are invited to bid ideas for the solution of a specific issue or around a detailed topic, and encouraged to think innovatively or radically in their approach. The first Grand Challenge centred on global health, as many have since, including the lack of vaccines for AIDS and malaria, and attracted around 1,600 proposals. Of these, 43 were so promising that they received funding of a collective $450 million, mostly five-year grants. This was more than double what Gates and the foundation had planned to support. When looking back in 2010, Gates himself laid into how the quest for radical ideas has certain consequences for the end results. 'We were naïve when we began', he repeated as all the involved scientists were brought together in Seattle at the end of the first Grand Challenge grants, and open about how he had underestimated the time necessary to take a new product from the lab to clinical trials to low-cost manufacturing to acceptance in developing country contexts.[12] Of the initial grants, one-third were renewed. When repeating the Grand Challenges scheme in 2007, the foundation shifted its approach from multi-million grants to smaller ones of around $100,000 with the possibility to have existing grant-holders add new goals to their current ones, saving the foundation and the grantee resources and administration. The Grand Challenges have continued since then and in 2014 the Gates Foundation partnered up with a series of new co-donors from the field of bilaterals, including Brazil, Canada, the US and the UK. Of the 2,091 grants awarded thus far by this group, 893 have been given to grantees based in the US, 239 to Canada, 127 to the UK and 66 to Australia. Among developing countries, grantees in India have received the most at 92 grants awarded, whilst Kenyan grantees account for the largest share of the African grants at 86.[13]

By 2006 the Gates Foundation had become the biggest philanthropic foundation in the world with endowments of $30 billion, but more cash was soon to arrive, prompting cheers but also stressful times in the foundation. On a Monday afternoon in the New York Public Library, Warren Buffett, the US investor so successful that he has claimed the nickname of Oracle or Sage of Omaha, stood up and presented five envelopes in front of approximately 200 philanthropy executives, scientists, students and reporters. All of them containing large gifts for individual foundations, the first four were given to ones in the name of his three children and his late wife Susan (amounting to approximately $6.4 billion), whilst the fifth and by far largest was gifted to the Bill and Melinda Gates Foundation. News had already broken the day before in *Fortune*, but a formal ceremony seemed to have been in place, in the heart of New York City. Upon receiving what would amount to at least $30 billion for his foundation, Bill Gates presented Buffett with a copy of Adam Smith's *The Wealth of Nations* and proclaimed that Buffett would be known not only as the world's greatest investor, but as its greatest investor for good. Comparing the process of selecting Bill and Melinda Gates as those to conduct philanthropy on his behalf with picking a spouse, Buffett exclaimed that 'I'm happy with the ones I'm marrying here'. The first unlikely meeting between a technology nerd and an investor who did not use email occurred 15 years earlier in July 1991. Their friendship has endured since, with some referring to it as the biggest billionaire 'bromance' in history.[14] Naturally, Gates sits on the board of Buffett's company Berkshire Hathaway. Upon pledging to donate shares of Berkshire Hathaway, Buffett likewise became the third trustee of the Gates Foundation alongside Bill and Melinda. Buffett and his wife had set up a foundation already in 1962, the Susan Thompson Foundation, that had been distributing hundreds of millions of dollars in the decades leading up to the 2000s, but it seems to have been Buffett's trust in Melinda and Bill Gates' ability and eagerness to distribute their fortune to charity that made him gift more than $30 billion to their foundation. Every year from July 2006 onwards, Buffett gives a set of annually declining (by five per cent) Berkshire B shares (in July 2006 amounting to approximately $1.5 billion and in 2016 increasing to $2.17 billion). Though Buffet claimed it was unrelated, it may have helped his decision that Gates announced earlier the same year, in mid-June, that he would be phasing out his responsibilities at Microsoft and devoting most of his time to the Gates Foundation, effective from June 2008. Though giving up his day-to-day role, Gates would continue his role as the company's chairman.

For the foundation the gift had enormous implications over and above the natural awe of receiving such an amount of money, not least seeing as it would have to double its annual spending over the course of a few years. In the spring of 2006, as rumours of a potentially massive gift from Warren Buffett surfaced (some months before the public announcement), a complete restructuring was made of the foundation, introducing three new programmes or divisions: the United States programme, the Global Health programme, and the Global Development programme. The reorganization meant creating a new high-level position as president within each of the programmes (Sylvia Matthews for the Global Development programme, Tadataka Yamada for the Global Health programme, and Allan Golston for the US programme) but, aside from this, the organizational tasks ahead for each of the areas were quite different. Global Health had already functioned separately for many years; the United States programme was new but integrated two longstanding programmes into one: the North West Pacific programme and the Library programme; and Global Development was to tie together and scale up a number of issues that had only been explored and experimented with in an internal group called 'Strategic Opportunities' in areas such as financial services for the poor, agricultural development, and water and sanitation. The Global Development programme would go on to see an immense scaling up of both financial and human resources in the following years, but so would the foundation in its entirety. The size of potential grants has always determined the level of authority involved in approving them in the Gates Foundation, but with the reorganization came also a substantial financial decentralization, i.e., an increased grant-making authority was given to the Presidents of each programme. To accommodate Buffett's gift, but also to respond to the rising criticism of the foundation's investment practices, the foundation was split into two in October 2006, and the Bill and Melinda Gates Foundation Trust was set up, adding further work to the already large task of reshaping the foundation. The legal documents governing the trust obligate it to fund the foundation for whatever amount it needs to accomplish its charity activities. As such, money is formally transferred each year, from the trust to the foundation, in the amount deemed appropriate by the foundation. We will return to this shortly.

Up until 2006 the foundation had only had two board members or trustees, Melinda and Bill. Even though Buffett was added as a third, the foundation decided to formalize a system of advisory boards, further answering increasing criticism of lack of accountability and critical feedback in the foundation. A panel of experts was set up for each of the programmes, with members chosen by the foundation. That same year the foundation also announced that it would shut down 50 years after the deaths of its three trustees. As mentioned, Bill joined Melinda at the foundation in July 2008, officially in a full-time capacity, yet he continuously served as the chairman of the company's board until February 2014, and has since continued to serve on the board, with some claiming he spends at least a third of his time with the company.[15] He also remains the largest individual shareholder in the company today, with approximately 4.5 per cent of the shares. In September 2008 Jeff Raikes (another former Microsoft executive) succeeded Patty Stonesifer as the CEO of the foundation, beating more than 150 candidates for the job. Whereas Stonesifer received a nominal wage of only $1 per annum, Raikes earned almost $1 million, perhaps signalling an increasing wish to professionalize foundation leadership (though all of it went to his own foundation). By the time Bill Gates entered the organization, it had become what some interviewees referred to as an 'Organizational mess'.[16] Having to adapt to Buffett's gift had meant a constant state of scaling up, and the foundation had become a pressure cooker, as one foundation employee described it, running at full steam. Employees were frustrated because the chaos was hampering the effectiveness of their work, making coordination with other teams impossible, and limiting attention from leadership. And the immensely fast scaling up meant that teams were constantly changing their portfolios, with employees moving from one side to the next, and then back again. The foundation had always been vocal about how it would constantly be changing and challenging its own perspectives and strategies, yet these organizational dynamics were not desirable nor productive. Gates himself famously sent round a blistering memo with wording to the effect of 'Everything is screwed', pointing to substantial changes and overruling earlier leadership decisions.[17] What followed then was a state of paralysis, with programme officers afraid of acting, facing potential grave consequences if they did something considered wrong by Gates or foundation leadership. It is difficult to say whether bringing in Raikes was a direct consequence of this situation, but he was a long-time leader under the auspices of Gates in Microsoft, and visibly came with a mission of bringing order to the organizational chaos. Just as he did in Microsoft, Raikes ran annual business reviews in the Gates Foundation, evaluating the performance of the foundation and its departments.

The endowments of the foundation, managed by the trust, suffered substantial losses that year due to the volatility of the world financial markets, i.e., what came to be known as the 2008 financial crisis. Losses in investments amounted to $7.8 billion and, as a consequence, endowments of the foundation declined to $29.7 billion while $4.6 billion was given out in grants. But the foundation was quick to bounce back, both in securing an investment income of around $4 billion the following year, but also in not letting the financial crisis become an excuse to scale back its grant-making. Instead, it increased this with some 100 million dollars, surely an important sign to the outside world of not letting charitable activities or development work pay the price for fluctuations in the global market. The increase was also followed by a series of messages from the foundation to public donors in which these were urged not to cut back their development aid despite facing growing levels of financial austerity. The year 2009 saw a continued scaling up of grants made to global development, increasing with 47 per cent to $677 million, while grants to global health remained steady at around $1.8 billion. This year was also when decisions were made in the foundation to open a European office in London and, starting in January 2010, Joe Cerrell (who was formerly director of global health policy and advocacy) moved to the UK to head a team of initially ten people who would build closer ties between the foundation and European governments and development organizations.

Towards global political influence

By 2012 net assets were almost at $32 billion with grant expenses amounting to $2.6 billion, and the foundation was now ready to move to new heights, both in Seattle and globally. Four years earlier, in mid-July of 2008, Melinda Gates and Patty Stonesifer, along with Seattle Mayor Greg Nickels, had broken ground on what would eventually become the Gates Foundation's new headquarters.[18] Across from Seattle's most famous landmark, the Space Needle, the 12-acre campus would bring together the different parts of the foundation, scattered across the city, and come to serve as a metaphor for an organization with growing ambitions and a more coherent approach to achieving these. The first real office of the foundation was a two-storey tan and grey concrete building facing Seattle's Lake

Union, which it moved into in 1999 when the two smaller foundations were united under one roof as the Bill and Melinda Gates Foundation. Ironically, it used to be a cheque-processing plant, not far from what the foundation was in fact doing.[19] Since then, it expanded to at least five different locations across Seattle. The new headquarters, inaugurated in May 2012, is radically different in appearance and manifestation. Almost entirely clad in glass, the headquarters provide 60,000 usable square metres across two massive buildings, with construction room for a third if the foundation should come to need it in the future.

In the beginning of that year, before moving into the new headquarters, the foundation implemented a restructuring of its global programmes to strengthen its operational set-up and adopt new ways of working collaboratively with part-ners. Recognizing that it was working increasingly in silos, and that the focus on solving specific problems in isolation had often prevented the foundation from stepping back and looking at the interrelationships among these issues to develop more holistic efforts, a more integrated approach to the global programmes was initiated. The initiative for the global restructuring came not least from Raikes, who had witnessed the fragmentation of the foundation's programmes. It did take the co-chairs some time to warm up to the restructuring, as it would see large parts of the Global Health programme move to that of Global Development. The aim of the restructuring was to increase the foundation's impact by creating a more integrated organization that would advance the capabilities of its staff, build productive collaborations and create predictable, streamlined processes for making and managing its grants.[20] The approach moved from several distinct pro-grammes and multiple regional presences to a realignment of the teams that make up the global programmes. The Global Policy and Advocacy division was created as a new entity, bringing together several different teams all working on issues of advocacy and policy, and it would now come to hold responsibility over in-country teams. The organizational changes meant that the foundation's divisions grew to five: the reimagined Global Development division (under Chris Elias, for-merly of PATH), the reimagined Global Health division (under Trevor Mundel, formerly of Novartis), the United States programme, the new Global Policy and Advocacy division (under Geoff Lamb, formerly of the World Bank), and the Global Communications division created in 2010.

A year later, in 2013, Jeff Raikes stepped down as CEO of the foundation, surely to be remembered for his task of managing the foundation's growth as it vastly increased its grant-making and its organization across almost all cylinders. On 18 December the Gates Foundation revealed that Susan Desmond-Hellmann had been appointed as the next head of the foundation. The first CEO of the foundation not related to Microsoft (though she does sit on the board of tech-related Facebook), she came from a position as chancellor of the University of California, and before that working for biotech company Genentech for 14 years. Used to a high degree of public scrutiny from her time in academia, Desmond-Hellmann made it clear early on that she intended to emphasize humility and embrace constructive criticism.[21] She did so during an event several months after her hiring, as it seems to be tradition that new CEOs are, understandably, given time to delve into the foundation's work before appearing publicly. In her first years, aside from getting under the skin of the foundation, focus has been on trying to steer the large bureaucracy that is the foundation today from a 'Rule-based culture to a culture that trusts our employees', not least after Melinda Gates had proclaimed early in her hiring that too many people were weighing in on decisions, slowing down the foundation.[22] Desmond-Hellmann also quickly halved the foundation's budget for external management consultants, a solution used widely to fill capacity gaps in the foundation, including for tasks that would be considered strictly internal in many other organizations. Whilst somewhat publicly outspoken about the foundation's priorities, there is no doubt the CEO position will remain one of running things internally (almost resembling the responsibilities of a Chief Operating Officer, though one such is also appointed in the foundation), whilst Bill and Melinda set priorities and handle most high-level publicity-related tasks themselves.

The year 2015 was a defining one for the foundation's global ambitions with a Financing for Development (FfD) summit in Addis Ababa in July, a MDG summit at the UN General Assembly in New York in September, where a new set of development goals for the following 15 years would be decided, and the UNFCCC climate high level meeting in Paris in December with what appeared to be a final shot at addressing climate change at the international political stage. Then again, a lot was at stake for everyone in 2015, which already before its start had been deemed one of the most important years for multilateralism. Things started slow in Addis Ababa with the Third International Financing for Development conference, following up from Monterrey, Mexico, in 2002 and Doha, Qatar, in 2008. Whilst some had astounding expectations, and with good reason as we knew trillions of dollars would be needed to attain a new set of development goals by 2030, the general feeling was that Addis needed first and foremost to form a good start for an important multilateral year, so as to not stall progress early on. This was largely achieved by not radically rethinking the proposed outcome document, nine months in the making. Discussions on tax (which all along seemed to be the centre of attention in Addis Ababa), and a last-minute proposal by the G77 group to upgrade the UN expert committee on tax to a new UN intergovernmental body that would give all countries a seat at the table, were perhaps the biggest 'threats' to a silent-but-not-satisfied ending to the conference that would sap momentum. The EU member states and the rest of the richest parts of the OECD blocked the proposal with arguments that tax matters belonged in the OECD, an obvious move that, whilst certainly true in terms of political effectiveness, also preserved power in the developed part of the world as opposed to opening up for global influence in the UN.

Unsurprising, the Gates Foundation was in Addis Ababa as well. The foundation knows very well that a persistent aid regime in which governments continue to support global development with significant resources is a dire necessity for its own work to be truly effective. Whether as direct partners, as the critical mass allowing the foundation to focus on niches, or through their ability to eventually scale up foundation activities, government donors and their ODA greatly allow or give way for foundations to work as they please. Though not represented at as high a level as we have sometimes come to expect from them, the Gates Foundation nonetheless had a strong presence in the Ethiopian capital. Mark Suzman, President of Global Policy, Advocacy, and Country programmes in the foundation, was especially active, being a panellist at several side events including ones on a new multi-donor trust fund to support maternal and child health, and one on creating investment opportunities at scale. The foundation had two aims with their presence then, firstly to advocate for and maintain or create ground for as strong a set of ODA commitments as possible, and second to launch a set of initiatives themselves or to make public pledges to others. One of these new initiatives was a partnership with the Islamic Development Bank to create a blended financing facility called The Lives and Livelihood Fund. The fund provides financing for the 30 least wealthy countries in the Islamic Development Bank's membership by providing a combination of grants and concessional loans. It specifically focuses on the three areas of improving health (combatting infectious diseases and supporting health systems), increasing agricultural productivity (particularly for smallholder farmers), and building basic infrastructure (power generation, water supply, forms of digital banking, etc.). Combining $500 million in grants ($100 million of these pledged by the Gates Foundation) with $2 billion of IsDB's ordinary capital resources, it will initially run over a five-year period until January 2021. Another Gates contribution was made to the establishment of the Global Financing Facility (GFF) in support of Every Women Every Child, a multi-donor World Bank trust fund designed to support reproductive, maternal, newborn, child and adolescent health. The GFF aims to mobilize at least $12 billion over the next five years for four front-runner countries – the Democratic Republic of Congo, Ethiopia, Kenya and Tanzania – and the Gates Foundation committed $75 million. Finally, the foundation pledged $75 million to create CHAMPS, a network of disease surveillance sites in developing countries whose main role is to gather data on how and why children are getting sick and dying, and where they are located.

Addis Ababa, of course, was only the start to a fast-paced year and, not many months later, the UN General Assembly followed in New York, where a new set of development goals for 2030 would be ratified. Even his holiness Pope Francis was present; the first time a pope would address such a large gathering of world leaders at the UN. For the Gates Foundation, however, UN development goals were not a case of love at first sight, just as the eventual SDGs were not necessarily the outcome hoped for by Gates and the foundation. Like most of the philanthropic environment, Gates was initially a pronounced sceptic of the Millennium Development Goals, perceiving them as fundamentally constraining the work of the foundation and largely as just a set of hollow government promises, never truly realized: 'The MDGs were hardly the first time someone had declared that children shouldn't die. And the UN had passed many resolutions calling for things that never came to pass. Why would this time be different?' is how Gates described his initial view of the MDGs in 2013.[23] Looking back to the end of the last millennium, the now late billionaire Nicolas Hayek, who earned his fortune on Swatch watches, recalled how 'One day Kofi Annan brought me, Ted Turner, Bill Gates and two other billionaires together and asked each of us to put $1 billion into a fund. Everyone except Turner refused. The United Nations doesn't need me; the UN needs to get itself respected'. For a long while Gates very much shared Hayek's view. Something happened over the years, however, that would bring the Gates Foundation closer to the MDGs and the UN. Gates himself explained that 'It's hard to pinpoint exactly when it happened, but over time Melinda and I moved from cautious optimists to full-throated fans'.[24] Perhaps the gradual increase in the prominence of the MDGs and a more thorough reading of their ambitions made Gates and his foundation realize that they in fact largely reflect Gates Foundation priorities such as health and education, even in a framework that reduced complex issues to simplified indicators and variables. As Gates later noted himself, 'Unlike so many vaguely worded international resolutions, the MDGs came with concrete numbers'.[25]

It comes as no surprise, then, that Bill Gates and the Gates Foundation have greatly preferred a post-2015 agenda that built on the MDGs, rather than casting these aside and creating a new and broader framework. From the start of the emerging post-2015 discussions, Gates held that they should 'Build on what made the current goals so successful—starting with the fact that there were only eight MDGs, which let the world zero in on the most important areas'.[26] This view was accentuated when Gates spoke at the World Economic Forum in Davos in 2013, telling the international society about the MDG framework: 'Leave it alone'. The Open Working Group on the SDGs report to the UN General Secretary and the proposed 17 goals and 169 indicators then did not evoke either admiration or consent from Gates or the Foundation. Aside from the welcome but expected focus on health and education, the proposed SDGs seemed to have been far too political in nature for Gates: 'When the UN reaches agreement on other important goals like mitigating climate change, it should consider whether a different set of actors and a separate process might be best for those efforts'.[27] He also made a rather interesting point in the context of the Gates Foundation's focus on developing new technologies, vaccines and ways of combating poverty, that areas within which proven instruments capable of producing results had not been developed should not be part of the SDGs. The argument becomes less surprising when we understand it as a way of focusing on a set of conceivably less political and more technical areas such as health and education, as opposed to the political nature of building democratic institutions: 'For example, improving governance is a worthy end, but do we have the tools to make it happen? It's not clear'.[28] Instead of disputed and deeply politically sensitive goals, measurability should be the central concern: 'Many of the potential new goals don't have unanimous support, and adding many new goals, or goals that are not easily measurable, may sap momentum'.[29] One of the political issues in the SDGs on which the Gates Foundation and Bill Gates himself have been relatively silent is inequality. Inequality has been central to the post-2015 agenda, and it received its own standalone goal in the new SDGs, but it has never been a prominent part of the philanthropy environment, with very limited attention from foundations. Since 2004, only 251 out of four million registered US grants have used the word 'inequality'.[30] No matter how we see it, however, inequality is a manifest fact of this world. A 2016 Oxfam report found that 85 individuals now hold as much wealth as the poorest half of the world's entire population.[31] The ambiguous relationship between inequality and philanthropy is quite apparent, as the vast majority of foundations have been founded and are governed by incredibly wealthy individuals, all obvious representatives of the increasing inequality.

In May of 2015, some months before the world's leaders would ratify the SDGs, the Gates Foundation hosted its annual Global Partner's Forum at the Westin Hotel in downtown Seattle, recounted in the introduction to this chapter. The overarching theme of the meeting was the forthcoming SDGs and scepticism was certainly in the air, not least towards the seemingly all-encompassing nature of the approaching 17 goals. Many speakers at the meeting poked fun at the SDGs, referring to them as a 'fantasy', a 'train wreck' or an unworkable and 'encyclopaedic' wish list.[32] The message seems to have been that the proposed SDGs were far too complex, unhelpful and wrong in their broad priorities and that they should be replaced by a much simpler, health-dominated framework, more akin to the MDG approach of the last 15 years. From the stage, Mark Suzman jokingly referred to the SDGs as 'No targets left behind', and Bill Gates himself referred to them as analogous to the Bible, adding that he would prefer to start with something simpler, 'Like the Ten Commandments'.[33] Suzman later explained that these statements had not been made in an attempt to undermine the UN agenda, but were rather about trying to figure out how to draw up a set of SDGs that would succeed. Likewise, rather than waging any form of all-out war against the SDGs and the UN system, the Gates Foundation has promoted a much narrower, more measurable and perhaps more pragmatic agenda, as opposed to the grandeur of the adopted SDGs. Pragmatic also in the sense of an agenda mainly promoting the priorities of the foundation within health and education, much as a large number of the MDGs did: 'Global health is a fantastic investment. It should be a top priority on the world's agenda. Figuring out how to deliver on the Sustainable Development Goals will require many tough decisions, but this is not one of them',[34] as Gates explained it. This view to a certain extent challenges the more UN-aligned opinion of the 2015 Partnership group of foundations, a group of foundations coming together with the aim of supporting the SDGs specifically, and is likely one of the reasons why the Gates Foundation rarely participated in panels and events during foundation dialogues with the UN on the SDGs. Eventually, of course, the new SDGs and the Agenda 2030 were adopted in late September in New York, and there was not a single bad vibe to trace as Bill and Melinda Gates stood up among world leaders, on the floor of the UN General Assembly Hall, and clapped vigorously as the Danish Prime Minister ratified the new agreement from the platform.

After New York and the UN General Assembly, all eyes turned on Paris and the outlook of perhaps finally reaching an agreement on how to address climate change. As the UNFCCC meeting approached, the Gates Foundation had its focus locked on bringing together business and political leaders for a new public–private partnership that could bring substantial funds to the table. Gates prepared well and visited French president Francois Hollande at the Élysée Palace as well as White House staff over the summer that year to lay the grounds for the partnership. Hollande and US President Obama promised to assemble a coalition of governments to double their spending on energy R&D. The funds provided by the partnership would not be spent broadly on climate change adaptation and mitigation, but very specifically on energy research and development, with Gates proclaiming at the December meeting that he was 'Surprised that the climate talks historically haven't had R&D on the agenda in any way, shape or form'.[35] Gates, on the other hand, managed to get several of his fellow billionaires on board, including Jeff Bezos of Amazon, Jack Ma of Alibaba, and Mark Zuckerberg of Facebook. When the partnership was launched in Paris in December 2015, under the name of the Breakthrough Energy Coalition, the involved governments promised $20 billion for energy R&D whilst the billionaires pledged to invest $2 billion in clean energy start-ups, with Gates providing half of that sum alone. For Obama, Gates' positive reputation in India seems to have been an important catalyst for his involvement, and a tool for the President to nurture the US–India relationship, finding common political ground with Indian Prime Minister Narendra Modi around energy investments, a common ground direly needed if India was to sign a climate agreement in Paris. In fact, the idea of the partnership was solidified in a meeting between Gates, Modi and Hollande in New York in September of that year, on the margins of the UN General Assembly.

The Gates Foundation of today

Over the course of its almost 20 years of existence, the foundation has been through a frenetic growth spurt from a lean family-run charity to a beasty bureaucracy, establishing itself as a major global political force. Over the last decade, Gates Foundation staff and administrative expenses have grown by a factor of ten. When the foundation moved into its first headquarters in 1999, it employed 130 people, of which 110 were only engaged in wiring public libraries across the US, leaving 20 people for everything else. Today, it employs almost 1,500 people (the vast majority of whom work in the Seattle headquarters), and its annual administrative expenses have grown tenfold from 2002 to 2012 (see Figure 4.1) and today amounts to more than $550 million. It supports grantees in 50 US states and in more than 100 countries, with offices in Seattle, WA, Washington, DC, New Delhi, Beijing, London, and representatives in Addis Ababa, Abuja and Johannesburg. Despite forming a burgeoning bureaucracy, the foundation today strikes a curious balance that sees it sometimes act with the agility of a lean and executive-driven organization, when *inter alia* co-chairs singlehandedly decide on new priorities and make grant pledges in the hundreds of millions of dollars without much internal consultation, and sometimes with the rigidity of a bureaucratic nightmare that sees grantees unable to establish contact with the foundation for several months. When the foundation opened its doors in

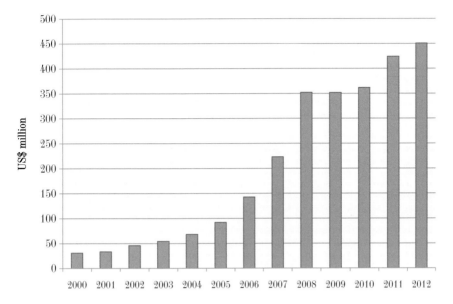

Figure 4.1 Programme and administrative expenses of the Gates Foundation, 2000–2012, US$ million. (Source: Gates Foundation annual reports 2000–2012.)

1999, Bill and Melinda would personally approve every grant above $1 million. Now the rule of thumb seems to be that Bill and Melinda do not get personally involved in deciding on grants unless they are somewhere above $40 million dollars. Yet, in certain cases where grants touch key areas of emphasis for either of the co-chairs, they may be found to micromanage.[36]

The foundation currently provides grants within three main programmes or divisions: the Global Development division, the Global Health division and the United States programme. The United States programme was essentially the first work of the foundation as it began supporting libraries and education efforts in the US Northwest Pacific in 1994. Today, the programme focuses on K-12 education, 'Postsecondary success', and projects in the state of Washington by supporting 'The development of innovative solutions in education that are unlikely to be generated by institutions working alone and that can trigger change on a broader scale'.[37] It is by far the smallest of the three large areas of work for the foundation, though it has hosted some of the largest grants in the foundation's history including $1.37 billion awarded over 20 years to the United Negro College Fund, providing scholarships for African-American and other students. In the US in particular, it is also the work of this programme on education that has garnered perhaps most attention, both among academics and the broader public.

Global health was the second area of intervention for the foundation as it began providing grants here in the late 1990s, but it soon emerged as its primary area of work. People who were involved in its early stage of engagement describe it as 'One big candy shop for global health and medical scientists', intellectually led by the trio of Bill Gates Sr, Bill Foege and Gordon Perkin.[38] When the Gates Foundation entered into global health in the late 1990s, and specifically immunization by founding the Global Alliance for Vaccination and Immunization or Gavi in the year 2000 with an initial grant of $750 million, it caused equal amazement and controversy. The reaction was not surprising, given that immunization rates were declining and organizations like UNICEF had difficulty in attracting funding for children's vaccination. Gavi was constructed as a private–public partnership, forming an unquestionable response from Gates who considered the existing organizations, including the WHO, too bureaucratic and inefficient. It has since been criticized by organizations such as Médecins Sans Frontières (MSF) for not properly handling the balancing act of making the initiative work for both businesses and the poor. The criticisms concern the fact that fully vaccinating a child today costs 68 times more than it did a decade ago, and that some children's vaccines seem to be overpriced.[39] An example is the important pneumococcal vaccine protecting children from pneumonia (the most lethal illness for children under the age of five in developing countries), which is priced at $60 per shot. GlaxoSmithKline and Pfizer, the only two producers of the vaccine, have made over $19 billion in revenue since introducing it in 2009.[40] For Gavi, the push for new vaccines is inevitably connected to the potential for overpricing, not least enabled by its Advance Market Commitment in which donors commit funds to guarantee the price of vaccines once they have been developed, thus creating incentives for vaccine manufacturers to invest in new vaccines but perhaps also pushing up prices. The foundation maintains its seat on the board of Gavi, as one of four permanent members, along with WHO, UNICEF and the World Bank. Since 2000 the foundation has provided more than $2.5 billion to this global public–private health partnership. It also sits on the board of the Global Fund to Fight HIV/Aids, tuberculosis and malaria, to which it has contributed more than $1.5 billion. Overall, the foundation is involved in an incalculable number of health-related initiatives and projects today. Some have even found that '[A]ll the key contributors to global health have an association with the Gates Foundation through some sort of funding arrangement'.[41] It has long been involved in setting the health agenda of G8, and participates in a self-made H8 group that also includes the WHO, the World Bank, Gavi, the Global Fund, UNICEF, the UN Population Fund, and UNAIDS. Selection of priorities naturally also means rejection of others, and the foundation's work necessarily shapes the broader priorities of others, whether deliberately or unintentionally. Not least when it comes to the so-called vertical interventions or programmes, which are essentially large-scale investments in narrow issues that, for the most part, are pursued in isolation. These have long been criticized for diverting focus away from health systems building, disrupting policy and planning processes in recipient countries by often being single-disease focused.[42]

Since venturing into this field, the foundation has provided well over $18 billion in grants to issues of health and vaccination, through the approach of harnessing 'Advances in science and technology to save lives in the developing countries'.[43]

Specifically, the current Global Health division includes teams focusing on discovery and translational diseases; enteric and diarrheal diseases; HIV; malaria; 'neglected tropical diseases'; pneumonia; and tuberculosis. In 2011, Trevor Mundel was hired as President of Global Health, coming from a position as head of global development in Novartis, one of the world's biggest pharmaceutical companies. He succeeded Tachi Yahamada, formerly GlaxoSmithKline, and before him Richard Klausner, who resigned after three years in the midst of allegations of financial fraud in his prior engagement with the National Cancer Institute, as well as Gordon Perkin, who had spells in the Ford Foundation and in WHO prior to coming to the foundation. With Mundel in place, the Global Health programme began a transitioning process of becoming a 'virtual pharma', narrowing the scope to focusing on supporting the biomedical and drug industry in developing new products, while the implementation and delivery responsibility for health projects have been moved to a newer department under the Global Development division called 'Integrated Delivery'.

In April 2017 the foundation announced a new initiative on global health research and development that went somewhat under the radar in the mass media, but nonetheless may come to have immense consequences for its work and for the field of global health. The foundation is establishing a non-profit medical research organization that will bear the name 'The Bill and Melinda Gates Medical Research Institute', with the overall aim of accelerating progress in translational science (literally the translation of scientific discoveries into potentially viable medical products). Its initial focus will be on enhancing the product development pipeline for malaria, tuberculosis, and enteric and diarrheal diseases, which in layman's terms means the institute will engage in innovating, designing and inventing novel forms of drugs, vaccines, diagnostics and medical devices. Once such devices have been developed, they will be transitioned to manufacturers and partner-developers that can take them forward into late-stage development. The institute will be co-located in Seattle and Boston and initially headed by Penny Heaton who leads the foundation's Vaccine Development and Surveillance programme.[44] She will lead a process of hiring up to 120 full-time scientists and maintaining an annual operating budget upwards of $100 million as a start. In essence, the creation of a separate medical institute working as an extension of the Gates Foundation is a significant break with foundation practices. Foundations, including the Gates Foundation, are increasingly taking part in designing projects and grants along with potential grantees, but have then largely left the actual execution of projects and grants to the grantee, while mainly monitoring and evaluating on the sidelines. The new institute essentially takes over the process of project execution and product development in the case of global health research and development. The foundation thus recaptures control over project design, funding and execution, with the only thing separating them from recipients being the current inability of the foundation to deliver such medical devices or inventions. It is another step towards an increasingly bureaucratized organization, but it is also one that greatly expands the ability of the foundation to govern and control projects, while providing substantial amounts of flexibility in pursuing successful vaccines, drugs or medical devices. Now it does not have to witness a grant slowly not deliver or fail over three years, but can instead quickly intervene and shift priorities or the direction of research. In the end this will lead to an even more dominant position for the foundation in global health. As David Bank wrote about Gates' desire for control during his Microsoft days: 'Control, for Gates, is not a matter of status or ego. It is more like breathing – essential to his very functioning. From his first forays into business as a teenager, he told his partners, I'm much easier to deal with if I'm in charge'.[45]

The Global Development programme is the newest area of intervention for the foundation and today its largest in terms of financial allocations.[46] As described, the programme was established in 2006 when the Buffett gift required the foundation to greatly expand its grant-making. It is an extremely diverse and fragmented programme that employs individuals with backgrounds in everything from the natural and medical sciences to anthropology and economics, and that aims to 'Identify and fund high-impact solutions that can help hundreds of millions of people lift themselves out of poverty and build better lives'.[47] Formally, it includes teams working on: agricultural development; emergency response; family planning; financial services for the poor; global libraries; integrated delivery; maternal, newborn and child health; nutrition; polio; vaccine delivery; water, sanitation and hygiene; and their reinvention of the toilet. Since 2012 this division has been led by Chris Elias, the former President and CEO of PATH, the Seattle-based organization that was one of the earliest grant recipients in the foundation's portfolio. The impatience of the foundation to achieve its goals has always been known to those who have partnered with it (Gates has said it clearly, 'I call myself the impatient optimist, because I want things to go faster'[48] – and Impatient Optimists is also the name of the foundation's blog), and nowhere has this been as clear as in the Global Development programme. As the programme was constructed following Buffett's immense gift, different teams and particularly the ag-team, as the agricultural team is known as colloquially, needed scaling up. Foundation leadership apparently had no time to waste, because, as one of them explained, 'You don't learn how to be big by being small'.[49] Over a few years from 2006, the ag-team went from zero to 100 employees, with initial budgets multiplying each year; 'It was almost like you could just add a zero to our budget each year'[50] as one senior programme officer has explained it. Across all new teams the rapid approach to scaling up was similar. Once the decision had been made of what issue areas to invest in, the foundation was able to use its high profile and financial strength to bring in a critical mass of, at least at the top, highly paid experts from the field.[51] This move includes hiring internationally recognized advisors, as well as individuals for programme officer positions, also often at a high level of expertise. In the ag-team such a scaling up meant the hiring of many different individuals with different professional training, coming from diverse positions and organizations, whether public aid agencies, private companies such as McKinsey, or research institutes. In the ag-team, interviewees who were involved during this process explained how such a dynamic or perhaps chaotic process meant that those who were already hired also utilized opportunities of mobility to shift between different teams. A culture of impatience thus formed, and people were increasingly unwilling to stick around, whether because of the composition of the portfolio allocated by leadership, or the impatience of driving one's career forward. Such a culture naturally entails that the projects established were often fairly short term in scope or, if long term, would see frequent rearrangements in priorities and goals as they changed hands inside the foundation. For much of this time the agricultural team was headed by the now late Sam Dryden who came to the foundation with work experiences from Monsanto, Union Carbide and Emergent Genetics. Today the team is led by Nick Austin, joining the foundation from CGIAR, a close beneficiary of the foundation. The foundation has given more than $700 million to CGIAR or the Consultative Group on International Agricultural Research, an influential organization driving agricultural (and particularly biotechnological) research across its 15 centres all over the world. The foundation also sits on the board of the organization.

At large, the story of the foundation's engagement in global agriculture compares well to its beginnings in global health. When it started approaching this particular field and announced its first major grants in 2006, international support for agriculture was at a low point. From 1985 to 2005 USAID's spending on agriculture decreased from 12 per cent of its budget to around 3 per cent. The largest Gates Foundation grant thus far has been founding and supporting AGRA or the Alliance for a Green Revolution in Africa with a $150 million grant in 2006, also with support from the Rockefeller Foundation, the founder of the original Green Revolution of the 1960s in India. AGRA aims to introduce 'technology packages' to poor farmers that will allow for an increase in agricultural yields, based on a crop-breeding approach that paves the way for genetic engineering technology. Former UN Secretary-General Kofi Annan was the first chairman of AGRA, a position that now belongs to Strive Masiyiwa, who is also a trustee of the Rockefeller Foundation. The founding of AGRA has not come without its controversies however, and critics hold that the reason why a green revolution similar to that in India has not been introduced in Africa is because the original revolution has been a failure, leaving Indian farmers in debt because of the high prices of seeds and fertilizers that in turn have compromised the local soil and environment, and that AGRA is making similar mistakes.[52] They hold that the technical approach of AGRA underplays how hunger is a deeply political matter of structural inequities and, rather than due to lack of food, it is caused by lack of access to the food already being produced.[53] The technical base is itself criticized for being on the wrong track, with genetic engineering potentially leaving smallholder systems more environmentally vulnerable and, finally, the process of forming AGRA has been criticized for not involving farmers, but mainly seed and fertilizer companies, philanthropic foundations and multilateral institutions.[54] The day after the Gates Foundation publicized the AGRA grant, Jacques Diouf, Secretary-General of the UN's Food and Agriculture Organization (FAO), called for support for a 'Second Green Revolution'. Similarly, after visiting Ghana in 2009, then US President Obama was quoted as saying that he was 'Still frustrated over the fact that the green revolution that we introduced into India in the '60s, we haven't yet introduced into Africa in 2009'.[55] During the same time, in the summer of 2009, G8 leaders committed $20 billion over three years to boost agricultural investments, with the fine print mentioning fertilizer and seed, grain storage vessels and plant variety research, most of these priorities of the Gates Foundation and its agribusiness collaborators. Around the same time in 2009, an advocacy report by the Chicago Council on Global Affairs (*Renewing American Leadership in the Fight Against Global Hunger and Poverty*), was co-authored by ex-Gates Senior Fellow and ex-WFP head Catherine Bertini. In the report Africa's hunger is mainly ascribed to technical deficits and it is concluded that the US needed to 'Reassert its leadership' in 'spreading new technologies' to increase trade and strengthen American institutions.[56] It seemed the Gates Foundation had certainly brought back some form of momentum to efforts in global agriculture. Unfortunately, donors failed to live up to their 2009 commitments and, as a follow up to the 2009 G8 declaration on agricultural investments, a G8 New Alliance for Food Security and Nutrition initiative was launched in 2012, once again aiming to accelerate agricultural production and lift 50 million people out of poverty by 2022. Similar to the private sector involvement in Gavi, the New Alliance provided seats on the leadership council to CEOs of companies such as Unilever, and agribusiness giants Syngenta, Yara and Cargill. 'The world's agriculture and food system is now outdated and inefficient'[57] Gates proclaimed that year in Rome, targeting specifically the United Nations agencies including the Food and Agriculture Organization, the International Fund for Agricultural Development and the World Food Programme, and particularly what he perceived as their inability to coordinate efforts. And he was not unsuccessful in convincing others that their approach was the right way to go. As *The New York Times* wrote in 2012, following exactly that meeting in Rome, 'There is not much mystery about what poor farmers need: simple inputs like fertilizer and improved seeds, as well as better access to markets and improved food storage'.[58] The foundation's approach to global health and agriculture demonstrates well how it is able to direct research and policy agendas by sheer financial force, and provision of grants to specific (in these two cases, underfunded) areas. The entrance into new areas seems often to be preceded by scoping and planning, identifying underfunded areas of interest while mapping who is doing what and how. What follows such a relatively humble approach, then, are often forms of attack from all sides. Grants are provided to organizations involved in the areas where approaches are found productive, while advocacy grants are given to ensure that talk about the issue in question increases. And not only talk but the right kind of talk that may draw in other donors and attract positive attention to the issue, and talk by the right people, including researchers, NGOs, politicians, media, etc.

The last of the four divisions of the foundation is that of Global Policy and Advocacy. Though a fairly new division, it was formed by bringing together several people and parts of teams that were already working on advocacy and government relations. Over its first years the budget of the division increased to several hundred million dollars in a process of massive scaling up that was largely a reflection of increasing acknowledgement of the need to strengthen this side of the foundation's work to increase impact. The foundation itself describes how seeing as its

Resources alone are not enough to advance the causes we care about, we engage in advocacy efforts to promote public policies that advance our work, build strategic alliances with governments and the public and private sectors, and foster greater public awareness of urgent global issues.[59]

Though it formally presents itself as only engaged in two areas, tobacco control and development policy and finance, the advocacy efforts of the foundation, vastly increasing over the last ten years as we have seen, covers an astounding breadth of political and strategic issues across all of the issues the foundation is engaged in. For global development specifically, these include advocacy for public donors to sustain ambitions of ODA but also government relations with countries in the Global South, as well as heavy investments in partnerships with NGOs, academia, international organizations and the media to shape agendas of research and reporting. As a registered private foundation, the Gates Foundation is legally prohibited from lobbying in the US, but these rules are easily bent. The foundation is not allowed to directly communicate with US government officials about specific legislative proposals, but they can safely speak to representatives about issues as long as there are no mentions of specific legal actions. They can communicate about pledges and commitments, about administrative rules and regulations, any form of judicial decision or government activity so long as it is not subject to legislative vote or approval, and are also allowed to directly distribute materials such as white papers or reports. Furthermore, foundation staff are allowed to speak with government officials about legislative proposals or actions if they do it in relation to programmes that are jointly-funded by the government and the foundation. Gates Foundation staff can thus fully discuss any legislative proposal related to programmes in which the US government is also involved, such as Gavi, the Global Fund to Fight AIDS, TB and Malaria, or its joint work on agriculture or polio. The Gates Foundation has always been mindful of walking right up to the line of what is legally permissible, and have gone to great lengths to ensure that its lobbying and advocacy activities were as direct and impactful as possible without crossing the line. Institutional safeguards in the foundation have included careful training of employees who are engaged in advocacy efforts, strong internal policies and a department tasked with monitoring advocacy activities and ensuring their legality.[60] But the elasticity of the legislation concerning foundation lobbying is such that very few, if any, conceivable messages or meetings cannot be conducted on the right side of the law. Gates Foundation staff may easily take representatives or government officials out for dinner and emphasize how USAID should push for a much stronger stance on global health research and development, so long as they do not talk about specific pieces of legislation.

The Trust and investment practices

The Gates Foundation has an endowment of approximately $40 billion, representing a greater value than the GDP of more than half the world's countries. As with the vast majority of private foundations, these funds do not sit passively in a bank somewhere but are actively invested to ensure a return and increase the assets of the organization, thus potentially expanding its grant-making. Up until 2006, the foundation's endowments were exactly there, in the foundation, but around this time the endowments were taken out of the foundation and put into the Bill and Melinda Gates Foundation Trust. As such, the foundation now has a two-entity structure in which the Foundation distributes money to grantees, while the Trust manages additional amounts of endowment assets. Every year then, funds equalling the desired level of grant-making of the foundation are transferred from the Trust. Investing approximately $40 billion is bound to attract public scrutiny, but it did not truly do so until when, in 2007, the *LA Times* had a reporter working fulltime for three months to review the investment portfolio of the foundation. The reporter found that the foundation was investing in oil companies, chemical companies, pharmaceuticals pricing drugs far beyond the reach of AIDS patients, and many of the world's major polluters including Royal Dutch Shell, Exxon Mobile Corp., Chevron Corp. and Total of France.[61] The newspaper concluded that they had found at least $8.7 billion worth of investments in companies that directly countered the foundation's charitable goals. The response was quite interesting for a charitable organization that aims to support poor people in the developing world. The foundation held that because of the two-entity structure they could not, nor would they be willing to, control what the Trust was investing the endowments in. Gates himself held that this tactic of setting up a system of scoring investments: 'That's not our role. That's more of a governmental role',[62] and that divesting from corporations that countered the foundation's aims was unreasonable, because 'We wouldn't have any direct effect there'.[63] The foundation did eventually announce it was planning a systematic review to determine if it should cut its financial ties to countries that are doing harm to society.[64]

The answer to the controversy that the foundation per se does not handle its own investments, while misguided, is technically true. The foundation's endowments are invested by an external holding and investment company called Cascade Investment LLC (also referred to as Bill and Melinda Gates Investments), based in Kirkland, WA, and employing around 100 people. The company only handles the foundation's endowment and Bill's own funds, and is said to have ensured the Gates family and the foundation an annual nominal return around 11 per cent.[65] Michael Larson leads the under-the-radar company, succeeding Andrew Evans as Gates' moneymaker in 1994. When a *Wall Street Journal* article in March 1993 reported Evans to have been convicted on charges of bank fraud, Gates replaced Evans with Larson.[66] Everything concerning Cascade Investment is secretive, and Larson has only ever given a single public interview (to *Fortune* in 1999), allowing the company to move beneath the public radar. Employees often sign pledges of secrecy upon leaving and are generally asked to abstain from telling anyone for whom they work.[67] In principle, Larson decides what to invest in, though he has apparently been asked to run a conservative scheme (aiming for a five per cent nominal annual return), as the Gates' plan to continuously donate money to the foundation makes it unnecessary to run an aggressive scheme. From 1999 to 2006 the investment portfolio earned an average of 8.53 per cent a year for the foundation.[68] However, as already mentioned, the invested endowment suffered greatly during the 2008 financial crisis with the foundation losing almost $8 billion. The annual return has since increased to an even greater level. Today, and surely also as an overdue response to the sustained criticism of its investment practices, the foundation has an 'investment philosophy', which it describes as the following:

> Bill and Melinda do guide the managers of the foundation's endowment in voting proxies consistent with the principles of good governance and good management. When instructing the investment managers, Bill and Melinda also consider other issues beyond corporate profits, including the values that drive the foundation's work. They have defined areas in which the endowment will not invest, such as companies whose profit model is centrally tied to corporate activity that they find egregious. This is why the endowment does not invest in tobacco or Sudan-related stocks.[69]

The two really off-limits investment areas thus remain tobacco and Sudan-related stock (though it has also divested from G4S after controversies over its prison contracts in Israel and Palestine). While the foundation continues to invest in fossil fuel companies such as Exxon and BP, it has significantly scaled down these activities, divesting billions away from ExxonMobil and Royal Dutch Shell over the last years.[70] It also divested the majority of its shares in McDonalds Corp., and Coca Cola Co., approximately worth $1 billion for each, in late 2014. Still, the approximately $26 billion invested by the Trust in corporate stocks and bonds includes notable corporations from mining (Rio Tinto, Barrick Gold, Freeport McMoran, Glencore and Vale), agribusiness (Archer Daniels Midland, Kraft, Mondelez International, Unilever), chemical and pharmaceuticals (Wallgreens Boots Alliance, GlaxoSmithKline, Merck, Novartis, Novo Nordisk, Pfizer), beverage, fast food and retail (Walmart, Coca Cola, Arcos Dorados [McDonald's franchisee], Pepsico, Diageo, SABMiller), as well as coal and oil (Anglo American, BHP Billiton, Shell, Conoco Phillips, Petrobras),[71] ranging from miniscule investments (Mondelez International investments only amounts to approximately $1.5 million) to massive ones (more than $700 million is invested in Walmart and almost $450 in Coca Cola). Together, they naturally call into question the foundation's efforts in global health and development. In addition to the questionable nature of some of these investments, ones that may actually come to counter the mission of the foundation, an issue regards the practice of providing grants to companies in which the foundation's Trust has corporate stock. As an example, the foundation jointly funds a project with Coca Cola in which 50,000 local farmers in Kenya are trained by US-based Technoserve (that works with business solutions to poverty) to produce for, e.g., Coca Cola's supply chain.[72]

Grantees

The Gates Foundation supports a vast volume of grantees of all sizes and forms. From $50 to the Mount Rainier, North Cascades and Olympic Fund to billion-dollar grants to international organizations (see Table 4.1 for an overview of some of its largest grants). The Gates Foundation is certainly not a community foundation, and though it does provide grants to its immediate vicinity in the Pacific Northwest, it is for the most part supportive of what we might deem elite institutions, as opposed to grassroots organizations. Likewise, its way of achieving influence through grants is largely based on a top-down approach that sees it target the most influential people and work with them to eventually have these individuals themselves further diffuse the ideas of the foundation as opposed to the foundation having to advance them. This is reflective of the impatience of the foundation, an attitude that would largely lead them to go to the top for quick change instead of targeting organizations at lower levels who would likely engage in more incremental and slow-paced (albeit perhaps also more lasting) forms of change. And it is certainly not surprising seeing as its mission and ambitions are first and foremost ones that are difficult to attain swiftly through grassroots engagement (i.e., a broad base of constituents), such as federal or even international policy change.

Some years ago an analysis found that more than half of the foundation's spending had been provided to only 20 organizations, leading to a concentration of funds and influence in a narrow set of actors, particularly within the global health field.[73] Likewise, the vast majority of the foundation's largest grantees are based in the US or in Western Europe, just as we have seen for the foundation's Grand Challenges scheme. In 2009 the foundation commissioned an independent survey of its work with grantees. The survey found that grantees felt the foundation had a positive impact on knowledge, policy and practice in the areas within which it works, but there were concerns about the clarity of the foundation's goals and strategy and lacking ability to understand grantees' goals and strategy. The decision-making and grant-making processes were not considered transparent,

Table 4.1 Top ten largest grants from the Bill and Melinda Gates Foundation.

Grantee	Year	Issue	Amount
GAVI Alliance	2016	Vaccine delivery	$1,550,000,000
United Negro College Fund, Inc.	1999	Scholarships	$1,525,380,950
The Rotary Foundation of Rotary International	2009 and earlier	Polio	$985,210,000
GAVI Alliance	2011	Vaccine delivery	$953,600,000
GAVI Alliance	1999	Vaccine delivery	$750,000,000
The Global Fund to Fight AIDS, Tuberculosis and Malaria	2011	Global policy and advocacy	$750,000,000
World Health Organization	2009 and earlier	Polio	$676,345,891
The Global Fund to Fight AIDS, Tuberculosis and Malaria	2006	Global policy and advocacy	$500,000,000
Hispanic Scholarship Fund	2015	Scholarships	$417,215,300
GAVI Alliance	2009 and earlier	Vaccine delivery	$375,000,000

and its communication was inconsistent and unresponsive. Three years later, in 2012, a follow-up survey was made with some reporting a continued lack of clarity in communication and decision-making, as well as in how grants contributed to the larger goals of the foundation's programmes. One grantee stated: 'I can't figure out the organization—it's a puzzle. They're a matrixed organization, and it's unclear who reports to whom.'[74]

In all of the four large programmes and divisions of the foundation, the formal process of funding a new grant officially occurs something like this. Formally, potential grantees submit letters of interest or inquiry (LOI) about projects they would like to receive funding for. If an LOI looks interesting, the programme officer accepts it and requests a full proposal. If the full proposal falls in line with the foundation's strategy, or the preferences of the programme officer, the organization is asked to submit a full packet of proposal-related documents to the foundation. From here, an often long and iterative process begins where the programme officer and the grantee discuss the project, back and forth. If this process is successful and leadership consider the project ready, different teams start due diligence (handled by KPMG) and compliance review of the project, inquiring whether the proposal adheres to foundation granting policies (Legal Department), if the budget matches the project and is reasonable (Financial Planning and Analysis), and the communications department likewise doing their job.

In reality, unsolicited proposals are rarely if ever successful when proposed to the foundation, which instead works strategically and deliberately to identify potential grantees that can help the foundation achieve its stated goals. Long gone are the days when programme officers would sit and screen incoming proposals, picking out the most promising ones and eventually leaving grantees to handle the grants on their own. Programme officers will often have been in contact with potential grantees to discuss their probability of gaining funding long before the formal process of submitting a proposal is initiated. Here, concrete deliverables and performance metrics are worked out with the potential grantees, while applications are negotiated with foundation staff to make sure that they resonate with foundation leadership and thus have a higher chance of approval. Grantees essentially become contractors who are tasked with delivering certain outputs, functioning as vehicles for the ambitions and aspirations of the foundation. As one Senior Programme Officer phrased the meeting between the foundation and its grantees, 'We know where we want to go and we know what we want to achieve. What we ask of them is "can you get us there and how?"'.[75] While it is certainly a strength in controlling outcomes to set a tight strategic direction that dictates objectives of grants, it often also means that priorities are difficult to change and may remain static, not allowing for the grantee to readily adapt if needed. As for the foundation's involvement in grant design, a Seattle-based grantee explained how

> Everyone's talking about the overwhelming task that is completing an application for the Gates Foundation, but once we reach that point in time where we have to actually fill out all this stuff we have worked with foundation POs for a while to identify everything from milestones to size of the grant.

Some have earlier criticized the foundation's selection of potential grantees for being predominantly managed through informal systems of personal networks and relationships, as opposed to the technical peer-review we see at some founda- tions.[76] While this is certainly true, it regards some areas more than others and the astounding scope of the foundation's annual grant-making means not all grants are planned ahead or proactively selected by foundation staff only on the basis of networks.

There is also a strong element of recurrence in much of the Gates Foundation's work with grantees. If a grantee has been shown to deliver impactful results or perhaps even failed to do so but showed promise and effective management, it is highly likely that new grants will be provided to it through informal channels. As a European grantee explained,

> As we were finishing up what was promised to be delivered, we had a few new ideas that we presented to the foundation, which would build on our first grant. The POs were interested, and the process of gaining these two new grants was so much easier than the first one, seeing as we had proven ourselves able to deliver, more or less effectively.[77]

Still, the persistent efforts of foundation staff to engage with grantees to influence project design and implementation does not necessarily apply to all grantees and throughout implementation. Just as has been reflected in the last many grantee perception reports of the foundation, some of my informants expressed a dissatis- faction with the uneven communication from the foundation as grants were being implemented. Especially one grantee informant who voiced frustration about lacking responses from the foundation towards the end of their grant, making dis- semination and conclusion of the project difficult:

> Even in the last six months of the grant we did not hear from the foundation over a period of three months. You write one mail, you write two. How are we supposed to know what to do? You slowly begin to become frustrated or paralyzed, and eventually the grant loses importance in your organization, but you also know that as soon as they return, they will have some very dis- tinct ideas about what should be done and what should not.[78]

Organizational culture or why Bill Gates did not invent the iPad

One way to try and understand the organizational culture of the Gates Foundation is to appreciate the life of being a programme officer, the portfolio-managing employees that make up the vast majority of staff in the Gates Foundation, just as they do in the majority of the world's foundations. Programme officers are a cor- nerstone, if not the backbone, of the foundation industry. In the Gates Foundation they each handle their own individual portfolio of grants within a subject area, and typically one they have an expertise in (but not necessarily so). Above them are, in theory, team leaders or deputy directors, directors, programme presidents, and the trustees. Despite what might appear to be a low position in the organizational food chain, they have great agency and influence over the foundation's core activity – grant-making. Directors are given budgets that they distribute on to their deputy directors, who then allocate financial resources to each of the individual programme officers. Because of this, programme officers often become personally associated with specific issues. This has the very natural function of letting everybody know who is doing what (basic distribution of roles to facilitate compartmentalization), but it also often entails that when something is downsized or loses its priority, not just the issue but also the programme officer often leaves the foundation. Despite the personal association of issues to specific programme officers, grants naturally need to stay in specific thematic teams. Grants typically move then from programme officer to programme officer as individuals change positions. This has several implications. For programme officers, it means you may inherit bad or unsuccessful projects, or be forced (if not changing position on your own initiative) to give up successful projects, perhaps ones you have followed over the course of a long time. This can have grave consequences for your future career within the foundation. For grantees, it means uneven communication with the foundation and, more importantly, that the objectives and purposes of the grant may change. As the grant changes hands, its content and purpose may easily change with it, as each individual programme officer brings to the grant his or her professional worldview, experiences and approach to working with both grants and grantees. For some grants, this can mean radical changes, potentially disrupting impact. In a 2009 grantee perception report, one grantee was cited as saying that 'In the middle of our grant development, our primary contact changed. With this, also the focus and goals of our discussions changed'.[79] Foundation POs have told me similar stories of how they have left grants to colleagues, only to see them change form as the new responsible employee preferred corn over cassava and made sure the grantee implemented alterations to reflect this in project execution.

Two things appear particularly important to attain for programme officers in the Gates Foundation: grant-making money and the intellectual attention of leadership. The axis of power is described by many foundation employees as being grant-making, and the larger the budget and portfolio you may scrape together as a programme officer, the more influence you appear to be in possession of, strengthening your organizational position. The non-financial way to attain such influence is through attention and talk. As in most organizations, the right talk, and with the right people, provides you with great influence. The highest level of talk involves gaining the intellectual attention of the trustees – Bill and Melinda. Such attention could in turn lead to an increased priority of one's area.[80] While some interviewees claimed that the majority of the grants are initiated fairly quickly and have limited life spans, after which they are often killed off before they may reach a stage where impact is more likely to be achieved, others found that, while potentially problematic in terms of impact, smaller or shorter grants are often made for a very special reason. The smaller a grant is, the less leadership needs to be involved. Programme officers can thus act strategically, using their agency to make smaller grants that ensure them a higher degree of autonomy with less monitoring from further up in the system. This includes most grants below the threshold of $3 million. There are of course limits to this agency, and several interviewees underlined how programme officers can only manoeuvre within the boundaries of what is deemed acceptable by leadership and official strategies.

In theory, programme officers should be engaged in reviewing other officers' grants (as we will see in the next chapter on the issue of mainstreaming gender equality across grants), but many of my informants explained that, in reality, it is not seen as good practice to ask critical questions about other people's work. All programme officers work under great pressure to finalize grants, and the last thing one would want is for someone to question the premise of one of your grants. Some were of the opinion that mistakes or flaws were thus not properly addressed and resolved in grants because of fear of meddling in other people's affairs.[81] Others thought it underlined what seems to be an organizational rule of 'Lead, follow or get out'.[82] This refers back to the point about how the right kind of talk could ensure influence. If you want to reach the top do not ask questions about other people's work or the priorities of the foundation, several advised. As opposed to innovation, keeping up such a work environment basically cultivates a unification of thought, in which critical independent thinking is not appreciated but rather penalized, and one interviewee explained how she understood 'Why Bill Gates made Microsoft, but also why he did not invent the iPad'.[83] Being successful, it seems, does not necessarily rely on the impact of one's grants. This hardly comes as a surprise, but the issue of success and failure is interesting in a foundation like the Gates. Publicly, failure is often described as potentially a positive thing, as long as one learns from it. The foundation is very conscious about making sure it is always portrayed as 'Trying different things, and seeing which ones work', and the same is conveyed to employees, and especially the pro-gramme officers. All in all, the willingness of the Gates Foundation to learn from mistakes is often portrayed as unusual for foundations. The translation of this mantra into reality seems to be quite different across teams. One interviewee held that failure is not necessarily penalized, while several others said that the anxiety of failing was leading to a risk-averse conservative approach to grant-making. Such anxiety, of course, may just as well stem from employees' false assumptions about leadership expectations as it might originate from actual reactions or signals of these. To encourage more constructive self-critical dialogue inside the founda-tion, it often holds events called Failure Fest (sometimes referred to as Fail Fest or Fail Festival), where employees talk openly of their failures in order to learn from them. Unfortunately, one of those who decided to do so a few years back was fired shortly after.[84] While such action may be coincidental or even untrue, it can easily come to serve as a scare story to other employees on the consequences of having grants in your portfolio that do not achieve appropriate impact.

The competition amongst all staff, not just the programme officers, is fierce, as it is in most professional organizations. In essence, interviewees often explained how 'Everyone wants to work for the Gates Foundation'.[85] This is an interesting point, as the very same people also explained how substantial the foundation's turnover rate has been during some years, because many, apparently, are surprised by what appears to be high demands from leadership and a tremendously fast-paced style of work. The dynamic working environment but also the presence of individuals from across fields of work and research with a tremendous level of expertise prompted some of my interviewees to describe how 'Working for the Gates Foundation feels a bit like being Alice in Wonderland. Tumbling down the rabbit hole, you never know what you're gonna expect', and that the distinctive trait of employing numerous individual Senior Fellows and Advisors meant the foundation 'Sometimes felt like the Dominican Republic national baseball team. It has all the star players, but they often seem to focus more on their individuality, with bad cooperation as a consequence'.[86]

When I talked to my interviewees about the organizational culture and the work environment, almost all of them found their way to mentioning Microsoft. Sometimes as the first thing in the conversation, and sometimes as a late realization of what they had just described. There is no denying the Microsoft legacy. From 1999 to 2014 the foundation was essentially led by former Microsoft executives, from Patty Stonesifer to Jeff Raikes. Pointing to the cultural similarities between Microsoft and the Gates Foundation in 2008, former CEO Jeff Raikes highlighted the focus and vision for how 'Science and technology can change the world and do it a very positive way'.[87] Microsoft, of course, does not have a positive reputation for its work environment. One of the infamous initiatives is that of 'stack ranking', requiring each team leader to declare a certain percentage of the employees as top, good, average, below average and poor, on a bell curve. Each year then, someone had to be rated poorly, even in situations of everyone performing well, and be let go or reassigned. Such fear-based management has been identified by some as the reason why innovation was apparently crippled in Microsoft, as employees were competing against each other instead of other companies.[88] Even Melinda Gates, who was employed in Microsoft from 1987, has later called the culture of the company 'Acerbic', explaining that she had considered leaving the company.[89] This approach to performance evaluation was not abandoned in Microsoft until 2012, but it is not one that has been brought over into the Gates Foundation, at least not formally. Many of the interviewees, however, do tell stories of authoritarian leadership, a remarkably vocal Bill Gates, sometimes using his executive powers to fire an entire team.[90] While most people think of Bill Gates as a harmless software nerd, it was his fierce and relentless ambition that drove Microsoft forward and gave him a reputation as one of the most ruthless CEOs in corporate America. He is known for his 'Conquer-the-world capitalist nature', often described as a poster boy of cutthroat capitalism,[91] and it is widely acknowledged that Microsoft, at least for its first decade and more, mirrored the person Bill Gates. In Microsoft, Gates' ambitions were beyond belief as he continuously drove the company towards deals that would buy up every single emerging competitor, in almost all of its fields. In the late 1990s, as this tactic was at a high point, Walt Disney's Michael Eisner proclaimed that 'The common wisdom is that the person to worry about the most right now is Bill Gates', while Robert Murdoch followed suit that 'Everybody in the communications business is paranoid of Microsoft, including me'.[92] The ambition for Microsoft was to dominate all industries with their software, from healthcare to banks to newspapers. While the comparison with Microsoft's well-known work environment issues is probably very real, it should of course be assumed in moderation. Rather than as a unique case for the Gates Foundation, this can be considered the way many US corporations work, especially those affiliated with Silicon Valley. The stories about Microsoft, Amazon and many other similar companies are plentiful, and they are not all pretty. The Gates Foundation may sometimes appear to be a development actor like an NGO or a public aid agency, but it is first and foremost a private foundation started by one of the greatest capitalists in American history, headed for its entire lifetime by leaders at several levels with roots deep into the US private sector, whether in Microsoft, McKinsey, Merck, Pfizer or Monsanto.

The normative power of the Gates Foundation

The most obvious of all the Gates Foundation's ways of exerting influence, whether in the developing or in the developed world, is the vast financial power embodied in its multi-billion-dollar annual grant-making. Without any additional action, this material power is in itself able to direct or shift research and policy agendas around the world. But the foundation also has many other options at its disposal when it comes to advancing its aims and strategies, and the reach and power of the Gates Foundation extends far beyond its immense financial resources, whether we observe it from US domestic politics or from global development. With networks into the wealthiest parts of all the world's societies, and celebrity statuses equalled by very few, Bill and Melinda Gates have access to prime ministers, presidents or kings around the globe (which we will hear more about in Chapter 8). Strong ties to former and current democratic cabinets, senators and congressmen and women in Washington DC allows for an exchange of personnel and ideas, facilitating a spread of the beliefs and agendas of the foundation, ensuring financial and intellectual support within the US political spheres.[93] In the rest of the world, the foundation has increased its presence in international fora and organizations in the last years, with recurring appearances in the UN, the EU and the OECD, and with board memberships of many influential organizations including Gavi, WHO, the Global Fund and many others. The funding of media 'partnerships' in the US and Europe furthermore allows it to influence the spread of news and reports. Obviously, this influence and power would wane were it not driven by immense ambition and confidence, something the perpetually impatient optimists of the foundation are full of. As former CEO Patty Stonesifer explained, 'We encourage the taxes to go up in China, they did that'.[94] The foundation may have influenced the decision, of course, but it is difficult to imagine that pressure from the Gates Foundation should be enough to make Chinese leaders increase taxes. Two areas are of specific interest in considering the growing normative power of the Gates Foundation: the power of celebrity and the foundation's spread of people and ideas.

In the last years studies on the role of celebrities in development or poverty-alleviating efforts have increased.[95] The role of celebrities in speaking for causes or attempting to influence public policy, however, dates back centuries, as West[96] has shown with regard to American culture. Celebrities may interact with development through many different strategies: as forms of endorsements, marketing ideas or humanitarian issues aimed at the public such as Scarlett Johansson's controversial spell at Oxfam International;[97] in informal advisor-like positions to governments, such as U2 lead singer Bono on foreign aid or Leonardo DiCaprio on climate change; by providing resources themselves to aid causes; or perhaps in a role combining all three, such as the one Bill and Melinda Gates have assumed now for several years. Bill and Melinda Gates are not only trustees of their own foundation, into which they have poured billions and billions of dollars. They are also advertising banners aimed at the public when they speak out about the priorities of their work to newspapers and magazines, or they use their celebrity status to engage with, and advocate to, governments all over the world. Highly visible and wealthy philanthropists such as these two not only use their high media visibility and public support for awareness purposes but also for influencing development agendas and exerting political pressure.[98] As we have seen, it was not the ambition of the Gates Foundation to pursue global political influence when it was started in the basement of Gates Sr's house in 1994. But, as time has rolled on and the foundation has grown in size, scope and ambition, the celebrity status of the two trustees has increasingly become part of its advocacy plans. By 2004 the Gates had become 'More comfortable using their status as celebrities to call attention to the foundation's work',[99] Melinda slowly began participating in interviews and, not long after, Bill fully embraced his celebrity status by opening a Twitter account, by blogging about his reading and thoughts on a new webpage called 'Gatesnotes.com', and by marketing the ideas and priorities of the foundation at all the events he took part in, or in interviews he gave to national and international media. And he explicitly told foundation staff that they should use their influence as much as they used their philanthropy.[100] Former CEO Patty Stonesifer herself explained in 2007 how 'Ten years ago, if Bono had asked to meet us, we would probably have said no'.[101] Since then, it has been difficult to separate the two. The celebrity status of the foundation's co-chairs has also been used to incite other billionaires to give away their fortunes for philanthropic purposes. In 2010 Bill and Melinda Gates along with Warren Buffett brought together 40 of the wealthiest Americans who would go on to pledge at least half of their fortunes for charity, for this particular group amounting to about $600 billion. The commitment was quickly institutionalized and made public under the name of the 'Giving Pledge'. In the US, reactions to the pledge from the media and public were mixed. Despite seemingly aimed at distributing wealth from the mega-rich to education or other public services, the timing of occurring in the backwash of the financial crisis with the growing attention to income disparity that followed it made some question whether the end result would just be these fortunes ending up as foundation endowments with small portions given away.[102] This critique was certainly not downplayed by the miniscule amount of information being publicized about what the pledge is going to do, who will benefit from it, or how it aims to be accountable to the public.

A second normative tool of influence for the foundation is the movement of people and, often through them, ideas. The influence from such undertakings, of course, is not always the result of deliberate action, but this does not weaken its effect. Historically, individuals who have not had their training within philanthropy or global development, and instead being former industry or government insiders, have assumed the majority of the foundation's leadership positions. The number of Gates Foundation employees hired through networks in Washington, DC, or moving there after their terms in the foundation is substantial (it seems to be more of a revolving door between the two that sees people moving both from and to the foundation).[103] Of all the bonds to the 'other Washington' as it is known in the foundation (Seattle, of course, is in the state of Washington), those to political bodies, and to Cabinets of the Democratic Party in particular, are the strongest. Whereas the foundation showed little interest in getting involved with the Bush administration, within the first four months of Barack Obama's presidency alone at least four high-ranking Gates Foundation officials had been hired in leadership positions in the education, agriculture and state departments.[104] One of the interesting stories is that of Rajiv Shah. As a medical doctor (formerly serving in Al Gore's presidential campaign) with limited agricultural experience, Shah was hired by the Gates Foundation and eventually became Director of the ag-team, a position from which he would profit from a high level of intellectual attention from Bill Gates. After several years in the foundation, Shah was headhunted to the Department of Agriculture as undersecretary for research, education and economics in 2009. By that time, the position as administrator of USAID had been vacant for almost half a year. Only a few months after his arrival, a unanimous Senate promoted the only 36-year-old Shah to administrator of USAID. Once in office at USAID, Shah carved out a new way forward for the administration, emphasizing issues around science and technology, whilst creating a new global health initiative that spent $63 billion over six years, both points drawing clear lines to his work in the Gates Foundation. As a complement to Shah, Sylvia Mathews Burwell was announced as Secretary of Health and Human Services for the Obama administration in June 2014. Prior to joining the Obama administration Mathews Burwell was, amongst other functions, President of Global Development during her ten-year spell at the Gates Foundation from 2001 to 2011, and mentioned as a possible candidate to succeed Patty Stonesifer as foundation CEO before Jeff Raikes got the job. Before that, she worked for the Clinton administration. The same story can be repeated for education, where the first secretary of education, Arne Duncan, appointed former Gates employees or grantees among many of his key personnel, including Jim Shelton as Assistant Deputy Secretary for Innovation and Improvement, who was a former Programme Director for the education programme in the Gates Foundation.

Over the past years the foundation has also invested heavily in partnerships with NGOs, academia, international organizations and the media, with its advocacy budget increasing to more than $500 million in 2016. It has established a great leverage over the voice of civil society through its involvement with major NGOs such as ONE and Oxfam. In 2009 the foundation pledged $40 million to independent think tanks in the developing world, starting with

24 institutions in Africa. Despite the financial support being unrestricted, the Gates Foundation's director of policy and advocacy held that they 'Do hope and expect much of the work they do will support areas we at the foundation care a lot about, like health, agriculture and financial services'.[105] The engagement in so-called media partnerships has also increased in the last years, and the foundation now spends millions of dollars annually in support of both non-profits and for-profits. Organizations involved include ABC, National Public Radio, PBS, but also European ones such as the BBC or the *Guardian*. The foundation often asserts that all of the grants are provided with complete editorial freedom, but since the organizations are all asked to engage in positive news stories accounting for progress in the developing world, it becomes quite difficult to draw the line between media and advocacy.[106]

Notes

1 Gates Foundation. 2012. *Annual Report*. Seattle, WA: Bill and Melinda Gates Foundation.
2 This *article* seems to refer to the 1993 *World Development Report*, which focused on the interplay between human health, health policy and economic development with the title of 'Investing in health'.
3 Strouse, J. 2000. 'Bill Gates's money', *The New York Times* 16 April.
4 Sellers, P. 2008. 'Melinda Gates goes public', *Fortune* January.
5 Strouse, 2000.
6 Serwer, A. 1999. One family's finances: how Bill Gates invests his money', *Fortune* 15 March.
7 Gates Foundation. 1998. *Annual Report*. Seattle: Bill and Melinda Gates Foundation.
8 Strouse, 2000.
9 Ibid.
10 Hafner, K. 1999. 'Bill Gates and his wife give away $3.3 billion', *The New York Times* 6 February.
11 Wilhelm, I. 2004. 'A view inside the Gates', *Chronicle of Philanthropy* 11 November.
12 McNeil, D. G. Jr 2010. 'Five years in, gauging impact of Gates grants', *The New York Times* 20 December.
13 See www.grandchallenges.org.
14 See Lachance Shandrow, K. 2016. 'Bill Gates and Warren Buffett celebrate 25 years of billionaire bromance', *Entrepreneur*.com 6 July.
15 See Bort, J. 2014. 'Bill Gates is way more involved with Microsoft than anyone realizes', *Business Insider* 8 October.
16 Interview with Senior Fellow, Bill and Melinda Gates Foundation.
17 Interview with Bill and Melinda Gates Foundation consultant.
18 The site had been bought by the Gates already in 1994.
19 Strouse, J. 2000. 'How to give away $21.8 billion', *New York Times Magazine* 16 April.
20 Gates Foundation, 2012.
21 Paulson, T. 2014. 'New Gates Foundation chief to seek revolutionary simplicity', *Humanosphere* 30 June.
22 McGregor, J. 2015. 'The head of the Gates Foundation on combatting "CEO disease"', *Washington Post* 21 December.
23 Gates, B. 2013. *Dream with a Deadline: The Millennium Development Goals*. Gatesnotes.com, 18 September.

24 Ibid.
25 Ibid.
26 Ibid.
27 Ibid.
28 Ibid.
29 Ibid.
30 Smith, B. 2015. 'Philanthropy's difficult dance with inequality', *Alliance Magazine* 29 June.
31 Oxfam. 2015. *Even It Up: Time to End Extreme Inequality*. Oxford: Oxfam International.
32 Paulson, T. 2015. 'Gates Foundation rallies the troops to attack UN development goals', *Humanosphere* 6 May.
33 Ibid.
34 Gates, B. 2015. *Setting Targets to Save Lives*. Gatesnotes.com, 2 July.
35 Davenport, C. and Wingfield, N. 2015. 'Bill Gates takes on climate change with nudges and a powerful rolodex', *The New York Times* 8 December.
36 Interview with Senior Programme Officers, Bill and Melinda Gates Foundation.
37 Gates Foundation. 2016a. *'What We Do'*. Seattle, WA: Bill and Melinda Gates Foundation. Available at: www.gatesfoundation.org/What-We-Do, accessed on 13 July 2017.
38 Perkin was a former WHO employee who now ran a non-profit in Seattle – PATH – and quickly became Gates' go-to-guy on all things global health. At a dinner on the top floor of a Seattle downtown hotel, Perkin had Gates trying a new syringe that PATH had developed for single use (to avoid re-uses and thus the potential spread of diseases), injecting saline solution into a bread roll. Not long after, Gates made a $100 million grant to PATH that would see it attempt to make common childhood vaccines more readily available.
39 Medicins sans frontieres (MSF). 2015. *MSF Calls on GSK and Pfizer to Slash Price*. Geneva: Medicins sans frontieres 20 January.
40 Curtis, M. 2016. 'Gated development', *Global Justice Now* June.
41 McCoy, D., Chand, S. and Sridhar, D. 2009. 'Global health funding: how much, where it comes from and where it goes', *Health Policy* 24(6): 407–417.
42 Storeng, K. 2014. 'The GAVI Alliance and the "Gates approach" to health systems strengthening', *Global Public Health* 9(8): 865–879.
43 Gates Foundation, 2016a.
44 The strong crowding-in effect from the foundation's emphasis on global health will be greatly felt in the state of Washington where it resides. More than 12,000 people are now employed there under the broad umbrella of global health, across research, logistics and manufacturing, an industry amounting to $6 billion annually.
45 Bank, D. 2001. *Breaking Windows*. New York, NY: Free Press.
46 In sheer numbers, global development is actually the largest division in the foundation with $2,211,000 spent in 2016, compared with $1,197,000 in the global health division. But this balance is mainly so because delivery-related departments from global health have been moved into global development (as described earlier in this chapter), such as polio and vaccine delivery, combined representing 42 per cent of the entire global development budget.
47 Gates Foundation, 2016a.
48 Revkin, A. C. 2016. 'Bill Gates, the 'Impatient Optimist,' lays out his clean-energy innovation agenda', *The New York Times* 23 February.
49 Interview with Bill and Melinda Gates Foundation Director.
50 Interview with former Bill and Melinda Gates Foundation agricultural team staff.
51 See Anderson, I. 2011. 'The Bill and Melinda Gates Foundation: business versus bureaucracy in international development', discussion paper 3, Development Policy Centre, Australian National University.

52 Thompson, C. 2012. 'Alliance for a Green Revolution in Africa (AGRA): advancing the theft of African genetic wealth', *Review of African Political Economy* 39(132): 345–350.

53 Holt-Gimenez, E. 2008. 'Out of AGRA: The Green Revolution returns to Africa', *Development* 51(4): 464–471; Holt-Gimenez, E., Altieri, M. and Rosset, P. 2006. *Ten Reasons Why the Rockefeller and the Bill and Melinda Gates Foundations' Alliance for Another Green Revolution Will not Solve the Problems of Poverty and Hunger in Sub-Saharan Africa*, Food First Policy Brief No. 12. Oakland, CA: Food First.

54 Thompson, 2012.

55 Heim, K. 2009. 'Gates Foundation funds African think tanks', *Seattle Times* 11 May.

56 Chicago Council on Global Affairs, Independent Leaders Group. 2009. *Renewing American Leadership in the Fight Against Global Hunger and Poverty*. Chicago, IL: Chicago Council on Global Affairs.

57 Gates, B. 2012. 'Bill Gates: International Fund for Agricultural Development Governing Council', prepared remarks by Bill Gates, co-chair and trustee.

58 Gillis, J. 2012. 'Bill Gates calls for more accountability on food programs', *The New York Times* 23 February.

59 Gates Foundation, 2016a.

60 See Tompkins-Stange, M. 2016. *Policy Patrons: Philanthropy, Education Reform, and the Politics of Influence*. Cambridge, MA: Harvard Education Press.

61 Sanders, C. P. E. and Dixon, R. 2007. 'Dark clouds over good works of Gates Foundation', *LA Times* 7 January.

62 Guo, J. 2010. 'In interview, Gates describes philanthropic journey', *The Tech* 23 April.

63 Ibid.

64 Heim, 2009.

65 Das, A. and Karmin, C. 2014. 'This man's job: Make Bill Gates richer', *Wall Street Journal* 19 September.

66 Serwer, 1999.

67 Interview with Cascade Investment employee.

68 Gates Foundation. 2006. *Annual Report*. Seattle, WA: Bill and Melinda Gates Foundation.

69 Gates Foundation. 2016b. 'Our investment philosophy', available at: www.gates-foundation.org/Who-We-Are/General-Information/Financials/Investment-Policy, accessed on 13 July 2017.

70 Gates Foundation. 2015. *Annual Report*. Seattle, WA: Bill and Melinda Gates Foundation; see also Birn, A. 2014. 'Philanthrocapitalism, past and present: the Rockefeller Foundation, the Gates Foundation, and the setting(s) of the international/global health agenda', *Hypothesis* 12(1): e8.

71 Bill and Melinda Gates Foundation Trust. 2016 990-PF; see also *Global Justice Now*, 2016.

72 Curtis, 2016.

73 McCoy, et al., 2009.

74 Gates Foundation. 2009b. *Grantee Perception Report*. Seattle, WA: Bill and Melinda Gates Foundation.

75 Interview with Bill and Melinda Gates Foundation Senior Programme Officer.

76 McCoy, et al., 2009.

77 Interview with Bill and Melinda Gates Foundation grantee.

78 Interview with Bill and Melinda Gates Foundation grantee.

79 Gates Foundation, 2009.

80 Interview with Bill and Melinda Gates Foundation staff.

81 Interview with Bill and Melinda Gates Foundation staff.

82 Interview with Bill and Melinda Gates Foundation staff.

83 Interview with Bill and Melinda Gates Foundation staff.

84 Interview with Bill and Melinda Gates Foundation Senior Programme Officer.
85 Interview with Bill and Melinda Gates Foundation staff.
86 Interview with Bill and Melinda Gates Foundation staff.
87 Paulson, T. 2008. 'Gates Foundation again finds CEO at Microsoft', *Seattle Post-Intelligencer* 12 May.
88 Eichenwald, K. 2012. 'Microsoft's lost decade', *Vanity Fair* 24 July.
89 Sellers, 2008.
90 Interview with Bill and Melinda Gates Foundation staff.
91 Sellers, 2008.
92 Bank, 2001.
93 Interview with Bill and Melinda Gates Foundation grantee.
94 Guo, 2010.
95 Richey, L. A. and Ponte, S. 2008. 'Better (Red)™ than Dead? Celebrities, consumption and international aid', *Third World Quarterly* 29(4): 711–729; Fridell, G. and Konings, M. (eds). 2013. *Age of Icons*. Toronto, ON: University of Toronto Press.
96 West, D. M. 2008. 'Angelina, Mia, and Bono: Celebrities and international development', in *Global Development 2.0*, edited by L. Brainard and D. Chollet, Washington, DC: Brookings Institute Press, 74–84.
97 Samman, E., McAuliffe, E. and MacLachlan, M. 2009. 'The role of celebrity in endorsing poverty reduction through international aid', *International Journal of Nonprofit and Voluntary Sector Marketing* 14(2), 137–148.
98 West, 2008; Lundsgaarde, E., Funk, E., Kopyra, A., Richter, J. and Steinfeldt, H. 2012. *Private Foundations and Development Cooperation: Insights From Tanzania*. Bonn: German Development Institute.
99 Wilhelm, 2004.
100 Thompkins-Stange, 2016.
101 *The Economist*. 2007. 'Bill Gates' other chief executive', *The Economist* 18 January, www.economist.com/node/8550607.
102 Strom, S. 2010. 'Pledge to give away fortunes stirs debate', *The New York Times* 10 November.
103 Holtzman, C. 2009. 'Growing D.C. presence for Gates Foundation', *Puget Sound Business Journal* 17 May.
104 Interview with Bill and Melinda Gates Foundation staff.
105 Heim, 2009.
106 For a discussion of foundation support for journalism, see Benson, R. (2017). 'Can foundations solve the journalism crisis?', *Journalism*, doi.org/10.1177/1464884917724612.

5 The power of ideas

Global development has always been loaded with immensely powerful ideas, some changing over time, and some returning to fashion in almost predictable cycles.[1] These have justified actions and interventions by lending legitimacy, directed policy agendas, distributed resources, and entailed changes when taken up. The Gates Foundation has been exposed to and met many ideas foreign to it since it began considerably intensifying its international efforts in the mid-2000s. Some of these ideas have fitted well with its existing ways of thinking and acting and have gone through uncomplicated processes of institutionalization, over time becoming a taken-for-granted part of everyday organizational life in the foundation. But certain ones have never been able to find traction inside the foundation, perhaps because of compromising existing ways of working or by being too radical in their nature to ever find footing. In this chapter we will engage a set of ideas, practices or norms that have increasingly risen to prominence inside the foundation, despite facing a great deal of resistance, reconceptualization and reinterpretation along the way – those pertaining to gender equality and women's empowerment. In 2014 Melinda Gates was the author of an article in *Science Magazine* in which she claimed that the Gates Foundation cannot achieve its goals unless it can 'Systematically address gender inequalities and meet the specific needs of women and girls wherever it works, and that it intends to systematically increase its focus on women's specific needs and preferences.[2] For an organization considered a beacon for the natural sciences through its investments in *inter alia* vaccines and technologies, the adoption of such an immediately political and contentious priority poses interesting questions as to how ideas on gender equality and women's empowerment found their way to the foundation and rose to such prominence, and what the organizational consequences have been of this endeavour. The incremental and stable nature of many organizations means that these are not prone to change and even less so in response to the disruptive qualities of a set of norms and ideas such as those on gender equality that, in their ideal form, challenge dominant practices of patriarchal social relations, positions and advantages. Its inherent pursuit of an ideal state of equality means this set of ideas and norms are not passive scripts and rules but profoundly normative and political, and they accordingly have to fight their way to become genuinely ingrained in organizations, or rather someone has to fight for them. And someone has certainly had to in the Gates Foundation. Here, proponents of bringing in gender as a significant priority were faced with a difficult task of construing a perceived fit between this new idea and already dominant technological and impact-effectiveness logics of the foundation. This was an extensive process facing substantial amounts of resistance, where opponents, in both formal and informal spaces of negotiation, would resist the institutionalization of gender through a range of more or less sophisticated armaments, from counter-arguments, attempts at policy sabotage, to outright denying the alignment to leadership instructions. Not least because these ideas sometimes fundamentally challenged the foundation's existing ways of thinking and working in global health and development.

The decision that all Gates Foundation grants should be attentive to gender equality and women's empowerment brings into the light a fundamental divide in the work of the foundation: that between the lab and the real world, between developing a vaccine in Seattle, WA, and eliminating local gender disparities in a rural village in Sub-Saharan Africa. Between the natural and the social scientists, and perhaps even between Bill and Melinda, each representing different ways of thinking about human development and problem solving. What we sometimes seem to forget is that it is not the Bill Gates Foundation, but rather the Bill and Melinda Gates Foundation. And those who consider Melinda to be along for the ride, as the wife of Bill, could not be further from the truth. Of the two, Melinda was the first to be engaged full-time in the foundation, long before her husband joined the foundation in June 2008. Her approach to the foundation's work was, and continues to be, radically different from Bill's. Melinda once explained how, after the two had settled that they wanted to provide grants to combat diarrhoea in developing countries, she travelled and visited slums in India to understand the context of those affected, while Bill read a book on vaccines. Coming back to Bill, Melinda held that it was not enough to just focus on vaccines; they had to do something about the roots of the problem. They could do all the great science they wanted to, but if the root causes or structural conditions for why the illness occurred were not addressed, the vaccine would make little difference. As *The New York Times* columnist Nicholas Kristof has alluded to, 'Melinda has been more enthusiastic about gender issues and family planning, while Bill worried that metrics in the area are squishy'.[3]

In the next section we will hear an intimate empirical account of the everyday processes that took place as gender proponents tried to win over both colleagues and leadership and secure the institutionalization of these ideas and practices. This includes efforts to produce consensus, negotiations over frames, and the agency to construct change projects that resonated in the organization. From it we come to understand not just the specific case of institutionalizing gender equality and women's empowerment ideas, but also wider questions of organizational culture, staff and change in the Gates Foundation. In the last part of the chapter we will see specifically what happens as two immediately incompatible sets of ideas meet and have to contend, by witnessing the confrontation between gender equality and women's empowerment on the one hand, and notions of impact effectiveness[4] on the other. This discussion allows me to further an argument of how ideas and logics that in their ideal-type share very few fundamental traits are nearly impossible to blend without losing significant core characteristics of one or the other. Gender equality and women's empowerment may be framed through the logic of impact effectiveness to instrumentalize a focus on gender. But doing so means a loss of its key transformative elements, ultimately remaking or even betraying that very idea. In the Gates Foundation this means that work on gender equality and women's empowerment cannot simultaneously be structural and functional, political and technical, context-sensitive and scalable. First, however, a discussion of the idea set that comprises gender equality and women's empowerment follows.

Ideas and norms of gender equality and women's empowerment

The recognition of gender equality and women's empowerment as important in achieving development goals has greatly increased in the past decades, after having emerged as a point of emphasis in this particular field in the 1970s.[5] This inclusion or entrance has been attributed to a tripartite explanation combining: 1) strong intellectual and structural leadership from women's groups and NGOs in alliance with 2) the UN system that has long provided key fora for agenda-setting and norm development, and 3) economic support from bilateral donor organizations that eventually utilized a window of opportunity following the collapse of the Soviet Union and the growing attention to human rights to have gender equality included in this norm development.[6] The United Nations has long been the agenda-setting international organization on gender equality, and especially so in relation to global development. The most famous spaces for developing and debating norms on gender equality were undoubtedly the three world conferences from the 1970s onwards. The first of these was Mexico in 1975, coinciding with the International Women's Year that launched the UN decade for women from 1976 to 1985, and identified a set of key objectives on the advancement and equality of women. In 1985 the Nairobi Convention defined rights and obligations of states and international organizations based on principles of equality and non-discrimination, and broke new ground by presenting measures for achieving equality at the national level. By this time in 1985 127 UN member states had created national bureaucratic entities for women's advancement and their participation in development. The Beijing Platform for Action from 1995 aimed at accelerating progress towards achieving the Nairobi Convention by identifying 12 critical areas of intervention. In the Nairobi Convention it was determined that all issues should include women. The Beijing Platform changed this view towards a human rights perspective by arguing for equality between the sexes i.e., gender. Importantly, the Beijing conference formally introduced the notion of gender mainstreaming that would come to dominate the approach to gender equality in many donor organizations. Between Mexico in 1975 and Nairobi in 1985 a set of legally binding rules in the form of the Convention on the Elimination of Discrimination against Women (CEDAW) was ratified in 1979, referring to the prohibition of discrimination against women and active promotion of equality between the sexes. A few decades later followed the Millennium Development

Goals, whose third goal aims to promote gender equality and women's rights by mainly focusing on primary education. While an important part of the MDGs' success, the inability to explicitly address the systemic barriers to gender equality and a too narrow interpretation of gender equality has resulted in substantive critique of MDG3 specifically.[7] Finally, the SDGs ratified in 2015 includes a standalone goal on achieving gender equality and empowering all women and girls (SDG 5), after extensive discussion of whether to mainstream gender across all goals or have it as a single goal.

Co-occurring with the world conferences, a heated debate played out amongst different factions. The 1975 meeting in Mexico revealed a major split between a mainly Western women's group who sought a focus on discrimination, and groups from the South who preferred a focus on development and justice referring to both men and women. This quarrel led to the 'women in development' (WID) frame that combined arguments for equity and economic efficiency. As WID gained prominence, its scrutiny by development practitioners rose and the internal critique of the norm eventually led to the adoption of 'gender and development' (GAD) in key UN texts,[8] incorporating elements of socialist feminist theories and stressing women's self-empowerment through bottom-up development involving women's NGOs.[9] Recently, trends treating gender equality as 'smart economics' have arisen, rationalizing investments in women and girls from an efficiency point of view.[10] Developing or directly descending from the WID focus of the 1980s, this view holds the win–win assumption that synergies exist between gender equality and efficient economic development (not to be equated with the macrostructural theories of increasing gender equality through access to paid labour[11]). This tactic has been criticized for its apparent lack of an essentially political critique of 'What is wrong with the world' (the existence of structural discrimination of women).[12] Though feminism and development to a certain extent share some philosophies of transformation, the discursive contestation between the two has taken on a form of struggle for interpretive power.[13] One such relevant struggle lies in the analysis of women and globalization. Globalization is often considered a process 'out there' with a devastating effect on the locally lived realities of women's lives (victims), and little attention is given to the complex nature of (gendered) globalization processes. The consequence is dichotomous thinking giving way to universalisms about women and orthodoxies (representing fixed dominant discourses maintaining the status quo in Bourdieuan terms) such as the victim-heroine (the feminization of poverty and women as victims making them the instrument to combat the evil that is globalization), the global-local (global processes perceived as masculine economic processes of international production, invading the feminine local cultural domain of consumption) and the traditional-modern.[14]

Today, different interpretations and translations of the norms of gender equality and women's empowerment are encapsulated and committed to in central international agreements and human rights instruments including the UN Convention on the Elimination of All Forms of Discrimination against Women (CEDAW), UN Security Council Resolutions 1325, 19820, 1888 and 1889, the

Mexico 1975 and 1985 Nairobi outcome documents, the Beijing Platform for Action, the Millennium Declaration, the Millennium Development Goals (especially goal 3), the 2005 World Summit, the 2008 Accra Agenda for Action and Doha Declaration, the Sustainable Development Goals (particularly goal 5), and the ILO Conventions on working women's rights. Together, all these constitute a complex set of norms, ideas and practices on gender equality to which development organizations are expected to adhere if they are to be considered legitimate in the eyes of other organizations in this particular field, and a set of ideas that would come to question core convictions in the Gates Foundation but also experience substantial attempts at being manipulated or reinterpreted to a point at which its transformative character was lost.

Early foundation efforts on women's empowerment

The history of the pursuit of women's empowerment as a priority for private foundations unsurprisingly starts long before the Gates Foundation's decision to embark on work in this area. The Ford Foundation, often assumed as the most progressive of the traditional US foundations (not least inspired by its founder's own opposition to, e.g., Rockefeller and Carnegie, as we have seen earlier), began making grants aimed explicitly at enhancing the rights and opportunities of women in the early 1970s. Thomas Franklin, a former president of the foundation, later recalled how, up through the 1970s and 1980s, this concern had evolved from a very limited number of discrete activities to being a major influence on the foundation's work.[15] The focus on gender relations and women's empowerment also came to be reflected internally in the Ford Foundation, where the percentage of women staff members increased from 23 to 53 from 1973–1986. The point of departure in the 1960s was certainly not one to be tremendously proud of. Despite 'equal opportunity' being designated as the first concern of the foundation by its board of trustees in 1966, all of its senior officers and members of its board of trustees up until 1971 were men. Korey tells a fascinating story of how women's rights and empowerment made it to the top of the Ford Foundation's list of priorities[16] that serves well as a preamble for exploring how comparable (but also vastly different) processes took place in the Gates Foundation 30 years later. As the result of a groundswell from the lower reaches of the foundation, the issue rose to prominence by firstly focusing on the internal needs and rights of women employees in the foundation, and only after that evolving into a substantial area of international programming. During the 1960s the foundation did provide some support for birth control research, but the intent mainly revolved around limiting population growth in the developing world and did not concern itself much with the reproductive health and rights of women. Kicking off the internal quest for advancing women's position, 150 staff members signed and delivered a report to the then president of the foundation illuminating the obvious inequality between genders in senior positions and on the board. After a few months and meetings, the president agreed to establish a committee that would look into the issue. What followed included the election of two prominent women to its board, salary increases aimed at eliminating the gap between male and female staffers and a significant improvement of the foundation's maternity leave policy.

Eagerly pursuing women's rights inside the foundation, attention soon turned outward to the most important group of partners for any foundation: its grantees. A survey found how only six per cent of the Ford Foundation's grantees had women in high-level positions and, as a consequence, in 1974, current and future grantees were asked to remove 'restraints' with respect to hiring and promotion of women. A group of women staff members began meeting frequently at lunch, around 1971, to discuss the awarding of grants to research on women's issues. McGeorge Bundy, foundation president at the time, took very well to this new agenda and urged the board of trustees to increase grant-making to it, attempting to translate a feminist agenda into formal policy.[17] A temporary Task Force on Women was established with the aim of delivering reports to the board, and after its mandate had finished it continued in the form of a formal 'Coordinating Committee on Women's Programs' that would gradually shift the attention of grant-making on women's issues outwards towards international grant-making. The committee was later closed down and succeeded by a 'Women's Program Group', headed by Susan Berresford (who would eventually go on to become president of the foundation), during a time where budgetary allocation to women's issues accounted for almost ten per cent of the foundation's grant-making, equal to $20 million. By the 1980s then, the outreach and support of the foundation to women's issues, mainly taking the shape of support to education and research (but also networks among women's groups as well as health and agricultural issues), had become extensive. With this story of initial institutionalization of gender and women's issues in the Ford Foundation, we move on to explore how such processes have taken place in the Gates Foundation, 30 years later and under very different circumstances.

How ideas on gender equality found their way into the Gates Foundation

In 2008 the Gates Foundation publicized an umbrella priority covering all of its work done in agriculture – gender equality and women's empowerment. From that moment, all agricultural grants had to explicitly address gender concerns to be considered for support. 'Whatever the idea, the proposal must address the gender gap and find a way to meaningfully support women in the field' as then Senior Fellow of the Gates Foundation and former head of the UN's World Food Programme Catherine Bertini expressed the new requirement for grantees at a London seminar.[18] The approach of the Gates Foundation would be exploratory. The foundation held that it was new to gender issues, and the purpose was to test ideas, seeing what would work and what would not, to hone the approach and increase effectiveness,[19] as we have heard it so often. The first organizational strategy made to guide the foundation's work was the 2008 *Gender Impact Strategy for Agricultural Development*, outlining that the foundation targeted women because of the role they play as the majority of smallholder farmers in the South, rendering it as a form of 'smart economics'. As a follow up to the 2008 *Gender Impact Strategy*, the Gates Foundation publicized an orientation document in 2012 with the name *Creating Gender-Responsive Agricultural Development Programs*. Much like the 2008 gender strategy, the orientation document builds on the assumption that ignoring the role of women in agriculture will hamper the success of the foundation's work. A few years later in 2014 the foundation's work on gender and women was finally cemented as Melinda Gates authored an article titled 'Putting women and girls at the center of development'. In it she expounded how the foundation intends to 'Systematically increase [its] focus on women's specific needs and preferences and on addressing gender inequalities and empowering women',[20] based on the understanding that the foundation cannot achieve its goals unless it can 'Systematically address gender inequalities and meet the specific needs of women and girls' wherever it works. Immediately following the article, the foundation announced a 'Grand Challenge' on 'Putting women and girls at the center of development', inviting partners to apply with project proposals on the topic. These three different illustrations from 2008, 2012 and 2014 represent opportunities to observe how the priority of gender equality and women's empowerment is framed and formulated in the organizational foreground, but not much more. Of course, the focus on gender equality had not just come out of the blue when the first strategy was officially launched in 2008, nor was the decision to make an orientation document in 2012 an uncomplicated one, or the launch of the Grand Challenge a coincidence. Much work has continuously been put into establishing this set of ideas as a priority within the foundation's teams, such as the agricultural team. As the attempt was made to institutionalize this set of ideas in the foundation, flowing back and forth between different organizational actors and levels, it went through processes in which its meaning and use was struggled and negotiated over.

Emergence

In its early life, as we have seen, the Gates Foundation largely functioned as a research and development (R&D) organization, predominantly supporting the development of new vaccines by providing Western research and pharmaceutical companies with funding, with little view to the much more complex and political processes of delivering such products in the developing world.[21] In such a context, not much thought seems to have been given to gender equality and women's empowerment and vaccines were widely considered a universal technical tool that did not require different contextual considerations to be developed. It was not until the time of Warren Buffett's 2006 gift equalling more than $30 billion to the foundation that changes happened that made the organization conducive to the entrance of such ideas. Some time before the gift, Sylvia Matthews, a former deputy CEO of the foundation, had been put in charge of a group called 'Special Initiatives', with the aim of exploring and identifying new potential strategic areas of intervention for the foundation within different areas of global development. As news of the Buffett gift surfaced in 2006 then, foundation leadership had already decided to embark upon making global development a third pillar of the foundation, alongside global health and the US programme. Financial services for the poor (FSP), water and sanitation, as well as agriculture, were to be its centres of attention. We are most interested in what happened in the agricultural team or 'ag-team', as it is known colloquially in the Gates Foundation, because of its to-be position as the centre of gender activities in the global development programme. Heading the new area of agriculture was a young doctor with little prior experience in agriculture, but already with a few years of experience in the foundation, Rajiv Shah. Following his appointment, he did what seems to be the norm in the foundation in situations of preparing to engage in new areas of intervention and reached out to different experts and organizations with knowledge of agriculture.[22] One of those experts was Catherine Bertini, a former World Food Programme Director. At a World Food Prize panel on agricultural development in 2006, Shah announced that the foundation was looking to move into this specific area, and would applaud all forms of advice. Being the last in line, Bertini addressed the Director and, quoting Abigail Adams, told him to 'Remember the ladies' and that failure to do so would mean they would waste a lot of money, quickly.[23] The effectiveness concern seems to have especially intrigued Shah, and he subsequently spoke with Bertini about issues of women in agriculture in private. Apparently convinced by Bertini's argument, Shah shortly thereafter invited her to join a staff meeting to present her arguments. Not much time passed before she was offered a position in the foundation and in mid-2006 Bertini joined the ag-team as a Senior Fellow, with the aim of building up an approach to gender equality and women's empowerment. The message from foundation leadership was basically, 'You have done this in WFP before and though you can't replicate that, go in the same direction'.[24]

Bertini would soon prove instrumental in gathering support and intellectual attention to the issue of gender equality, driving forward a gender equality agenda with the aim of putting structures into place that would secure the institutionalization of this concern.[25] Having witnessed the questionable effects of institutionalizing gender equality efforts in a top-down manner in WFP, Bertini seems to have been more focused on the lower levels of the foundation. According to staff present at this time, the initial ambitions for institutionalizing the ideas were quite clear: establish an above junior-level gender programme officer position with a substantial portfolio of gender-specific grants, and provide the responsible person with a strategy that would see him or her mainstream gender equality across all grants in agriculture, spreading the importance of gender equality to colleagues throughout the ag-team. Shah was fairly swiftly convinced to create a dedicated position of gender responsible programme officer at an above-junior level, as well as to agree to the preparation of a new gender equality strategy for agriculture. Before Bertini's entrance into the foundation, however, things had already been stirring. One of Rajiv Shah's team leaders, a former World Bank employee, had several years of experience in the field, particularly in Sub-Saharan Africa, providing him with an appreciation of including a focus on gender equality and women's empowerment in agricultural work.[26] The team leader was eager to include gender equality as a significant component of the foundation's work on agriculture and made one of the first hired ag-team programme officers, and the first woman hired in the ag-team, responsible for developing initial thoughts on the issue. She did not have much prior experience in working professionally with gender equality, not from an agricultural point of view nor any other area related to development issues. Like Rajiv Shah had done himself, she reached out to different organizations such as the International Center for Research on Women (ICRW) and the International Food Policy Research Institute (IFPRI) for advice and guidance on how to approach the issue. Not much time went on, however, before Bertini entered the organization and began to drive forward her own work of institutionalizing these new ideas.

During this process of emergence there can be no doubt as to the importance of Bertini's efforts in importing notions of gender equality and women's empowerment into the organization, facilitated by Shah's acknowledgement of bringing in the concern. But other factors had to be conducive to their arrival as well. The emergence of gender equality should accordingly be attributed to different individuals who simultaneously planted small seeds of the idea of gender equality, which at a certain point accumulated sufficient intellectual attention, resulting in the emergence of this new normative framework. We can see how individuals who had been embedded in multiple institutional or social structures were more likely to not take the prevailing institutional arrangements for granted, increasing the probability of them transposing practices from one organizational context to another. Several of the key individuals had longer spells behind them in organizations such as WFP, the World Bank and other institutions with long and notable histories of intervention in development contexts (including in the women's rights movement during the 1970s and 1980s), and with prior experiences in implementing gender equality in a donor organization context, positively influencing the likelihood of institutionalization, but also greatly shaping their particular approach to how it should be translated into the foundation. The experience from developing-country contexts and other development organizations is likely also the reason why the agricultural team was so conducive to the set of ideas on gender equality, as opposed to other departments such as those pertaining to health issues.

'Optimize, never equalize': internal negotiation

As ideas on gender equality and women's empowerment were slowly making their way into the Gates Foundation, and as the decision to try and develop a specific approach in the organization had been made at leadership level, processes of internal negotiation and consensus production increased. During these initial stages, a central mechanism for ensuring the concern as a foundation priority was work by the gender proponents to convince programme officers on the floor of the necessity to include it in their grants. Such negotiations took place in both formal and informal circumstances. The central formal arenas for negotiation were the recurring team meetings and occasional special meetings where only gender concerns were on the table. During these almost ritualistic gatherings, with participation from different organizational levels, opposition to ideas on gender equality were not truly verbalized. Employees critical of implementing gender equality ideas did not voice such criticism during formal meetings as leadership seemed positive towards it. 'Questioning leadership positions at meetings would be like questioning the leaders themselves. You don't do that around here' one interviewee explained, identifying a different course of action: 'Instead, the less visible way of obstructing the gender concern became to not ask your grantees for it, hoping it would slip pass leadership if they scrutinized your grant proposal'.[27] Opposition thus seems to have mostly materialized in the everyday practices of working with grants or grantees and, as such, the legwork that could pave the way for a formal, though perhaps artificial, consensus also had to occur in between larger meetings during intimate encounters between gender proponents and opponents.

In these intimate spaces of negotiation the proponents would confront other programme officers with what their individual reservations towards focusing on gender equality might be, aiming to collect and understand all the different positions of opposition in the ag-team. Such immediate counter arguments seem to have taken on different forms. Some accused the multiplicity of concerns already imposed on programme officers with arguments such as 'We already have so many requirements' and 'There is no time to screen proposals for gender issues'.[28] Others argued that the foundation should not impose different concerns on its grantees that did not necessarily fit with their individual way of conducting projects and that they 'Should trust the grantees that they know what they're doing'.[29] Yet again, others tried to argue that gender concerns were not applicable to their issue areas and would not make a difference in securing results, trying to convince the gender proponents to make it a demand that would only be relevant for some and not all. Bertini and the assistant tried to take all these concerns up collectively during formal team meetings and informal brown bags, confronting the individual counter arguments. Often, though, grants with no considerations of gender or women would slip past leadership screenings, likely attributable to the still not secure institutionalization of the ideas.

During this initial stage the gender proponents decided to begin working on a draft gender strategy for the foundation's agricultural work. Attaining the adoption of such a strategy would, they thought, be a major step towards institutionalization, as it would function as an institutional artefact able to empower the proponents with a reference point instructing that the inclusion of gender concerns in all grants was a top-down mandatory requirement.[30] As much as it would potentially provide the gender proponents with an important institutional weapon, however, it also provided opponents with an avenue for resistance. The strategy's drafting process in particular was long and cumbersome, moving through more than 50 early drafts. One reason for the heavy drafting process was the need for the gender proponents to treat the process as one in which ultimate success was not merely the adoption of a strategy: 'Making a glossy strategy with a strong gender language was not as important as trying to build a sense of ownership among those that were going to use it'[31] one interviewee explained, underlining how the negotiation process that went into making the strategy was as important as the strategy itself as an outcome. But it also resulted from opponents attempting to impede or drag out the process, taking the shape of two different approaches on each end of a spectrum of resistance. Some opponents practiced a strategy of non-intervention or indifference, anticipating that not responding to circulations of drafts would either suggest to leadership that the interest in the subject was at such a low level that it should not be institutionalized, or facilitating the draft to easily run through, allowing for the adoption of a strategy that did not have any support on the ground. Others practiced a different approach to resistance: 'Some of us who didn't think this concern should be added as a requirement for everyone in their grant making quickly agreed that ignoring the drafts was untenable and instead began to overflow it with comments'.[32] Heavy response to drafts then, and often in many different directions, made life exceedingly complicated for the gender proponents and reaching a consolidated version seemed almost impossible at times.

In May 2007, after almost a year of initial work to introduce gender issues as a necessary component in agricultural grants, a new programme officer was hired specifically to handle grants on gender equality and women's empowerment, and overlook the mainstreaming of this concern across the team. This new programme officer was young, bright, and quickly predicted to face a great future in the foundation, coming in from the Millennium Challenge Corporation. Her age and experience may not have formally lived up to the relative seniority of her position, but Bertini's influence seems to have been strong, and the new gender responsible person was given a grant portfolio beyond what many senior employees in the foundation handled (reportedly around $50 million). In addition to building up the grant portfolio, the new programme officer was essentially handed a draft of the new gender equality strategy that the gender proponents had been working on. The programme officer seems to have been conscious about framing the new gender equality endeavour within the dominant logics of the foundation. In presenting it to colleagues, she would essentially frame it as something 'Right and smart' to do, not in a moral sense, but rather through the aim of increasing impact and results. Institutionalizing gender equality notions should thus not be perceived by the programme officers as a new requirement being imposed, but rather as a logical extension of the foundation's mission and nature. To convince her colleagues and grantees, she would use the tool that all the foundation's work is built on, from the domestic US programme to global health – data. Numbers and statistics play a fundamental role in all the foundation's endeavours, and she would use World Bank and FAO data to frame the change-project within the logics of the foundation, construing an obvious reason why a particular focus on gender equality and women's empowerment was a necessary component of any sound agricultural grant: you need it to create measurable results. In an organizational culture where individuals are judged by the measurable results of their grants, such wording should be sweet music to the ears of any group of programme officers. Eventually, the strategy was released as the 2008 *Gender Impact Strategy for Agricultural*

Development, introduced earlier. The gender proponents considered it to have been 'Generally positively received'[33] by the programme officers, in spite of its mainstreaming character, which tasked the gender-responsible programme officer with keeping an eye on the grant proposals of colleagues (essentially allowing him or her to intervene directly in the work of others). To a large extent, however, the consensus produced by the necessity to target gender equality because of its instrumental ability to increase the effectiveness of projects, seems to have been a fairly artificial one. Of course not everyone swallowed the 'bait', and some predictably continued to resist by not asking grantees questions related to gender equality, and by attempting to bring agricultural grants past leadership that were not considering the role of women or gender. One interviewee explained how 'Sometimes, leadership would scrutinize these programme officers' grants and ask questions about missing gender components but most of the time, they would pass through unnoticed'.[34]

Ultimately, the gender proponents worked to create a coherent vision for change that appealed to, and could win over, the different actors needed to implement it. To achieve this they attempted to frame their change project of implementing gender equality with logics that aligned with the values of other important organizational actors. This was especially impact effectiveness and efficiency concerns coupled with notions of technology, all issues or logics that had been prominent in the foundation since its beginning, and around which the culture of the organization had been built, and continues to be built. As a foundation employee described it 'We had to add the Bill Gates mind-set: "I don't want any of this baloney about politically correct statements. I want efficiency and effectiveness"'.[35] Doing so meant they could bring in a new set of logics that would otherwise have appeared as being in conflict with the existing ones. This was an especially important tool for actors such as the programme officers, who do not possess very high degrees of formal authority (i.e., decision-making competencies when it comes to foundation priorities). To attain this, the gender equality proponents drew on both their properties as actors and on their institutional positions. Bertini used Shah's intellectual attention to realize gender as a foundation priority, and her reflexive qualities to frame the change project within the dominant logics of the foundation. Likewise, the programme officers made crucial decisions that influenced under whose leadership gender equality would remain, where and how to implement which measures and, importantly, the actual contact with other programme officers on the ground that had to be convinced of the change project (using their organizational positions). But such successes are not achieved easily. The gender equality proponents succeeded in mobilizing allies and cultivating alliances along the way, but not without organizational struggles and shifts in the approach of whom to form alliances with. They were faced with opponents who benefited from an institutional status quo, and who did what they could to ignore or demolish the evolving gender equality regime in the organization. The institutionalization of new ideas and practices in development organizations, however, is never a straightforward endeavour without unintended consequences for actors' institutional work, and though the obvious conclusion remains that, eventually, ideas and practices on gender equality and women's empowerment have been institutionalized in the Gates Foundation (albeit in a very specific form), we should not equate this with an assumption that these concerns are included in all corners of its grant-making.

External negotiation

Processes of making new ideas and practices workable in an organizational context are not solely of an intraorganizational nature but just as much concern external relationships and influences, entailing necessary attention to interaction with the institutional environments of which the organization and its employees are part. These environments play both an apparent and a more latent role in shaping these processes. The latent role largely refers to how the institutional sense making and interpretations by individuals who are or have been embedded in other organizational contexts are shaped by these other environments. During both preceding processes, we could observe how experiences of Gates Foundation employees from other organizational contexts shaped the way they approached the institutionalization of gender equality ideas and practices in the foundation. The gender proponents' reflections on 'You will get nowhere by running around talking about women's rights' led to a focus on convincing programme officers to apply gender equality norms in their work by repeating a mantra of 'Optimize, never equalize'. This decision was not least shaped by their prior experiences and challenges of having to institutionalize similar ideas and practices in other contexts. Just as the specific translation of these ideas was shaped by such experiences, so too was the approach to institutionalization that saw the gender proponents work from the bottom up as opposed to previous attempts of working from the top down.

The more apparent role and process of direct interaction with the institutional environment, here illustrated by relations to two groups of actors, grantees and peer organizations, requires some further explaining. Starting with the group of peer organizations, three instances appear important. First is that of the initial period of organizational genesis for the agricultural team, during which it made contact with other organizations in the field in an attempt to gather advice and experiences on the issue of agriculture in the developing world. Here, as we have seen, gender emerged as one of several key issues that slowly turned into a foundation priority. The decision to turn to the field and gather experiences, avoiding missteps already taken by others, and lessons learned for how to best approach the issue is a recurring strategy of the foundation when it ventures into new potential areas of intervention. After a decision is made to explore a novel issue, either foundation employees with expert-level knowledge or external consultants are assigned to explore what is being done and by whom, in the particular field. The second illustration occurred in the drafting of the first gender strategy from 2008, as a late draft was sent to six different organizations in the field, perceived to be progressive in their work on gender equality and women's empowerment, including the Nike Foundation and IFPRI. These organizations were asked to provide 'peer review' of the strategy and responded with different comments similar to their individual preferences such as 'Focus on girls', or 'Focus on rights', though with neither of these two pieces of advice making it substantially into the strategy in the end.[36] The third instance is largely a recurrence of the first. Sometime during 2011, gender equality issues began to move outside of the agricultural team, something not often occurring up until this time. The Director of Family Health began asking questions about gender equality to his team: 'Are we doing anything on women's issues?'[37] He was subsequently given time to audit grants across several teams, eventually identifying a range of missed opportunities to include a gender focus that might have increased impact. Alongside a hired consultant, he began a three-phased approach by interviewing employees across more than 20 teams in an attempt to gain insights into whether and how people were thinking about gender equality in the foundation. The second phase, then, was studying the evidence, learning what was out there, and particularly from what they characterized as 'rigorous' studies, often based on randomized-controlled trials (not least because the Director came from a medical and health science background). A consultant involved in this exercise recalls how 'We realized we were late to the party and that people had been dancing since at least the 1980s. But we also found too much weak evidence based on anecdotes and jargon, and with a huge pilot graveyard of projects that had resulted in nothing'.[38] This experience-gathering included not only exploring the literature but equally importantly visiting around 12 peer organizations to discuss how they approached their work on gender equality. The result, obviously, was that no one could provide a cheat sheet for how to institutionalize this concern, with everyone having different opinions of what to do and how, and the only thing in common being that there is no easy answer to the question of best practices. This work, coupled with Melinda Gates' growing attention to gender equality, eventually led to the 2014 article in *Science Magazine* and the foundation-wide prioritization of gender equality and women's empowerment, not least illustrated by the following Grand Challenge that focused on exactly this issue.

The outcome of appropriation to and negotiation with the other external group of actors, the grantees, is perhaps more tangible. As the first gender strategy was launched in 2008 and the Gates Foundation made it public that all agricultural grants supported now had to take into account the role of women, the response from many grantees was one of scepticism. The majority of these were doing technical or R&D work on, e.g., seeds, and did not understand how and why they should think about women and gender ('The Technoserve guys in particular just did not get it' as an interviewee described of one grantee with obvious problems of accepting a gender focus[39]). Foundation programme officers faced an arduous task of trying to convince them that developing seeds was just as much about delivery as it was scientific development, requiring them to think about the farmers who would use them, the majority of whom were women. But, unlike the majority of the programme officers, many of the grantees were not quite buying into the focus on gender equality and women's empowerment as a 'smart' move to increase impact and results of their products. To satisfy the foundation's demands for gender sensitive applications, 'some grantees would include general writings about the issue, and some would even go on Wikipedia and copy/paste text on women' without truly considering the specific impact of their product on women and vice versa, a programme officer explained.[40] Those of the foundation's programme officers that were conscious about gender issues did not tolerate such superficial efforts, and would demand grantees improve their thinking before funding could be considered. Others cared less and did not address such insufficiencies.

Responding to critique from grantees that the foundation's approach to gender equality was too prescriptive, the gender-responsible (now senior) programme officer began work to prepare a new orientation document that would lay out a less strict and more open-ended approach for grantees to work by. The idea of the orientation document was to introduce gender equality at an early stage in discussions on grants, and to provide grantees with increased room for manoeuvring on how to approach gender equality in their projects. By bringing up the orientation document in early talks, the programme officer was hoping for grantees' thinking on gender equality to emerge throughout the process, as opposed to screening nearly finished applications and applying a checklist approach. The jeopardy of opening up the way individual grantees should approach gender equality for interpretation by these, of course, is that it increases the risk of the aim becoming diluted. For many grantees, the open-ended approach entailed that 'Gender equality efforts would most often refer to hiring of more women in grantees, and rarely did a deeper gender analysis form the basis of grantees' interventions' as one programme officer described it.[41] The adoption of the orientation document accordingly appears largely as a negotiation with the external environment, resulting in a pragmatic appropriation to the demands and opinions of the grantees. We see how the negotiations and consensus production do not occur in an internal organizational vacuum but rather in the centre of different environments that the organization may be considered part of, each influencing or furthering specific translations or approaches to gender norms. The normative environment of the Gates Foundation had both direct and indirect influence on its translation of gender equality norms. Indirectly by having shaped the experiences of individuals that would eventually be engaged in the translation process in the foundation, and directly by intervening in policy drafting processes, as we saw with the interaction with grantees and the subsequent light appropriation to the opinions of this group.

Clashing logics in the foundation: between gender equality and impact effectiveness

As ideas on gender equality and women's empowerment found their way into and entailed changes in the Gates Foundation, they gave rise to significant contestation and struggle between teams, management and employees. This was not least so because they in their basic form carry with them strong connotations of political, social and organizational change that did not fit well with other ideas already dominant in the foundation. One other set of ideas in particular was not very conducive to the entrance of gender equality in the Gates Foundation, and represented opposite ways of thinking and working – that we might refer to as 'impact effectiveness'. In fact, this set of ideas is so strong in the foundation that we can refer to it as a logic. It not only forms a set of loose ideas floating around, but constitutes a strong vocabulary of action and discourse, providing organizing principles and criteria for legitimacy while greatly influencing the behaviour of individuals inside the foundation. This logic of impact effectiveness is part of a wider trend in which positivist thinking from the scientific and methodological core of the natural sciences has increasingly entered different areas of public policy in the last decades, and in particular organizations like the Gates Foundation. Here they have furthered evidence-based policy paradigms with special attention to notions of 'objective evidence' and 'knowledge hierarchies', aiming to shift policy-making towards objective and rational problem solving with an emphasis on efficiency and effectiveness. Significantly related to the managerialist ideas emanating out of the neoliberal paradigms of New Public Management, the intention is to reduce messy and complex realities to a set of logical causal chains, treating problems as bounded.[42] Evidence, in this line of thought, is a form of objective information that we have not yet acquired, but whose presence will fill the gap we need to have an impact in any given area, like the last material piece of a puzzle that reveals the entire picture.[43] The intellectual roots of this movement can be traced back to Britain's attempts at introducing payments by results in the mid-1800s and French experimental medicine around the 1850s, but it did not make its way into public policy before the 1960s and 1970s (especially in the US under the name of Management by Objectives), where it was seen as a rational and technical break with 'old-fashioned' ideological policies and instruments.[44] In the Gates Foundation, proponents of this logic in essence consider policy and implementation as something to be driven by notions of scientific evidence and rationality. Development interventions are seen as too dominated by notions of contextuality and politics, undermining the potential of policy to follow scientifically proven programmes and prescriptions. Truth is not relative, and it is possible to determine the outcomes of particular events as a linear cause–effect model.[45] The problem for global development has been the inability or hesitance to carry out systematic reviews that generate overviews of what works and what does not work, establishing solutions or axioms that may be applied across contexts and countries.[46]

In the Gates Foundation, the solution to these issues is one that incorporates different elements, central to all is the notion of control. Evidence as a form of control is needed to provide both accountability and improvement, the first concerned with how to prove that government or organizations are working effectively (basically as performance management), not wasting scarce resources, and the latter with what works under different circumstances (generating reliable knowledge that provides a basis for effective action). The solution becomes to construct a type of policy-making that is seen as depoliticized and technical in nature, in which evidence collection represents a scientific progress towards a higher state of knowing what works and what does not. The Gates Foundation and organizations like it are often very vocal about how their interventions are completely apolitical because of their 'scientific' nature, apparently able to provide them with objective solutions. Foundation employees certainly understand their fields of work, whether global health or global development, as very complex systems, but they are nonetheless often seen as systems in which one can understand the different mechanisms and their effects and consequences, allowing the foundation to predict the necessary actions to bring about change in social systems, i.e., a post-ideological approach to policy and governance. The answer for the foundation often becomes to apply a set of evidence-based and results-oriented tools and artefacts that basically function as technologies of power including: randomized controlled trials; systematic reviews; impact-effectiveness analysis; option appraisals, impact evaluation; reporting, tracking and disbursement mechanisms; progress reviews; performance measurement indicators; logical framework analysis; and payment by results. Greatly shaped by the logic of impact effectiveness, the foundation builds an understanding of change that pursues the highest possible return within the shortest possible time frame. Perceiving such change and its own role within it as being merely functionalist through a depoliticized and technical mode of operation. It is thus able to reduce policy issues to questions of evidence that can be acquired and measured in an objective sense, while displaying a hierarchical perception of knowledge, seeing quantitative above qualitative in a classic economistic evidence hierarchy, and a belief in the feasibility of generalization and scaling solutions across contexts.

In their fundamental form, ideas or even the logic of gender equality and women's empowerment (however incoherent we might see such as being, these can in essence also be understood as representing a logic in their fundamental form) forms a radically different interpretation of change, and it is no surprise that these two have struggled and continue to do so in the Gates Foundation. It understands the world as being in a state of structural gendered inequality in which men and women have unequal access to opportunity, across health, education, employment, power and decision-making, and many more areas. The main reason for this is a combination of cultural and social institutions and structures that reproduce and uphold inequality (from the family to the state).[47] Gender equality and women's empowerment is both a private and public issue then. Without acknowledging the family, it is impossible to make any real progress, making the domestic sphere of great importance, including issues such as: unpaid work typically not being considered as a productive activity (and thus invisible); unequal gender division of caring work; allocation of income; and constraints on women's movements outside of households.[48] The logic thus combines the structural relational aspects of gender with a call for the transformative needs of women. Solutions to these issues are largely understood as transformations on a societal scale, more heavily focused on structures that cannot easily be modified by way of policy change. It holds that gender equality cannot be achieved unless we consider the gender implications of all public policies, i.e., gender mainstreaming-type arguments; that women's standards of education and skills should be improved to make them more competitive with men; that women's access to employment and incomes should be increased; and that measurement and visibility of, e.g., domestic labour and unpaid care work should be enhanced, so that reproductive labour is not considered a 'naturalized' attribute of women, potentially undermining their rights to an equitable sharing of household resources.[49] It is the responsibility of governments, therefore, to set in place instruments that alleviate women's inequality to men, and to make policies that are sensitive to variations among women. But there are also more deep-seated elements to the logic holding that solutions are not only different policies and laws, but that we are essentially dealing with deeper social and cultural problems that need addressing. Those of a more transformative nature hold that it is not only women's conditions that are a problem, it is their position (in a patriarchal society reproducing gender inequalities), and the ensuing objective becomes to focus on the structures that uphold inequality, centring on the strategic and long-term transformative needs of women. To some, gender equality as a relational issue and a matter of structural inequality is something that can be addressed by institutions, governments and wider society.[50] To others, forms of gender justice and equality cannot be promoted or achieved by working through already unequal and patriarchal institutions that are themselves part of the problem, forming a system of gender inequality reproduction.[51] In essence it is a logic whose change perception is focused on (long-term) structural change, though complemented by more short-term engagements through policy instruments and projects, whose nature is by default political and social. It is widely based on recognition of the necessity to work from an understanding of different contexts, each with its inherent complexity, entailing how interventions must be individually fitted, and knowledge of best practices and effective measures is relative to circumstance. Interventions guided by this logic not only recognize the social, political, and cultural implications of the change it attempts to instil; it will seek to utilize such deep-level interference.

Just from these two small discussions on the differences between these two dominant ideas or logics, it comes as no surprise that their encounter in the Gates Foundation has been conflictual and challenging. Already to a great extent we have seen these logics meet in the foundation, as different individuals inside it, each furthering opposite logics, encountered or clashed in practice on the organizational floors. Yet, such backend discussions eventually result in frontend results, whether policies or strategies, that represent negotiated compromises between individuals and different part of an organization. In the next section we take a brief look at the two main gender-related strategies to come out of the Gates Foundation to date, to see what the outcome has been of the contestation already witnessed. The purpose is to show how ideas do not always peacefully co-exist or complement each other, and to look at what the consequences have been in the Gates Foundation for the way it understands and practices gender equality.

Clashing logics in the organizational discourse

The first organizational strategy made to guide the foundation's work on gender equality and women's empowerment was the 2008 *Gender Impact Strategy for Agricultural Development*, as already discussed. As a gender strategy its objective was to 'Ensure that the practical needs and strategic interests of women and girls are considered in each proposal' from grantees, and furthermore that understanding the complexities of gender roles would help refine the foundation's project goals and design. Introducing gender equality as a specific requirement for all future grants provided by the Gates Foundation was not presented in the organization as the promotion of a political agenda, but rather as a matter of effectiveness.[52] At least three tools for strengthening the gender integration in the foundation's grant making were introduced with the new strategy: 1) a gender checklist, 2) proposal and review templates, and 3) the necessary project components list. The last is of greatest interest to us as it presented potential grantees with an overview of key components, based on the perception of change that 'Addressing gender will improve the impact of all agricultural projects', on the basis of which proposals were to be reviewed to determine if they demonstrated an effective commitment to gender integration. First, the participation of women in each project should be 'At the optimum level'[53] to produce the greatest impact on the reduction of hunger and poverty. The foundation explains the inclusion of 'optimum level' with the rationale that 'Past efforts to mainstream gender have often relied on notions of equality or quotas which do not always yield the greatest benefits'[54] and, as such, gender inequality towards a majority of men or women may be found preferable so long as it leads to 'Optimal project effectiveness'.[55] This provides grantees with quite substantial amounts of flexibility in deciding on the gender-equality outcomes of specific activities, but it also embodies the viewpoint that sees gender mainstreaming serving as a tool for effectiveness through women's empowerment as opposed to advancement of the equity beliefs of gender equality, very much a functionalist or instrumentalist perception of change. Secondly, projects were expected to strive towards increasing opportunities for women in income-generating activities, learning, and participation in decision-making processes. Interestingly, such a focus is more clearly aimed at transforming existing structures and institutions to increase women's participation, without an all-out attention to effectiveness, though it may be implicit that increasing the participation of women will automatically lead to an increase in effectiveness. Third, new projects should reflect the importance of gender dynamics within the community where they work, within the grantee itself and among the wider international community as evidenced by the inclusion of appropriate gender strategies throughout the project design, implementation and evaluation, furthering the importance of contextuality. This third component carries with it an explicit belief that 'Increased understanding of gender dynamics will dramatically increase the impact and effectiveness of grantees' programs'.[56] making gender policy not only a requirement for funding, but a critical element of success, and leveraging awareness of gender opportunities and constraints as a way to create high impact delivery. Though vaguely formulated, this component is interestingly followed by the point of view that improvements in agriculture can reduce gender constraints. Such an inverted argument is noteworthy because it assumes that an increase in agricultural productivity will entail increased gender equality and empowerment of women. The last component of interest sets out the importance of hiring women inside the grantee itself and among its implementing partners, especially with a view to leadership roles, as including women at all levels of project implementation 'Will likely improve successful implementation of projects, improve uptake of new technologies, generate innovative approaches, and reduce the number of projects that fail on account of failure to address the needs of the vast majority of smallholder farmers'.[57] Such considerations provide women with taken-for-granted, superhuman-like capabilities, while representing an almost Rostowian belief in the ability of technology to progress society and the lives of women. On the other hand, grantees are asked to 'Consider the constraints on time many women have; child rearing, gathering water/firewood and the restrictions and difficulties they often have when traveling', and 'The labour and time implications of the proposed work of the project [needs to] have been considered from the perspective of women and girls', accentuating women as victims of their own lives.[58] In essence the strategy targeted women because of the role they play as the majority of smallholder farmers in the South, rendering it as a form of 'smart economics'. To empower women it valued the importance of not just women themselves, but their families, communities and also the men in their lives. Despite an emphasis that a transformational and effective approach must also improve equity between men and women, the woman, 'she', was still at the forefront of the gender work proposed by the strategy. The perception of women, as we see above, moves incoherently from one extreme to another as the foundation draws heavily on victim/heroine dichotomies. Women are frail and vulnerable, yet, at the same time, they possess superhuman-like powers to save not only their families from hunger and poverty, but also the communities and even the countries they live in, by way of increasing agricultural production.

As mentioned, the foundation publicized an 'orientation document' in 2012 with the name *Creating Gender-Responsive Agricultural Development Programs*, as a follow-up to the 2008 *Gender Impact Strategy*. Much like the 2008 gender strategy, the orientation document builds on the assumption that ignoring the role of women in agriculture will hinder the success of the foundation's work.[59] First, without the inclusion of women the foundation considers households less productive, because women farmers are thought to miss critical knowledge, skills and assets all contributing to increased household productivity, they do not have the same access to productive inputs as men and, if they had, household productivity would increase by 20 per cent. The orientation document consequently considers empowerment of women to entail a 2.5 to 4 per cent increase in agricultural output for developing countries. Second, new approaches are not adopted if women are not targeted and empowerment sought, and without access to education or information women cannot influence research agendas and in turn are less likely to adopt new practices and technologies, because men are understood as predominantly producing knowledge and technologies relevant for men. Third, nutrition is not prioritized, because men are considered less likely to reinvest income in the health of the family. The orientation document occasionally refers to the role of women and men, but little attention is given to the role of men, other than their enclosing effect on women, family life and agricultural productivity. Interestingly, the document correspondingly appears basically uninterested in gender equality per se, with a much stronger women-centric focus in play. Women are, as we also saw in the 2008 strategy, described as both victims and heroines. Restrained by their men, they do not have access to similar resources and decision-making processes, and are victims of many other disempowering feats. Meanwhile, emancipatory actions would benefit not just the women but also their families, as well as local and national agricultural productivity. Such beliefs interestingly cut across the public/private dichotomy, targeting and aiming to transform not just the role of women as farmers, but women as mothers and head of families. They are considered a technical tool, with which it is possible to increase effectiveness of projects and thus impact. Men, on the other hand, are not deemed much worth in either of the spheres, whether unable to handle financial issues or automatically reducing the yields from their land by way of their mere presence.

The consequences of contending logics

Where are we getting to then after all this? The purpose of drawing up these clear lines of difference between these two logics or sets of ideas is to show that such do not easily meet and fuse in organizations. If we look at Table 5.1 below, it quickly becomes apparent that the two idea-sets of 'gender equality and women's empowerment' and 'impact effectiveness' in their intrinsic or ideal-type nature share very few traits, from perceptions of temporality, to processes of change and mode of operation, to that of evidence and knowledge. Such differences ought to render different forms of blending near impossible but, as we have seen in the empirical part, this is certainly not the case.[60] What is impossible, however, is for these two different logics or sets of ideas to blend without letting go of significant core characteristics of one or the other, and that is exactly where we are getting to. In essence, it means the Gates Foundation cannot truly pursue the transformative

Table 5.1 Key differences between gender equality and impact-effectiveness logics.

	Logic of gender equality and women's empowerment	*logic of impact effectiveness*
Diagnosis	Structural gender equality; gendered unequal access to institutions and services	Development interventions too dominated by contextuality and subjective value politics
Prognosis	Societal transformations; addressing social and cultural problems of gendered inequality	Policy and implementation to be driven by scientific evidence from which axiomatic solutions can be derived as implemented across contexts, allowing for added control
Change and temporality	Structural; non-linear; long term	Functional; linear; short term
Scale and knowledge	Contextuality; relative	Generalizability; hierarchy
Mode of operation	Social; political	Technical; depoliticized

nature of the gender logic if it is coupled and combined with impact-effectiveness ideas. The preference of impact effectiveness logic for, e.g., randomized controlled trials and their inherent positivist logics to the study of gender norms and relations will necessarily entail a shift towards large populations and quantifiable data that may be compared across other cases, increasing the generalizability of the intervention studied. But the reductionism of such approaches means that the end result cannot account for the complexity of how, e.g., cultural and institutional structures reproduce gender inequalities, undermining the potential for applying a transformative approach. Utilizing women as a category or technical tool for boosting agricultural production through empowerment cannot be done in a depoliticized way or be released from the social world, as it necessarily remains a matter of redefining the relationship between men and women.

As the Gates Foundation has entered into international political life and particularly the field of global development, it has brought with it new ideas and normative frameworks that may incite change and question the legitimacy of established thinking. But it has also been confronted with strong norms and ideas already present in the field and that have secured prominence over time through iteration in international agreements, and in the discourses and practices of established organizations. In the foundation, the gradual entrance and institutionalization of ideas and practices on gender equality and women's empowerment have entailed significant challenges to organizational, programmatic and policy orthodoxies. Eventually, these ideas have emerged as an almost foundation-wide priority with an inherent political or social character significantly different from the technological and self-perceived apolitical logics of the foundation. Through substantial organizational and institutional work by different groups of actors, however, a resonance between these new ideas and the established and almost path-dependent logics of the foundation was made. At least to the degree of a perceived fit between the two. Ideas of gender equality and women's empowerment, like all ideas, certainly have an inherent elasticity to them, meaning they can be turned and bent to serve the purpose of those doing so. Yet they cannot be soundly blended with a significantly different set of ideas such as those of impact effectiveness without betraying one or the other's core characteristics. The logic of gender equality and women's empowerment may be framed through the logic of impact effectiveness to instrumentalize a focus on gender. But doing so means a loss of key transformative elements of the first. It is near impossible to couple a targeting of cultural or institutional structures for the sake of increasing gender equality with a fast-impact focus on increasing the agricultural productivity of women. In the Gates Foundation this means that work on gender equality and women's empowerment cannot simultaneously be structural and functional, political and technical, context-sensitive and scalable, but that key choices are made as these ideas meet in the foundation, with the strong logic of impact effectiveness stripping the foundation's approach to gender equality of its gender-transformative potential. From the logic of impact effectiveness, the next chapter moves on to discussions of a similarly powerful logic governing the work of the Gates Foundation since its genesis; the notion of social progress through technological innovation.

Notes

1 Some parts of this chapter have been adapted from Fejerskov, A. M. (2017). 'The influence of established ideas in emerging development organisations: gender equality and the Bill and Melinda Gates Foundation', *The Journal of Development Studies* 53(4): 584–599.

2 Gates, M. 2014. 'Putting women and girls at the center of development', *Science* 345(6202): 1273–1275.

3 Kristof, N. 2015. 'Bill and Melinda Gates's pillow talk', *The New York Times*, 15 July.

4 Impact effectiveness is often used interchangably with the similar notion of cost effectiveness.

5 Kardam, N. 2004. 'The emerging global gender equality regime from neoliberal and constructivist perspectives in international relations', *International Feminist Journal of Politics* 6(1): 85–109.

6 Kardam, 2004.

7 Kabeer, N. 2005. 'Gender equality and women's empowerment: a critical analysis of the third millennium development goal 1', *Gender & Development* 13(1): 13–24; Aikman, S., Unterhaler, E. and Challender, C. (2005) 'The education MDGs: achieving gender equality through curriculum and pedagogy change', *Gender & Development*, 13(1): 44–55; Painter, G. 2004. *Gender, the MDGs and Human Rights in the Context of the 2005 Review Processes*, Report for the Gender & Development Network. London: Gender & Development Network.

8 Andersen, M. 1993. 'The concept of mainstreaming: experience and change', in *Focusing on Women: UNIFEM's Experience with Mainstreaming*, edited by M. Andersen, New York, NY: UNIFEM.

9 Razavi, S. and Miller, C. 1995. *From WID to GAD: Conceptual Shifts in the Women and Development Discourse*, UNRIS Occasional paper 1. New York, NY: United Nations Development Programme; Krook, M. and True, J. 2012. 'Rethinking the life cycles of international norms: The United Nations and the global promotion of gender equality', *European Journal of International Relations* 18(1): 103–127.

10 See Plan International. 2009. *Because I Am a Girl: The State of the World's Girls 2009*. Surrey: Plan International.

11 Seguino, S. 2007. 'Plus ça change? Evidence on global trends in gender norms and stereotypes', *Feminist Economics* 13(2): 1–28.

12 Chant, S. 2012. 'The disappearing of "smart economics?" The World Development Report 2012 on Gender Equality: some concerns about the preparatory process and the prospects for paradigm change', *Global Social Policy* 12(2): 198–218; Chant, S. and Sweetman, C. 2012. 'Fixing women or fixing the world? "Smart economics", efficiency approaches, and gender equality in development', *Gender & Development*, 20(3): 517–529.

13 Cornwall, A., Harrison, E. and Whitehead, A. 2007. 'Gender myths and feminist fables: the struggle for interpretive power in gender and development', *Development and Change* 38(1): 1–20.

14 These are also related to the *private/public dichotomy*. In this classical feminist discussion, the two spheres of private and public are considered deeply interrelated because of the role of each in supporting and maintaining the other. Feminists have struggled to broaden out the definition of 'political' to include personal and intimate issues such as violence against women, reproductive rights, sharing of work between sexes, etc. This division is a key dimension in the conceptualization of how to maintain and contribute to gender equality. See Pateman, C. 1987. 'Feminist critiques of the public/private dichotomy', in A. Philips (ed.) *Feminism and Equality*. Oxford: Blackwell.

15 Korey, W. 2007. *Taking on the World's Repressive Regimes: The Ford Foundation's International Human Rights Policies and Practices*. Basingstoke: Palgrave Macmillan.

16 Ibid.

17 McGeorge Bundy is an interesting persona, not least in the context of the Ford Foundation's work on women's empowerment. Bundy moved from a position of dean at Harvard College to serve as the White House assistant for national security affairs under John F. Kennedy and Lyndon Johnson from 1961–1966. According to Nielsen (Nielsen, W. 1972. *The Big Foundations*. New York, NY: Columbia University Press) many in Congress had come to believe that Bundy played a key role in the Bay of Pigs and in the escalation of the Vietnam War, and saw his tenure at the Ford Foundation as an attempt to reminisce, transforming from a hawkish strategic planner to an activist domestic reformer almost overnight.

18 Bertini, C. 2008. 'The Agricultural Initiative at the Bill & Melinda Gates Foundation', speech delivered at a 21 July ODI and Oxfam event in London, UK.

19 Interview with Bill and Melinda Gates Foundation staff.

20 Gates, 2014.

21 Interview with former Bill and Melinda Gates Foundation Senior Advisor.

22 Interview with Bill and Melinda Gates Foundation staff.

23 Interview with former Bill and Melinda Gates Foundation Senior Advisor.

24 Interview with Bill and Melinda Gates Foundation Senior Programme Officer.

25 Interview with Bill and Melinda Gates Foundation Senior Programme Officer.

26 Interview with former Bill and Melinda Gates Foundation Programme Officer.

27 Interview with former Bill and Melinda Gates Foundation Senior Advisor.

28 Interview with Bill and Melinda Gates Foundation Senior Programme Officer.

29 Interview with Bill and Melinda Gates Foundation Senior Programme Officer.

30 Interview with former Bill and Melinda Gates Foundation Senior Advisor.

31 Interview with Bill and Melinda Gates Foundation Senior Advisor.

32 Interview with Bill and Melinda Gates Foundation Senior Programme Officer.

33 Interview with Bill and Melinda Gates Foundation Senior Programme Officer.

34 Interview with former Bill and Melinda Gates Foundation Programme Officer.

35 Interview with former Bill and Melinda Gates Foundation Senior Fellow.

36 Interview with Bill and Melinda Gates Foundation consultant.

37 Interview with Bill and Melinda Gates Foundation consultant.

38 Interview with Bill and Melinda Gates Foundation consultant.

39 Interview with former Bill and Melinda Gates Foundation Senior Fellow.

40 Interview with former Bill and Melinda Gates Foundation Programme Officer.

41 Interview with Bill and Melinda Gates Foundation Senior Programme Officer.

42 Lapsley, I. 2009. 'New public management: the cruelest invention of the human spirit?', *ABACUS* 45(1): 1–21.

43 Denzin, N. K. 2015. 'The elephant in the living room: or extending the conversation about the politics of evidence', *Qualitative Research* 9(2): 139–160.

44 Sandersson, I. 2002. 'Evaluation, policy learning and evidence-based policy making', *Public Administration* 80(1): 1–22.

45 Eyben, R. 2010. 'Hiding relations: the irony of "effective aid"', *European Journal of Development Research* 22(3): 382–397.

46 Sandersson, 2002.

47 Verloo, M. and Lombardo, E. 2007. 'Contested gender equality and policy variety in Europe: introducing a critical frame analysis approach', in *Multiple Meanings of Gender Equality: A Critical Frame Analysis of Gender Policies in Europe*, edited by M. Verloo. Budapest: CPS Books, 21–50.

48 Chant, S. 2007. *Gender Generation and Poverty: Exploring the "Feminisation of Poverty" in Africa Asia and Latin America*. Cheltenham: Edward Elgar.

49 Ibid.

50 Chant and Sweetman, 2012.

51 Cornwall et al., 2007; Wilson, K. 2015. 'Towards a radical re-appropriation: gender, development and neoliberal feminism', *Development and Change* 46(4): 803–832.

52 Interview with former Bill and Melinda Gates Foundation Senior Advisor.

53 Gates Foundation. 2008. *Gender Impact Strategy for Agricultural Development.* Seattle, WA: Bill and Melinda Gates Foundation.
54 Ibid.
55 Ibid.
56 Ibid.
57 Ibid.
58 Ibid.
59 Bill and Melinda Gates Foundation. 2012. *Annual Report.* Seattle, WA: Bill and Melinda Gates Foundation.
60 As has also been proved repeatedly elsewhere, see, for example, Liebowitz, D. J. and Zwingel, S. 2014. 'Gender equality oversimplified: using CEDAW to counter the measurement obsession', *International Studies Review* 16(3): 362–389.

6   The Global South as a laboratory of experimentation

Across all the issues occupying the attention of the Gates Foundation, a stream of emphasis runs through that sees it further notions of societal progress through experimentation and technological innovation. And that almost with the determination as if it was a global tech corporation whose very market position and core business depended on it. Whatever the nature or scope of a problem, the solution is often articulated as the necessity to harness technological innovation in the name of progress. These two notions of technology and experimentation are obviously not new to development. For decades, technology transfer embodied development assistance from rich to poor countries and was perceived as the key element in catalyzing economic and social advancement. Today, however, more than 60 years after development cooperation was institutionalized among Western donors, the way technology is perceived and advanced by the Gates Foundation (and other foundations along with it) is fundamentally different. Early science and technology efforts in development cooperation centred on the transfer of established technologies and hardware from developed to developing countries. Inventions that had proved their worth in Western countries were looked at in an effort to send them south and have them bring about the same forms of change in the worse-off parts of the world, something they rarely did. Contrary to this notion of transferring known innovations and technology, the contemporary aspirations of the Gates Foundation centre on 'live' experimentation and innovation in developing countries, attempting to quantum leap development through precarious technological experimentation, the social and political consequences of which are rarely understood.

There can be no doubt of the profound ability of novel technologies to transform economies and people's lives for the better. But they can also reinforce existing inequalities or radically change the trajectories of societies for the betterment only of an elite few, through their inherent disruptive qualities. This chapter reflects on the renascent role of technology in global development as we see it advocated by the Gates Foundation to understand how its experimentalist technology aspirations aim to influence and structure human life and relations in the Global South. Despite being widely claimed by their advocates, arguments for development work to focus on experimentation and technological innovation are not apolitical or driven by an objective analysis of issues and solutions of development. They are deeply normative claims and practices that ought to be explored and examined, whilst not being fatalist about the implications of technology for development, raising questions such as technology and development for whom and for what? And with what consequences?

Technology and global development

At least since Solow's[1] influential work, it has been acknowledged that technological progress and innovation shapes (if not determines) productivity and the rate of economic growth for societies, especially those in transition. Technology crosses borders through a variety of formal and informal channels, including technology transfer, trade, foreign direct investments, and migration of labour.[2] Early development cooperation thought and practice was driven by a belief that economic growth could flow from developed to developing countries by introducing similar forms of technology that had come to shape decades if not centuries of especially agricultural and industrial work in the West. President Harry Truman's inaugural speech to the US Congress in 1949 pronounced this opinion that would soon materialize in colonial and post-colonial relations to the developing world: 'We must embark on a bold new program for making the benefits of our scientific advances and industrial progress available for the improvement and growth of underdeveloped areas'.[3] Capital flows were not considered sufficiently efficient in themselves and a material–physical dimension in the form of diverse technology transfers was pursued by many donors. For one of the immanent promoters of development cooperation, Denmark, the first organizational set-up devised to govern this new issue (in 1962) was named the 'Secretary for technical cooperation with developing countries'. Likewise, and among many other examples, up until its 2011 merger with two other government bodies the German aid agency was the 'German Technical Cooperation'.

The majority of technology transfers during the 1960s, the first decade of formalized development cooperation, mainly included capital intensive and 'modern' technologies, thought to help economic growth in developing countries take off.[4] For many donors, including the World Bank, the US, Great Britain and France, the strategy essentially became to couple financial aid with technical assistance (experts from the donor countries) who could prepare and execute projects by utilizing modern technology, especially within the physical infrastructures of roads, ports, and electricity.[5] By the 1970s, the lacking or negative impact of such technologies was increasingly recognized as large parts of the population were bypassed in the perceived technological progress that did not 'trickle down' as expected. Dependency theorists began arguing for the increasing reliance of developing countries on developed countries, a dependency created by technology transfers, and the so-called 'white elephants' began to emerge. These, of course, were the failed infrastructure and technology transfers in which the local needs and capacities had not been taken into account, leading to the transfer of electricity-driven wells to villages without electricity and the like. Focus then turned towards so-called appropriate (or intermediate) technologies, understood as the most effective and acceptable forms of technology in any given social context.[6] After a good few decades, this material dimension of development cooperation was gradually toned down through the 1990s as more immaterial concerns of human development, including education, health and gender equality, increasingly took centre stage, not least with the growing role of the United Nations.

Today, we see a second coming of technology in global development, materialized in at least three streams of thought and practice. The first is the link between technology and climate adaptation and mitigation, which is increasingly foregrounded in discussions in the United Nations Framework Convention on Climate Change (UNFCCC), as well as work surrounding the Technology Facilitation Mechanisms, adopted with the new Sustainable Development Goals in New York in 2015, and related mantras of 'ICT (information and communications technology, ed.) for development' or 'Knowledge for development'.[7] Gates is not least involved in this work through the Breakthrough Energy Coalition discussed in Chapter 4. The second, related to the first, is an increasing emphasis on the potential of South–South technology transfer, not least pertaining to the idea of appropriateness between technology and social context, as recent decades have seen a (re)turn in the geography of technological progress towards China, India and other Asian economies.[8] Third, and most important here as it serves as the object of this chapter, we witness increased focus on societal progress through technological innovation and experimentation from certain private foundations and donor countries. For some, developing countries have been thought to have a relative advantage over developed countries because imitation and adaptation of existing technology is less expensive and risky than creating them.[9] In this third and principal direction of contemporary technology and development cooperation relations, however, this seems to be reversing as the Global South is increasingly articulated and utilized as a live laboratory for technological innovation and testing, especially by private foundations.

The techno-politics of philanthrocapitalism

Private foundations have historically played a significant role in the diffusion of science, technology and value systems from industrialized to developing countries, as we have seen throughout this book. As architects of international networks of scholars and institutions that have produced and disseminated knowledge, they have influenced social and cultural policies on an international scale. But they have also engaged directly in the experimentation and diffusion of science and technology to the Global South. Early examples include the Rockefeller Foundation's export of Western medicine (and medical educational infrastructure) to Asia and particularly China from the 1920s and onwards, with which it hoped to spark a technological transformation of Chinese society.[10] At the opening of the Peking Union Medical College in 1921, predominantly sponsored by the Rockefeller Foundation, John D. Rockefeller Jr exclaimed that this new institution would absorb 'The best that is known to Western civilization not only in medical science but in mental development and spiritual culture'.[11] The intent was to train a limited group of scientifically oriented medical doctors through a strong hospital and laboratory-based research tradition, who could then go on to educate other doctors, driving forward a Western medical revolution in China. Unfortunately, in the decades that followed, the results seem to have mainly been the creation of an expensive medical care system for urban elites, with rural populations generally unable to access such systems or reap the benefits of the foundation's efforts. Another example is the foundation's deep engagement in genetically modifying crops in both Latin America and in Asia, aiming to introduce 'modern' agricultural technologies, already discussed in length. Also worth mentioning is the Carnegie Foundation's work in East and Southern Africa, similarly beginning from the 1920s, to conduct educational reforms (a large part of it implemented by the Phelps-Stokes Fund that had as its primary purpose 'The education of Negroes both in Africa and the United States'[12]), as another attempt from private foundations to diffuse ideas and practices of science to the Global South.[13]

Over the past decades, as we have learned, a new generation of philanthrocapitalists have emerged, seemingly shifting philanthropy from altruistic charity to strategic social impact investment. Largely affiliated with neighbouring fields of social entrepreneurship and venture philanthropy, the basic logic of this movement remains that business thinking and market-based methods hold the key to save the world, not least because traditional ways of solving social problems are perceived to have failed.[14] These new individuals and foundations largely hold Silicon Valley as their epicentre, at least culturally or intellectually, embodying an important factor in explaining their faith in technology and innovation. For most of these philanthrocapitalists notions of technology and innovation have made and shaped their careers, and these have accordingly come to form the basis of their philanthropic activities. While not a part of this chapter, it is also important to stress that the experimentalist approaches of private foundations can be felt not just in the South, but also deeply among marginalized groups in the North.[15] Over the next sections, the technology and innovation-centred discourses and practices of especially the Bill and Melinda Gates Foundation are presented.

The Gates Foundation and technological innovation for development

The Gates Foundation, epitomized of course by Bill Gates, is a paradigmatic promoter of approaches that see technological innovation as the central driver of societal progress in the developing world.[16] The foundation invests more than $500 million annually in health and medical research specifically (including drugs, vaccines, and medical devices) and has invested more than $530m in innovative agricultural research and development since 2008. Gates himself generally considers innovation as 'The most powerful force for change in the world',[17] fundamentally able to shift the trajectory of development. He does not consider it to have played as big a role in development as it could have, and maintains that though development aid may spur innovation, the real expertise of such 'Lies with the private sector'.[18] Essentially, the world will need to 'Invent to really make a dramatic difference'[19] on issues such as agriculture in the developing world. Agriculture is conceived by Gates as an example of a market that simply does not work for the poor and one in which change is predominantly to come from innovation in digital technology.[20] And Gates believes that the number of people who can spur innovations is much greater than in the past, something that will be defining in creating 'A new era in development'.[21] Speaking to future generations in their 2016 annual letter, Bill and Melinda Gates make it clear who will drive poverty-alleviating efforts in the future: 'Some of you will become engineers, entrepreneurs, scientists, and software developers. I invite you to take on the challenge of serving the poor'.[22] Engineers, entrepreneurs, scientists and software developers will be the ones driving forward global progress and development. These views are mirrored in the foundation as well. In describing itself, the foundation talks of 'Applying new thinking', 'Finding solutions' and 'Funding innovative ideas', whether in the form of 'Innovative financing mechanisms', 'New techniques' or 'innovative technologies'.[23] The co-chairs see the foundation's key role as 'Investing in innovations that would not otherwise be funded. This draws not only on our backgrounds in technology but also on the foundation's size and ability to take a long-term view and take large risks on new approaches'.[24] Optimistic about societal progress over the next 15 years, the two exclaim in their 2015 annual letter that we will see major breakthroughs for most people in poor countries, and that these breakthroughs will be driven by innovation in technology.[25] The framing here is one that considers poverty to be an engineering problem (with perceived causal links between a problem and its resolve), in which the innovation of new technologies is the main road to solving human misery. Despite the inherent complexity sometimes acknowledged in some of the many quotes used above, it is a linear conception of development solutions. According to Gates, 'Cutting through complexity to find a solution runs through four predictable stages: determine a goal, find the highest-leverage approach, discover the ideal technology for that approach, and in the meantime, make the smartest application of the technology that you already have'.[26] In this view, international interventions such as those furthered through global development are systems or processes in which we can understand the different mechanisms and their effects and consequences, allowing us to predict the necessary actions to bring about change in social systems.

The Global South as a live laboratory of experimentation

Proceeding from the above, a central issue is how the transfer of established technologies is substituted by technological or solution innovation that takes the shape of experimentation, and considers the Global South as a form of live laboratory in which failure of technical and social experiments is not in itself problematic. Bill Gates himself has described the work of the foundation as more like Microsoft at age three than at age 33, highlighting the experimental focus or nature of much of the work engaged in. The foundation holds that its role in global development and health is 'Funding a range of ideas with different levels of risk that they could fail'.[27] This is basically so because 'Finding the best ways to help people improve their lives takes many years of research and experimentation'.[28] Innovation, high-risk engagement and experimentation apply not only to technology, but extend far into the private and social realms of people in the Global South, according to the foundation:

> High-risk innovations require the invention of new tools. Some are at the frontiers of science, such as finding a new drug and running a large trial to see how well it works. Other high-risk efforts involve changing social practices, such as persuading men at risk of getting HIV to get circumcised.[29]

The most obvious examples of technological experimentation in the context of the Gates Foundation are perhaps its endeavours in the innovation of new toilets or condoms. The first was essentially launched as a contest to reinvent the toilet with parameters including suitability for a single-family residence in a developing country and the ability to output waste as drinkable water and turn faeces into energy. The cost of the winning toilet was $1,000. Consider the costs of maintaining it for a family, or the consequences of installing such an expensive toilet in a village in which people live off $1 a day. In 2014, When Bill Gates recalled 10 years of Grand Challenges' funding for cutting edge technology and innovation, his humbling message was that out of the numerous projects sponsored for a total of $1 billion, none had made a significant contribution to improving health in the developing world. But less popularized efforts, such as the innovation of new seeds, are also important technological endeavours of the foundation. Within agriculture, the foundation's most well-known project to innovate technology is likely the Alliance for a Green Revolution in Africa (AGRA), discussed earlier, introduced in 2006 with a grant of $150 million together with the Rockefeller Foundation who founded the original Green Revolution. The original 'Green Revolution' was not so much a coherent framework for agricultural development as a diverse set of interventions across the developing world that took on many forms. For the Rockefeller Foundation, this work started in Mexico, where in 1941 its Natural Sciences Division began a project to develop new modified varieties of corn and wheat, in particular as regards high-yielding capacity, headed by plant pathologist George A. Harrar. Twenty years later, Harrar would go on to become foundation president. Similarly, AGRA today aims to introduce 'technology packages' to poor farmers that will allow for an increase in agricultural yields, based on a crop-breeding approach that paves the way for genetic engineering technology. The founding of AGRA has not come without its controversies, and critics hold that it is on the wrong track, with genetic engineering potentially leaving smallholder systems more environmentally vulnerable. The process of forming AGRA has also been criticized for not involving farmers, but only seed and fertilizer companies, philanthropic foundations and multilateral institutions.[30] Responding to criticism, the Gates Foundation reiterated that it was 'Learning all the time' and that a state-of-the-art project on cellular feedback from local farmers would soon allow them to communicate with more than 10,000 stakeholders. Though AGRA is a relative newcomer, it builds upon and forms part of a quasi-public institutional architecture for agricultural research that dates back almost a century and includes organizations such as the Consultative Group on International Agricultural Research or CGIAR, where foundations both serve as members and as core funders, including foundations governed by biotechnology and agribusiness companies. The CGIAR has long been a central proponent and funder of genetic crop improvement and had the Gates Foundation as a major funder. Bill Gates himself has often defended these priorities by referring to the debate of for-or-against Genetically Modified Organisms as an ideological battle between those in favour of technology and those opposing it.

The Gates Foundation's deep engagement with the global pharmaceutical industry means it is also entangled in certain questionable practices furthered here. Seeing as the costs of developing a new drug today amounts to billions of dollars, the vast majority of which is spent on Phase III clinical trials, the pharmaceutical industry has increasingly turned to the developing world in conducting such trials at much lower prices. Clinical trials are essentially tests on large groups of human subjects, to monitor effectiveness and side effects of new vaccines and other drugs, who all have to be identified, registered, tested and compensated under the applicable regulatory regimes in a given country context. As governments in the developed world are raising the regulatory bar, the pharmaceutical industry is increasingly looking towards 'emerging markets' (i.e., developing countries), and have been incited by companies such as McKinsey & Co. to do so.[31] Here, clinical trials are cheaper and speedier, and regulations far more relaxed, whilst patient recruitment is easy with struggling public health sectors and high poverty entailing a lack of resources or access to specialized medicines and treatment. South Africa and India in particular have surged as favoured places to conduct clinical trials because of these very factors.[32] Both countries are also amongst those where Gates-funded organizations and specific projects have conducted trials over the past years, some with great controversy.[33] In India in 2010 a Gates-funded and PATH-conducted clinical trial of an HPV (Human Papilloma Virus) vaccine, developed by GlaxoSmithKline and Merck, allegedly caused the death of seven adolescent girls and severe side effects or autoimmune disorder for at least 1,200 girls (in a trial of 23,000 girls between 10 and 14 years of age). Whether the side effects were caused directly by the trial may be uncertain given the context, and more important here is that an Indian Parliamentary Committee found that PATH 'Had violated all laws and regulations laid down by the government in a clear-cut violation of human rights'.[34] The investigation claimed the trial had been characterized by widespread disregard of ethical norms, with village girls forced into the trials or involved through forged signatures. The controversy that surrounds the side effects of such clinical trials are conspicuous, but so too are placebo-controlled studies (which many Gates-funded grantees conduct) when executed in a developing country context, in which test subjects are either given the test drug or a placebo. In these cases, it is difficult to avoid questions such as whether poor people with little access to specialized medicines or health care are easily recruited because they lack insight into the conditions of a trial, and in fact expect tested medicines but receive placebo?

Aside from concrete projects, institutional environments are increasingly consulted and used by foundations to facilitate experimental efforts in global development, including so-called 'Social innovation labs'.[35] These have been funded by the Rockefeller Foundation since 2013 and have been used by the foundation to develop new tools and resources for issues such as improvements in the livelihoods of small-scale fisheries. According to the foundation, social innovation labs consist of three ingredients – diverse stakeholders, experimentation and learning by doing, and unique tools and processes – and are best used when a problem affects many stakeholders and sectors and can change in unexpected ways.[36] These 'labs' are perceived in opposition to what the foundation deems 'Traditional problem solving', in which the problem is clearly defined and confined to a single sector or organization. Likewise, where a traditional planning approach is thought by the foundation to take at least a year to implement its first pilot programme, the social innovation labs can begin prototyping and experimenting with solutions as early as within two months. In such 'lab' contexts, subject expertise is often considered unnecessary or even counterproductive, because of the disruptive ambitions. In their explanation of the nature of social innovation labs, the Rockefeller Foundation tells a story of how a venture capitalist and an SMS expert came together to design solutions for small-scale fisheries and coastal communities, benefitting from the fact that they had no prior knowledge of the issue, and were thus not restrained by notions such as prior experience or norms of the field.[37] This certainly gives way for disruptive qualities. As a report funded by the Rockefeller Foundation explains it, 'Social innovation is about profoundly changing or transforming a system rather than adapting or improving it'.[38] Their point of departure is that 'When present solutions do not work, we need to develop new solutions. As it is impossible to predict what works, we need to experiment'.[39] Here, poverty is no longer just considered an engineering problem (as presented in much of the Gates Foundation's discourse) in which we can predict which levers to pull in order to gain the wanted effect. Rather, it is a scientific problem in which solutions can only emerge from experimentation, because of its inherent non-linearity and complexity.

These experimental lines of thought are deeply connected to another core Gates Foundation mantra, namely that of constructive failures. In the eyes of the foundation, failure can be a very positive project outcome as long as it may learn from the failure, deducing from it new approaches or leaving behind those that have proved unsuccessful. The foundation maintains that 'Failure is critical to success. When we discover what doesn't work, we gain scientific knowledge that eventually will help us learn what does work. And the feedback from failures helps us continually set new priorities'.[40] As the former CEO Jeff Raikes explained upon taking office in 2010, 'Almost by definition, good philanthropy means we're going to have to do some risky things, some speculative things to try and see what works and what doesn't'.[41] One grant-making tool that relies on a high degree of experimentation, risk and potential failure is the aforementioned Grand Challenges, in which potential grantees compete for foundation funding within the context of a specific issue. Here, the forms of ideas, technology and forms of innovation hoped to be developed 'Are all unproven, and we expect that the vast majority of them will fail'.[42] As mentioned earlier, the vast majority of them seem to have failed. To an extent, this frankness is admirable and a welcome breath of fresh air to traditional and especially public aid agencies where admittance of failure is often completely absent. This difference may very well lie in the fact that whereas aid agencies essentially handle tax-payers' money, that is funds of the public, and thus have to pretend that all of these are spent effectively without any mistakes being made, foundation endowments are essentially the big pockets of one or a few high net-worth individuals. In the context of development, however, and thus interventions in the Global South, we are not dealing with an isolated lab in which the consequences of failure do not move beyond the time and resources of researchers. Experimentation and failure affects the lives of real people – from the individual to thousands or more – and often people living in deep poverty.

Problematizing the new techno-politics of global development

There can be no question as to the potential of technology to progress society, stimulate economic growth and spur social development. But this is not a given nor likely the most probable outcome of most forms of technological innovation, not least when conducted as forms of experimentation or trial and error in which consequences and impacts of the technologies are not known or necessarily foreseeable. In the former section, we looked at the way technology and innovation is framed within the thought and practices of the Gates Foundation's approach to global health and development. We came to appreciate the philanthrocapitalist conception and application of technology in development, from perceiving poverty as an engineering problem to forms of technological experimentation as an attempt to accommodate perceived complexity and non-linearity of both development challenges and solutions. In practice, the focus on corporate private influence on and delivery of social progress is coupled with a belief in the ability to literally hack societal advancement. These concerns raise questions such as who can legitimately experiment with other people's lives, and whether such legitimacy can be achieved by way of large funding potential and good intentions? This is problematized next, starting with a critical look at the laboratory metaphor.

The laboratory metaphor

In 1973 Schumacher proclaimed that 'There is nothing in the experience of the last twenty-five years to suggest that modern technology, as we know it, can really help us to alleviate world poverty'.[43] The same cannot be said of the 40 and more years that followed since he published his influential work. In fact, the Gates Foundation will likely say that its advancement and application of technology in developing countries is an answer to Schumacher's call for technology that 'Lightens the burden of work man has to carry'.[44] Instead of a transfer of appropriate technology per se, however, we seem to be dealing with a gradual appropriation of the technologies transferred through a trial and error process in which the Global South appears as a live laboratory of experimentation. The developing world as a laboratory for the West has a long history to it, as is clearly shown in Tilley's[45] and others' work on the colonial undertakings to decide and govern the territoriality of the African continent. During the second part of the 19th century, colonial powers attempted to structure human life in Africa, a watershed moment not just for geopolitics (and the Eurocentric shaping and forming of African states) but tangibly for African citizens through, *inter alia*, the physical–material implications of border demarcation. The current approach to the Global South as a laboratory is somewhat different, however, in that it largely bypasses any notion of the state and seeks to directly affect local populace and communities.

The differences between a laboratory and the Global South are abundant and they do not deserve comparison. It is obvious, however, that while the variables and influences of a lab are often predictable, manipulable, and may be changed to the liking of the scientist, the variables of the Global South are – as any society (or social process) inhabited by human beings – non-linear and complex beyond any scientific comprehension. We cannot determine reactions and consequences beforehand as we are not dealing with a lab, or lab rats, but rather real people, the trajectories of whose lives are deeply influenced and potentially disrupted by technology, the exact consequences of which we do not and cannot know. This is not to say that laboratories do not also accommodate political practices and are value neutral.[46] But what remains is that these forms of experimental approaches to technological innovation in the Global South (deliberately or not) influence social, cultural, and political practices and action in indeterminate and unforeseeable directions, providing foundations with an uncontrollable ability to greatly influence the lives of people who rarely have a choice of consent as to their involvement. Private foundations such as the Gates Foundation often excuse controversial impacts on the local populace by referring to themselves as 'learning organizations' still readily learning from mistakes and failures. This articulation of developing countries as a legitimate or acceptable space to fail is highly problematic when we consider the consequences of failure that influence the lives of actual citizens.

The main contradiction between private diffusion of innovation, as furthered by the private foundations, and public generation is that

> While much public funding of research is aimed at common goals, such as better health and a cleaner environment, since the means of distribution is the market, there is no explicit mechanism or criterion built into most S&T (science and technology, ed.) programmes to make sure that both advantaged and disadvantaged share in these benefits.[47]

In work affiliated with forms of development cooperation or aid, the difference between these two often means that instead of supporting sanitary systems or health reforms, i.e., the building up of health systems for the general public's good, funds from private foundations are provided to Western companies to try and innovate isolated technological hardware such as a new toilet or a new condom, when what is needed may be large-scale waste management efforts and sexual and reproductive health education and information.[48] Such recalibration is seen in the approach from vertical global health initiatives like Gavi, favouring a narrow and technical approach to global health that mainly sees it fund vaccinations. In Gavi, but also in the World Health Organization, the Gates Foundation has been instrumental in gradually pushing the organization and its donors away from supporting national health systems to these types of vertical and technical engagements that favour relatively quick fixes such as vaccines.[49]

Technological experimentation, democracy and the uselessness of subject expertise

Technological innovation indisputably supports the socio-economic foundations of societies and communities. In the West we have come to consider technological artefacts as the inevitable products of progress. Technological innovation and economic development have proceeded hand in hand over the last century, and the technologization of everyday life is as inevitable in developing countries as it unavoidable in the developed. However, as in the case of economic growth, technology and innovation are not sufficient to satisfy the minimum requirements of human lives and may easily exacerbate existing (and create novel) forms of inequality. As Rogers[50] reminds us, 'When a system's structure is already very unequal, it is likely that when an innovation is introduced (specifically if it is a relatively high cost innovation) the consequences will lead to even greater inequality in the form of wider socioeconomic gaps'. Of course, technologies are not dead hardware only becoming corrupt through questionable intentions or practices. They are deeply political, especially those of the philanthrocapitalist private foundations that can be understood against a backdrop of neoliberalism as a hollowing of the state and refocusing on corporate and private responsibility.[51]

Critical thinking on the social and political consequences of modern technologies has a long history in the contemporary social sciences – the breadth of which cannot be covered here – with central thinkers such as Lewis Mumford[52] or E. F. Schumacher,[53] but also someone lesser known such as Günter Anders, whose thoughts on technology are relevant and only beginning to be explored.[54] In his time, Anders developed a critical theory of techno-politics, especially referring to the nuclear condition, which was global and activist in orientation.[55] His is a peculiar story. Anders studied under Martin Heidegger, where he met his first wife Hannah Arendt. His main work, though never translated into English, is considered to be the first volume of *Die Antiquiertheit des Menschen* (translatable to 'The obsolescence of human beings', published in 1956). It was in large part the experience of living in the Cold War US that influenced his thinking on technology and modernity, observing the immense progress in technological innovations, the like of which we are witnessing today. Central for Anders was the political nature of technology, breaking with instrumentalist views on technology that saw this as a neutral instrument of good or bad, and the argument that existence itself is governed by technology. According to Anders, technology shapes the trajectories of social relations not least by introducing new forms of dependencies. For him, those who equated technology with social progress were the worst (in his view, shaped by but departing from Marxism, they were counter-revolutionaries), reproducing and strengthening only the dominant class' control over resources and power.[56] However far away, Anders' writings and perceptions of technology and its implications for man are peculiarly close to how the disruptive qualities of technological innovation are framed as progress within the philanthrocapitalist movement. Like Anders, his contemporaries were perceptive in articulating a critique of technology and innovation as salvation to the human race, challenging core elements of philanthrocapitalist conceptions of the same. Mumford[57] referred to this perception as one considering 'The machine as a norm, to which all other aspects of human life must conform', denoting how technology is thought of as a tool to change social practices because of the inherent value it is thought to represent. Adaptation of social practices is thus only a necessary condition or step towards properly utilizing technology designating the adjustment of man to machine, not machine to man. This is a core element of philanthrocapitalist technological experimentation in which inappropriate technologies are considered a matter of habituation for the local populace, not recalibration of the hardware itself. Unfortunately, these thinkers, while forwarding a view to the entirety of the planet and humanity, gave little actual thought to the Global South in their writings.[58] Their observations on technology nonetheless help us to question the techno-optimism as we see it renascent today in philanthrocapitalist conceptions by arguing against any conception of human salvation by technology.

These concerns also position debates on democracy and accountability dead centre. The deeply ambivalent relationship between democracy and technology is a core theme in science and technology studies and has been so for decades.[59] Technology and democracy, just as science and democracy, are not opposites, and may in fact greatly invigorate each other. This co-constructive association cannot be taken as a given however, and there is a need to ask how the practices of technological innovation and experimentation as forwarded by philanthrocapitalists affect the relationship between democracy, participation and accountability. It is extremely difficult, if not impossible, to balance equality and innovation within capitalism.[60] If we consider democracy in the context of technological interventionism, at the very least some form of participation and access becomes central, and it comes to mean something more specific: forms of access to and control over technology. The forms of technological innovation and experimentation accounted for here may be seen as bypassing democratic institutions because of the direct intervention of private foundations in developing countries. This makes other shapes of technological governance relevant, and fundamental to such is the question of consent, as the power to give or withhold it shapes degrees of participation.[61] During the processes of technological experimentation furthered by private foundations, the intended beneficiaries are almost always unable to exercise influence in other forms than ex post intervention. They neither have access to, nor are heard during initial design processes in which the technologies are developed – processes that mainly involve the funders and the (often Western) companies tasked with innovating a new product or technology. Since they are not directly involved in the processes of innovation, or even in decisions about having these technologies intervene in their communities, they may only be able to react to how the technologies are already shaping their lives. Furthermore, participation not only refers to the design or innovation processes themselves but also to the opportunity to determine whether technology should be considered an answer to the problems encountered in their lives and their communities in the first place.[62]

This moves us further to discussions of expertise. The difference between a group of Western scientists building a new toilet for the Gates Foundation and the local Indian populace who refuse to use it may be explained by the notion that innovations in the form of artefacts are flexibly interpretable (i.e., employing a social constructivist view on technology), and that different social groups accordingly will relate differently to the same piece of technology. This essentially means that a technology developed in isolation from those who are supposed to benefit from it cannot be expected to wield predictable outcomes. In this case, though, we are not only dealing with forms of social construction. There is a difference in material circumstances as much as in social practices when we consider the providing and receiving ends of philanthrocapitalist technology from the West to the rest of the world. Expertise is a negotiated attribution, and everyone may simultaneously be considered an expert and a lay person in different ways.[63] Those who developed the new toilets of the Gates Foundation were experts in the technical processes surrounding the conversion of waste into energy, but they had little knowledge of the social practices in relation to which the toilets were to be used or of the financial, political and social constraints and consequences associated with giving out $1,000 toilets. As Jason Kass, founder of the organization Toilets for People, has explained it,

> The trouble is that the Gates Foundation has treated the quest to find the proper solution (to building a new toilet, ed.) as it would a cutting-edge project at Microsoft: lots of bells and whistles, sky-high budgets and engineers in elite institutions experimenting with the newest technologies, thousands of miles away from their clients.[64]

While a negotiated attribute, the asymmetries in knowledge and comprehension of technology between experts and non-experts is a significant issue for democracy.[65] Interestingly, as shown earlier, subject expertise is often considered unnecessary or even a hindrance in forms of 'social innovation'. Such forms of disruption from the established order of things and thinking can be very effective, but casting away prior knowledge or experience is seldom a good way to come up with effective solutions.

Final remarks

In this chapter I have tried to show the very tip of the iceberg of why the meeting between contemporary Western ideologies of technology and the Global South remain an immensely pertinent avenue for research on the social and political ramifications of modern technology. The aim has not been to explicate design paths in the technologies forwarded by philanthrocapitalists and propose alternative forms of hardware or solutions. It has rather been to accentuate some of the political and social ramifications of technological innovation and experimentation as it takes place with the Global South as a live laboratory. We should, of course, be careful of making any general diagnosis of democratic deficit in the work of foundations, just as we should not generalize these problematic elements to all attempts at using technology in global development. Related to this, critics of the arguments made here may perhaps inquire whether cautioning against technological innovation in the Global South means denying people in the developing world a modernity, taking from them the possibility of progress by questioning contemporary technology thought and practice in global development. The arguments made here are not ones against technology or progress, just as they are not about denying developing countries a modernity. Rather, they are arguments for letting citizens themselves decide what kind of modernity they see as worth pursuing, and they are arguments against assuming that technological innovation is necessarily analogous to democratic societal progress. One could choose not to assume that the problematic consequences sketched here are the intended outcome of philanthrocapitalist interventions, and if we consider technological innovation a complex and iterative process it becomes far more difficult to see how societal consequences can be intentionally inscribed in technological artefacts from the outset of their construction. Nevertheless, it is necessary to question the technopolitics of the Gates Foundation and like-minded organizations, and particularly their articulation and use of the Global South as a live laboratory of experimentation and as a free space to trial and fail. Perhaps one is even asking whether there is a need for deliberate political action to regulate such private action influencing the lives of citizens. As Zimmerman[66] describes it, 'Many complex technologies pose substantial hazards and risks to individuals, communities, regions, or even to the entire planet. To impose such risks on people without even their tacit consent is undeniably an act of tyranny'. Society is not a piece of software to be 'hacked', a system that can be manipulated like a computer programme. Without being fatalist about technology and its aspirations, it is important not to assume a straight line between the philanthrocapitalist conceptions of technological innovation and experimentation in the Global South and equitable or democratic societal progress. To truly understand how technology structures human life in parts of the world other than the West, there is dire need to explore further the experiments and applications of such artefacts and practices.

Notes

1   Solow, R. 1957. 'Technical change and the aggregate production function', *Review of Economics and Statistics* 39(3): 312–320.
2   Groizard, J. L. 2009. 'Technology trade', *Journal of Development Studies* 45(9): 1526–1544.
3   Truman, H. 1949. *Inaugural Address*, www.presidency.ucsb.edu, accessed 3 April 2016.

4 Rostow, W. W. 1959. *The Stages of Economic Growth: A Non-Communist Manifesto.* Cambridge, MA: Cambridge University Press.
5 Martinussen, J. and Engberg-Pedersen, P. 1999. *Bistand: Udvikling eller afvikling.* Copenhagen: Mellemfolkeligt Samvirke; Wilson, G. 2007. 'Knowledge, innovation and re-inventing technical assistance for development', *Progress in Development Studies* 7(3): 183–199.
6 Stamp, P. 1989. *Technology, Gender, and Power in Africa.* Ottawa, ON: International Development Research Centre; Schumacher, E. 1973. *Small is Beautiful: A Study of Economics as if People Mattered.* London: Blond and Briggs.
7 Cherlet, J. 2014. 'Epistemic and technological determinism in development aid', *Science, Technology, & Human Values* 39(6): 773–794.
8 Kaplinsky, R. 2011. 'Schumacher meets Schumpeter: appropriate technology below the radar', *Research Policy* 40(2): 193–203.
9 Ibid.
10 See Brown, E. R. 1982. 'Rockefeller medicine in China: professionalism and imperialism', in *Philanthropy and Cultural Imperialism*, edited by F. Arnove, Bloomington, IN: Indiana University Press, 123–147.
11 Brown, 1982.
12 Berman, E. H. 1982. 'Educational colonialism in Africa: the role of American foundations, 1910–1945', in *Philanthropy and Cultural Imperialism*, edited by F. Arnove, Bloomington, IN: Indiana University Press, 179–203.
13 Nielsen, W. 1972. *The Big Foundations.* New York, NY: Columbia University Press.
14 Bishop, M. and Green, M. 2010. *Philanthrocapitalism: How Giving Can Save the World.* London, UK: A & C Black; Edwards, M. 2010. *Small Change: Why Business Won't Save the World.* Oakland, CA: Berrett-Koehler Publishers; McGoey, L. 2015. *No Such Thing as a Free Gift.* London: Verso.
15 For this and the inability of private foundations to address inequality there, see Kohl-Arenas, E. 2015. *The Self-Help Myth: How Philanthropy Fails to Alleviate Poverty.* Oakland, CA: University of California Press; Morvaridi, B. 2015. 'Introduction' in *New Philanthropy and Social Justice: Debating the Conceptual and Policy Discourse*, edited by B. Morvaridi, Bristol: Policy Press, 1–17.
16 During Bill Gates' time in Microsoft, employees tending towards technical *absolutism* were usually referred to as 'Bill Guys'.
17 Gates, B. 2011. *Innovation with Impact: Financing 21st Century Development.* Report to the G20 Leaders. Personal report to the G20 Cannes Summit, November 2011.
18 Ibid.
19 Guo, J. 2010. 'In interview, Gates describes philanthropic journey', *The Tech* 3 April.
20 Gates Foundation. 2016. *Annual Letter.* Seattle, WA: The Bill and Melinda Gates Foundation.
21 Gates, 2011: 3.
22 Gates Foundation, 2016.
23 Gates Foundation. 2012. *Annual Letter.* Seattle, WA: The Bill and Melinda Gates Foundation.
24 Gates Foundation. 2010. *Annual Letter.* Seattle, WA: The Bill and Melinda Gates Foundation.
25 Gates Foundation. 2015. *Our Big Bet for the Future: 2015 Gates Annual Letter.* Seattle, WA: The Bill and Melinda Gates Foundation.
26 Gates, B. 2007. Remarks of Bill Gates, Harvard Commencement 2007. Accessed 15 April 2017: http://news.harvard.edu/gazette/story/2007/06/remarks-of-bill-gates-harvard-commencement-2007.
27 Gates Foundation, 2010.
28 Gates Foundation. 2008. *Annual Letter.* Seattle, WA: The Bill and Melinda Gates Foundation.
29 Gates Foundation, 2010.

30 Thompson, C. 2014. 'Philanthrocapitalism: appropriation of Africa's genetic wealth', *Review of African Political Economy* 41(141): 389–405.
31 McKinsey. 2011. *A Wake-Up Call for Big Pharma.* 15 April, McKinsey.
32 For a discussion on South Africa as a site of clinical trials, see Wemos. 2013. *The Clinical Trials Industry in South Africa; Ethics, Rules and Realities.* Amsterdam: The Wemos Foundation.
33 See Levich, J. 2014. 'The real agenda of the Gates Foundation', in *Aspects of India's Economy* No. 57. Mumbai: The Research Unit for Political Economy (RUPE).
34 Dhar, A. 2013. 'It's a PATH of violations, all the way to vaccine trials: house panel', *The Hindu* 5 September, www.thehindu.com/news/national/its-a-path-of-violations-all-the-way-to-vaccine-trials-house-panel/article5083151.ece.
35 For a study on the use of US universities as 'development labs' see Collins, C. S. 2017. 'Development labs: university knowledge production and global poverty', *The Review of Higher Education* 41(1): 113–119.
36 Rockefeller. 2014. *Understanding the Value of Social Innovation Labs: Solutions to Complex Social Problems.* Accessed 15 April 2017: http://visual.ly/understandi ng-value-social-innovation-labs-solutions-complex-social-problems#sthash.uKMftAzM.dpuf.
37 Rockefeller. 2016. *To Save Our Fisheries, We Need a New Approach.* Accessed 15 April 15 2017: www.rockefellerfoundation.org/blog/save-our-fisheries-we-need-new/.
38 Westley, F., Laban, S., Rose, C., McGowan, K., Robinson, K., Tjornbo, O. and Tovey, M. 2014. *Social Innovation Lab Guide.* Waterloo, ON: University of Waterloo.
39 Ibid.
40 Gates Foundation. 2007. *Annual Letter.* Seattle, WA: The Bill and Melinda Gates Foundation.
41 Blankinship, D. G. 2009. 'New CEO: Gates Foundation learns from mistakes', *Associated Press*, www.thestreet.com/story/10506452/1/new-ceo-gates-foundation-learns-from-experiments.html, accessed 15 April 2017.
42 Gates Foundation, 2007.
43 Schumacher, 1973.
44 Ibid.
45 Tilley, H. 2011. *Africa as a Living Laboratory: Empire, Development, and the Problem of Scientific Knowledge, 1870–1950.* Chicago, IL: University of Chicago Press.
46 Latour, B. 1987. *Science in Action: How to Follow Scientists and Engineers through Society.* Cambridge, MA: Harvard University Press.
47 Cozzens, S. 2007. 'Distributive justice in science and technology policy', *Science and Public Policy* 34(2): 85–94.
48 For a discussion of this issue and the role of private foundations in contemporary global heath see Moran, M. 2011. 'Private foundations and global health partnerships: philanthropists and "partnership brokerage"', in *Partnerships and Foundations in Global Health Governance*, edited by S. Rushton and O. Williams, Basingstoke: Palgrave Macmillan, 123–143.
49 Storeng, K. 2014. 'The GAVI Alliance and the 'Gates approach' to health systems strengthening', *Global Public Health* 9(8): 865–879.
50 Rogers, E. M. 1995. *Diffusion of Innovations, 4th Edition.* New York, NY: Free Press.
51 Calder, N. 1969. *Technopolis: Social Control and the Uses of Science.* London: MacGibbon & Kee; Schumacher, 1973; Moran, M. 2014. *Private Foundations and Development Partnerships: American Philanthropy and Global Development Agendas.* New York, NY: Routledge.
52 Mumford, L. 1934. *Technics and Civilization.* New York, NY: Harcourt, Brace & Company.
53 Schumacher, 1973.
54 Anders' work is increasingly turned to in contemporary international relations theorizing on political and social aspects of nuclear power and the 'nuclear condition', see Munster, R. and Sylvest, C. 2016. *Nuclear Realism.* Abingdon: Routledge.

55 Aradau, C. and Munster, R. 2011. *Politics of Catastrophe: Genealogies of the Unknown.* Abingdon: Routledge.
56 Anders, G. [1956a] 2002. *Die Antiquiertheit des Menschen 1: Über die Seele im Zeitalter der Zweiten Industriellen Revolution, 3rd Edition.* Munich: C. H. Beck.
57 Mumford, 1934: 317.
58 Munster and Sylvest, 2016.
59 Nahuis, R. and van Lente, H. 2008. 'Where are the politics? Perspectives on democracy and technology', *Science, Technology, & Human Values* 33(5): 559–581.
60 Papaioannou, T. 2011. 'Technological innovation, global justice and politics of development', *Progress in Development Studies* 11(4): 321–338.
61 Mol, A. 2002. *The Body Multiple: Ontology in Medical Practice.* Durham, NC: Duke University Press.
62 Ibid.
63 Bijker, W. E. 1999. 'Towards politicization of technological culture: constructivist STS studies and democracy', in *Science, Technology and Society: International Symposium*, edited by H. Ansal and D. C. Alisir, Istanbul: Istanbul Technical University, 37–47.
64 Kass, J. 2013. 'Bill Gates can't build a toilet', op-ed in *The New York Times*, 18 November.
65 Hamlett, P. W. 2003. 'Technology theory and deliberative democracy', *Science, Technology, & Human Values* 28(1): 112–140.
66 Zimmerman, A. D. 1995. 'Toward a more democratic ethic of technological governance', *Science, Technology, & Human Values* 20(1): 86–107.

7 From Seattle to the fields of India

Pursuing development through isolated technological innovations makes any organization prone to criticism for not properly comprehending the complexity of human and social forces at play.[1] The Gates Foundation is often targeted for its approach to global health and development, which its critics have deemed neoliberal, instrumental and narrowly technical.[2] Indeed, one such critique was advanced in the former chapter where the dangers of using the Global South as a live laboratory of technological innovation in the name of the poor were accentuated. Very seldom, though, do we hear empirical accounts of how Gates Foundation projects reach the ground and are implemented. In this chapter we will move from the high-rise landscape of Seattle to the fields of Odisha in Northeastern India, where the Seattle-based INGO Landesa works to ensure women's land ownership, through a Gates Foundation-granted project that I will refer to as the 'Women and Land' project.[3] By studying how the project is constantly reformulated and reinterpreted by the different organizations that fund and implement it, we will see why the Gates Foundation's strong ideologies and logics (whether of neoliberalism, impact effectiveness or something else) may in some cases never reach 'the ground', i.e., sites of implementation, impacting people in the developing world. The distance from Seattle to the state of Odisha is great, and all the objectives and meanings inherent in the project go through substantial processes of translation and renegotiation as it moves through the organizational system of development that is comprised of numerous organizations and individuals, each with their own distinct agenda, identity and ability to resist or object to other interpretations of what the project is and what it is supposed to do.

In the Gates Foundation, in Seattle, the 'Women and Land' project is perceived as a prime example of how 'Women can act as agents of economic growth', or as a 'Lever to increase agricultural growth and productivity'.[4] Here, women are considered far more effective than men and a guarantee for scientific progress since they are 'Much more likely to uptake innovative agricultural technologies and approaches'.[5] In Landesa's international headquarters in Seattle, WA, and in its Indian country office in New Delhi, on the other hand, the same project is lauded for its objective to establish a 'Responsive institutional delivery system' that can strengthen 'The legal aid for rural women' by working with local government to bring women into the 'Official system'.[6] Finally, from a narrative about social change, local employees in Odisha describe the aim of the Gates-funded project in a profoundly different way, as 'Bringing about socio-economic justice' by 'Improving and defending the rights of women' and spurring radical change in the formal institutions that reproduce such structural inequalities.[7] Consider the difference of interpretation of functions and objectives between the three different levels of the same project: from a (neoliberal) instrumentalizing of Indian women to increase agricultural productivity, to legal–institutional, to transformative and deeply political. In this chapter we come to understand how the exceedingly instrumental and borderline neoliberal approach of the Gates Foundation, that leads them to mainly further a set of narrow and reduction-ist project objectives (*how many plots of land did you succeed in supporting women to obtain?*), actually provides organizational and institutional space for actors to step in and define additional covert targets and tactics. Opportunities for reconfiguration and reinterpretation that may, in the end, if they are indeed used, open up passages for transformative change. By performing productive forms of institutional resistance, actors placed elsewhere in the organizational chain that encircles the project, removed from the Gates Foundation, essentially reconstruct it. This leads us to appreciate that things are not always as black and white as we think, and that, while the instrumentalist approach of the Gates Foundation in itself calls for criticism, the way it reduces complex realities to simplistic project targets (such as asking organizations to mainly report on how many new land titles have been ensured for local women, without determining how to reach such targets) actually provides room for other organizational actors to reconstruct projects and ultimately produce transformative effects.

Gates, Landesa, and women's rights

As we have seen, issues of agriculture, land and women rose as programme priorities in the Bill and Melinda Gates Foundation during the mid-2000s, as it rapidly expanded its areas of intervention following an approximately $30 billion gift from investor Warren Buffett in 2006. In the foundation the gift meant an immense expansion of programme areas from what had been a heavy focus on health globally (especially the development and distribution of vaccines) and edu-cation domestically. An entire new wing called 'Global Development' was added to focus on issues of agriculture, water and sanitation, financial services for the poor, and others. Within agriculture, attention to gender equality and women's empowerment would turn out to be a key priority, rising steadily over the years to a point where all grants have to include this perspective, at least in theory (as we saw in Chapter 5). Important here is how the Gates Foundation works through a modus operandi in which potential partners either contend for funding (through, e.g., the foundation's Grand Challenges) or projects are established on the basis of initial contact and discussions, often commenced by foundation programme officers drawing on professional networks or mapping of actors. It rarely, if ever, engages in forms of direct project implementation on the ground, and thus relies heavily on partners to implement and ensure the impact of its distributed funds.

This has naturally led the foundation to abundant partnerships, including with the US-established INGO Landesa, the case described in this chapter. An international NGO working almost exclusively with issues of access to land and land rights, Landesa was launched in 1967 as the Rural Development Institute by Roy Prosterman, a University of Washington Professor of Law. Supported by the US Government, Prosterman conducted his 'land to the tiller' programme in Vietnam from 1970–1973 as the Vietnam War raged, reportedly securing the land rights of one million tenant farmers, seemingly entailing an increase in rice production and a decrease in Viet Cong recruitment.[8] Since then, Landesa has worked across especially Africa and Asia and, according to its own numbers, has helped 120 million families with securing their land rights over the past 50 years. It now employs a couple of hundred employees in its international office in the US, and in India and China, and has gradually moved from an approach of sending out teams of lawyers from Seattle to now being much more locally grounded with national teams in the relevant developing countries. Over a period of ten years, Landesa has received around $25 million in grants from the Gates Foundation, including for specific purposes and projects, but also grants for general operating expenses and for efforts to support Gates Foundation grantees in integrating a gender angle in their grants. It launched the Landesa Center for Women's Land Rights in 2009 to focus its work exactly on women's access to land and land titling.

The Gates-funded 'Women and Land' project takes place in India, where it is implemented across different states (Landesa's work in India accounts for the vast majority of its project and programme efforts). In its project description, the objective of the project is to establish 'a responsive institutional delivery system to ensure women's access to and control over land'. It works across several Indian states, and here we will follow it through to the level of a particular one, Odisha. Access to land is a fundamental need in rural India as the principal determinant of rural income distribution, and particularly that of women, has been extremely limited, often constrained by a mixture of local customs, gender discrimination, ineffective institutions and inconsequential laws. Women in rural India are often resource-poor, lacking educational skills needed for gainful employment and, when they are employed, they receive lower wages than men, altogether limiting their economic independence and upward mobility.[9] According to Landesa,

> Deep-seated patriarchy is evident from instances like a) land beyond ceiling limit is recorded in the name of women so that male members have de facto rights over them; b) wherever land is registered in the name of wife/daughter, it is assumed to have belonged to her husband/father; c) while assessing family landholding, women's landholdings are considered as surplus; d) state revenue laws consider adult sons as separate family units, but not the unmarried adult daughters; e) state tenancy laws prioritise male's inheritance rights, but consider women's inheritance only in the absence of any male heir.[10]

Odisha, specifically, is among the poorest states in India with more than ten million people living below the poverty line and around half a million landless single women. It largely follows the national trend of rural India, with more than 80 per cent of women being dependent on agriculture, yet only 10 per cent having ownership over land. Land is so important here because, without it, it is impossible to get residence certificates that provide access to institutional credit in the form of bank loans, education, social benefits from the state, as well as school enrolment for children. The local governments in India have officially worked (though inconsistently and ineffectively) for some time to provide land to poor families no matter if the head of the household was considered a man or a woman. However, a single widowed (the vastly dominating category of landless women) or divorced woman is not considered head of a family and thus has no land rights, the presumption of laws not permitting this being that she will somehow be supported by her family. Historically, Odisha has been one of a few states attempting to legally abolish land tenancy, but this has almost always not referred to what has been formally known as 'persons of disability', where it just so happens that widows, divorcees and unmarried women are cynically included. Land tenancy or leasing can be problematic because tenants often have little or no protection in law, and thus may unexpectedly have their land revoked or the rent unfairly increased, but it often also remains the only option for single women to gain access to agricultural land. With a land allocation programme called Vasundhara, the government of Odisha started a process of allocating government land to rural families without homestead through the 2000s. However, there was no mandate in the programme for the inclusion of single women, and revenue officials largely bypassed these when enumerating the landless or those without homestead.

Landesa started working on the project in question in Odisha in 2009 by assessing precisely the Vasundhara programme across 88 villages in ten districts. The key purpose has been to provide technical assistance to set up Women's Support Centers (WSC) devoted to counselling women in their quest to achieve land ownership in each of Odisha's sub-districts or *tehsils*. Up until today, Landesa has helped the government set up more than 76 such centres across Odisha, starting in Ganjam District before moving on to Mayurbhanj, Koraput and Kalahandi and then on to others from there. To identify landless women, the WSCs rely on government *angawadi* workers (primarily child and mother healthcare workers) who visit villages and rural areas to check on pregnant women and newborns, but in doing so are also able to identify landless women and point them towards the support centres. The support centres act as exclusive cells for women in each *tehsil*, with a 'priority helpdesk' where a trained woman revenue officer supports women, particularly with a view to land-titling and social security entitlements, but also with options for much more, as we shall see later on. Using a Management Information System (MIS), inventories are made of single dispossessed women and used to facilitate service deliveries of land and social security, as well as livelihood support services, including the government's housing, sanitation, social security and livelihood programmes. The MIS database essentially produces village-wide lists of women for field verification by revenue officials. One list, the Ashrayi list, contains data on single women in the district who are landless, while another, the Sanjeevani list, contains data for processing social security services. All of this is information that might not have reached revenue officials or local government and thus not resulted in access to services for the women without Landesa's involvement. With the available data, processes of land allocation under different revenue laws can be started, including camp court, record correction and eventual preparation of *pattas* (plots of land), as well as disbursements of social security entitlements from block offices. Predictably, not all of the hundreds of thousands of women who have been identified are ultimately given land by the state. Nonetheless around 20 per cent seem to have been given land, the remainder being supported by Landesa to apply for other government programmes such as the food supplement programme.

The 'Women and Land' project as an instrument for economic growth and scientific progress

In Seattle the 'Women and Land' project is exceptionally praised among foundation staff as an ideal model of the power of working with a women-centric approach to increasing local economic and agricultural growth. The work Landesa is doing is considered 'A perfect example of how we can use GEWE (gender equality and women's empowerment) as a lever to increase agricultural growth and productivity'.[11] The lever metaphor is used to highlight the binary impact of the perceived approach of the project, namely more explicitly that 'Increasing the access of women to land then not only becomes about their lives but also about the impact they can have on a local and national level', or expressed similarly by another Gates Foundation employee as 'Empowering women through access to land would mean an increase in household productivity and thus also in national agricultural outputs'.[12] The instrumentalizing of women seems strong when other staff members similarly explain how 'Women become agents of economic development'[13] through the partnership with Landesa. Women are, in this line of thought, not merely able to provide resources for their families that ensure increased nutrition and the like, but also able to collectively boost economic and agricultural growth, and not only at a local but at a national level. Targeting women is not just important for immediate reasons referring to the women themselves, but serves as a key element in a successful management strategy, and has become 'A key part of our mission to create high-impact programs, the effectiveness of which Landesa's work illustrates really well'.[14] This notion of 'Societal progress through technological innovation' is one shared across the US philanthropic environment of which the foundation is part, and especially the new approaches of the philanthrocapitalists currently emanating out of Silicon Valley with an immense faith in technology,[15] as we have seen in the previous chapter. Similar to the influence from the philanthropic environment in the US, the organizational translation of gender equality and women's empowerment norms into the specific 'Women and Land' project largely seems to follow trajectories of some other peer organizations such as the World Bank, in which women are instrumentalized as agents of economic growth.[16] In this interpretation, women are also considered to constitute a guarantee of scientific progress towards a more efficient use of innovative technologies and approaches, as explained thus: 'With one hand we increase GEWE, and with the other, simultaneously, we move land into the hands of individuals that are much more likely to uptake innovative agricultural technologies and approaches'.[17] Just as women are considered more effective in farming than men, they also have an inherent quality that allows them to take up new technologies and thus secure social and economic progress through scientific means. Women are, for example, considered 'Much more likely to adopt improved varieties of seeds' than men are.[18]

Just as this interpretation is exceedingly clear about what purposes the project serves, there are instances where it becomes explicit what it is not considered to be, when staff explain how 'The ultimate aim of this work is to increase agricultural outputs to potentially reduce hunger and poverty, not necessarily to fight for cultural or social rights'.[19] Rights have a distinctive place in the Gates Foundation, meddling with which will have political consequences that the Foundation's leadership is not normally too fond of engaging with, though some projects do work explicitly on rights. Furthermore, as much as a lack of rights may manifest itself very concretely in practice as a lack of access, etc., rights are an abstract concept whose somewhat inherent immeasurability (or perhaps just complexity of measurement) makes it difficult for it to penetrate an organizational culture built up around measurement and evidence like that of the Gates Foundation. As shown in the Chapter 5, issues of gender equality and women's empowerment are treated very distinctly in the Gates Foundation, being thoroughly embedded in the organization's specific political, social and historical contexts where they have been met with and shaped by practices and rules embedded in the foundation's own institutional and organizational history. This significant organizational culture and history, but also the networks and epistemic communities within which the foundation is embedded, also greatly shapes the way it articulates and understands this specific project. Finally, the translation at play here may immediately appear dominant because it is representative of the organizational actor expected to possess more traditional forms of institutional or compulsory power and who also has full control of resources from project initiation and all the way through implementation. It manifests itself in internal documents surrounding the project, from grant proposals to concrete milestones and deliverables. Yet this is not as clear cut a relationship of power and subjugation as one might think, as we will see shortly.

The 'Women and Land' project as rational–institutional and legal equality

As we descend through the organizational system that constitutes the project at hand, we enter some of the intermediate levels situated between 'top' and 'bottom', however imprecise such categorizations are. These are the US office of Landesa and especially the national office in New Delhi where, for the first time, the lofty milestones of the project are confronted with the realities of the specific context within which it is to be realized. This is also a journey in which key components have gone through transformations as the project has been affected by Landesa's own distinctive organizational culture, capacities and experiences that are responsible for its realization. Landesa has a long tradition of centring on the legal and institutional frameworks of the implementation context, maintaining a strong belief in the necessity of working in partnership with local government and, importantly, spurring both legal–institutional and cultural change here to ensure the sustainability of the changes that have potentially been evoked. Predictably, then, interpretation of the project's core purpose and approach is shaped by such notions. Here, the purpose is widely understood as to 'Strengthen the legal aid for poor rural women', and 'Improving legal awareness at the local level of women's land rights'.[20] Revolutionizing the system for the sake of legal equality is important beyond concerns for increased productive and economic growth: 'Contrary to many other NGOs, we work in close collaboration with local government and state institutions, acting as catalysts by attempting to secure these concerns in the legal system'.[21] There are many reasons why the central aim here is articulated as the equal inclusion of women in the institutional framework and culture of local government. A central one seems to be that 'By helping them secure title deeds we can bring them into the official system, potentially having them benefit from government schemes and benefits only available to owners of land'.[22] Just like staff at these organizational levels, official Landesa project documents frame the work as establishing a 'Responsive institutional delivery system' and gender-sensitive institutional mechanisms within the local government structure to ensure a 'Gender-equitable governance of land tenure'. In practice this entails a focus not so much on changing cycles of operations as on the organizational culture and perspectives of state officials, the vast majority of whom are men: 'A central part of the project's work is capacity building the existing institutions and introducing to them more inclusive ways of working with access to land'.[23]

The decision as to whether women are eligible to engage in a process of potentially obtaining land from the state is one taken by an officer formally placed at the low end of the administrative hierarchy. Despite this position, he or she (these officers are overwhelmingly men) enjoys an astonishing degree of power by essentially being the gatekeeper of access to land ownership for millions of poor people across the state. A core focus of the project is to change the professional culture of these officers by encouraging a change of attitude towards considering women as equally entitled to own land as men, while also institutionalizing the concern that land ownership is not something to be determined by access to resources in exchange for bribes – another issue.[24] At this middle level of Landesa offices, the project's ideas and practices begin to be faced with implementation, which affects the process of translation more than any other context the INGO may be part of. As Levitt and Merry formulate it,

> India has a long and rich tradition of women's movements and concepts of rights are deeply embedded in the constitution and everyday social practice. In addition, India has embraced human rights, setting up a National Human Rights Commission in 1993 as well as ratifying several human rights conventions. Women's human rights discourses and approaches are added onto socialist ideas, Gandhian philosophy, Marxist theory and a variety of Hindu and Muslim religious traditions.[25]

This context is growing in importance, but the legal–institutional arguments are still dominant. Despite having an explicit legal–rational interpretation, we also see the first steps towards more socially radical interpretations of the project's purpose: 'Including landless women in the institutional framework opens up great avenues for transformation and can bring positive changes to their self-consciousness, identity and awareness of rights'.[26]

The 'Women and Land' project as societal transformation, women's empowerment and rights

We have moved from a widespread appreciation of women as agents of economic growth and increased agricultural productivity, and of the necessity for their local and national contexts to increase these, via an interpretation that represents a shift towards the rational–institutional and legal equality of the institutional framework that is prevalent in local government. Attention is now turned to what is distinctly the most substantial break with the Gates Foundation's interpretation of the project, one whose ideational resistance has tangible consequences on the ground. At the state level of implementation, interpretation of the project shifts radically towards a narrative of social change more than a concern for economic growth or agricultural productivity, an articulation mainly identifiable with respect to changes in society, changes in the women themselves and the introduction of a far more political account. For several of its local staff members in Odisha, the project is considered 'The first step on the way to social change',[27] especially with regard to the status of women: 'Through the project we want to transform the status of women. In rural Indian society today, a woman's life is worth zero. Absolutely zero. That needs to be changed'.[28] A central aim is to target the attitudes of men and their perceptions of women in society: '"If we give women land, they will just run away" some men claim when they learn of the project. It is this kind of dreadful imagining that makes it so important to change social norms',[29] as one of the employees explained it. Such cultural change is still partially linked to the formal legal aspects, when one staff member, for example, expressed how they 'Need to change the culture of local government, to institutionalize a recognition of women's rights'.[30] The allocation of land by the officer in question, whose job it is to determine if women are eligible for land or not, is, for example, 'Too much based on interpretations of law, and suffering from old-fashioned perceptions of gender roles and women; that is a culture we work to change'.[31] Aiming to introduce these fairly radical changes to an otherwise predominantly patriarchal culture is a mission not without controversy, something understood by the local staff of Landesa. As one employee put it,

> We understand that such work which targets fundamental culture and social structures in local society will always entail conflict. Conflicts may already occur between brothers or sons and fathers over land, and by insisting on the rights of women to own land, we add another component that may cause conflict. But we must accept that social change does not happen without conflict, as the status quo is challenged.[32]

But change is not just needed in the minds of men, as 'Traditional practices are prohibiting women from empowering themselves; it is simply internalized in them that they cannot learn. We are here to change such mindsets'.[33] Enlightening and empowering women through training and awareness-building regarding rights becomes a central concern of the project: 'We want to empower women by building their knowledge, and that to the point where men begin to talk among themselves saying, "We need to train now, because the women know more than we do"'.[34] In practice this is done through workshops on issues such as 'land literacy', as much an exercise in increasing the self-consciousness and awareness of the actual status of the women as an opportunity to teach them about the importance of land ownership. Rights also play a central part:

> We try to convince women of and build their own capacity to exercise their own rights. To them it is a matter of a mistaken self-consciousness that for the most part makes them doubt their rights. Rural societies here are so deeply caught in patriarchal culture that women themselves do not believe they have such rights to own.[35]

One staff member told me a brief story of how she had been in a village, trying to arrange a meeting among the women, when very few would utter anything more than a few words while hiding their faces in pieces of cloth. After a year and repeated meetings with the women, including ones on land literacy, the women of the village seemed to have grown in confidence and were now actively embracing their rights to own land by initiating land settlement processes with the local government. We may, of course, question a well-off Indian woman coming to a poor rural village and thinking it is necessary for her to spur such fairly radical cultural change, but the story illustrates well how these new and intended (and perhaps also unintended) consequences of the project reach far beyond increasing income generation and agricultural productivity into matters of social change.

Finally, as opposed to the technical and instrumental perception advanced in the Gates Foundation's interpretation, where political and social change is seen as problematic because of its inherent complexity and somewhat immeasurable nature, the project is here considered to have important political and social implications and is praised for them. Several staff members expressed how the ultimate goal of the project is 'Bringing about socio-economic justice', while others (as we saw briefly in the previous section) articulate the importance of 'Defending the social and political rights of the women'.[36] Defending the rights of women in order to spur socio-economic justice is strong language set in an unmistakably political framing. The difference between the interpretations of the project, at the different levels, is illustrated well in two different short films produced and used by Landesa in advocacy work with governments and shown to prospective funders and partners. Both videos include recorded material from the local Indian context, yet one was produced in the US headquarters and one in the local state office. The promotional short film produced in the US headquarters, which is used in communicating with donors there such as the Gates

Foundation, features a voice-over explaining how the acquisition of title deeds entails increased productivity, improved harvests and the possibility of making savings, while also providing an opportunity for the household's children to receive an education; it does not devote appreciable attention to the implications for the women themselves. Juxtaposed to this, the short film produced in the Indian state office, with images of the same Indian women, features a voice-over about the positive consequences of the organization's work for women's dignity and self-esteem, as well as in driving forward the pursuit of social justice, social transformation and equality.

Aspects such as emotions, contextual knowledge and connections play an important part in the translation at the Odisha level, as employees engage in fundamentally reinterpreting and translating the project's core functions and objectives to make it fit the local context. As a form of indirect resistance, they did not entirely follow the framings from higher up in the organizational chain, but instead changed the ideas and practices of the project so that they resonated with what they perceived as legitimate action. This entailed a much greater focus on strengthening and defending women's rights in a socio-political context, as opposed to the aim of increasing agricultural outputs, as articulated and pursued by the Gates Foundation. Women's ownership of *pattas* remained a question of socio-economic justice, and only secondly was increasing local agricultural outputs considered important. The majority of the employees in Odisha were locals who had been born and raised there, something that might explain the strong response to and connection with the local context. The Landesa logic of working through local legal–institutional systems of governance is still an important part of its practices at the local level, but instead of aiming to change local legislation, the actors here are much more concerned with transforming the organizational cultures of the local institutions to break with the widespread unequal access of women to state services. The organizational context and history thus wane considerably as we approach implementation on the ground, and the personal experiences of the employees is increasingly foregrounded, just as we see strong notions of agency in play. Through forms of strategic intervention, employees on the ground worked to undermine existing ideas and practices and introduce new ones that were legitimate in their eyes, and they worked to create hybrid forms in which new and old are melded together, basically using forms of 'social construction power'.[37] At the local level in Odisha we thus witnessed employees cultivating a collective understanding of the necessity of transformative change in the perception and practices of gender relations, far from the Gates Foundation's understanding of the project.

Consequences of the different translations

The translations between the different organizational levels that constitute the development project in question are multidirectional and occur continuously as the different levels meet, whether in project monitoring, reporting or evaluation. Yet there is still a downward directionality that situates implementation mainly at the bottom. What, then, are the consequences down here? Is it possible to trace not just ideational or discursive but tangible changes on the ground? The elephant in the room thus far has perhaps been the matter of palpable consequences, that is, ideational resistance materializing as altered practices. Infusing the same practices with radically different meanings not only has ideational consequences, it changes the practices themselves, and reinterpretation will often mean the adoption of different goals, functions or purposes.[38] For the 'Women and Land' project, I argue, there are also tangible implications at play as outcomes of the ideational resistance and reinterpretation. Three points in particular are relevant here. The first is an overwhelming focus on the importance of owning homestead land as opposed to agricultural land, as is observable in the project's implementation. For each individual woman, an estimate is made by the NGO as to whether she should be supported to pursue ownership of homestead or agricultural land. Prioritizing homestead land means valuing social identity, social security and community identity above the agricultural productivity potential. Acquiring homestead land naturally increases productivity if the baseline situation is one of no land, but there is substantial difference between the purposes of the two types of land. In the majority of cases, homestead land was chosen because of its positive social repercussions, which would grant the women a much more concrete position in their local communities. Had a strictly instrumentalizing logic aimed mainly at increasing agricultural output been strongest here, agricultural land would surely have been prioritized above homestead land, as the implications for productivity are far greater here. The second point is the attention given to informal institutional reform and changes in the organizational culture and perception of women in local government. As opposed to focusing only on the importance of poor people's access to plots of land, building the capacity of local government aims to change its perceptions of women and of their rights as landowners, equal to men. That is, applying a strictly formal institutional perspective would mainly mean seeking to change the structures guarding access to land by *inter alia* changing the decision-making process in which only a single, always male, officer makes the decision to grant a woman access to land to including a wider array of government actors in the decision. Alternatively, perhaps a quota could be set for a certain number of the decision-making officers to be women, so as not to have only men decide on the fate of women. However, in Odisha the work of Landesa goes beyond only securing changes to the organizational structures to include also a focus on organizational cultures by aiming to change the values and beliefs of officers working there. As one Landesa employee explained it, they 'Hoped to stimulate changes that go beyond just the legal framework, and deep into the officers' perceptions of women and their rights'.[39] The third point refers to interaction with women at different levels, which is dominated by a focus on their rights and empowerment, as opposed to concerns with local economic growth or agricultural outputs. In practice, the responsible officers appointed to support women, who are trained by Landesa but paid for by the state, aim above all to create awareness and enlightenment among the women of their rights. They also aim to facilitate a change in attitude regarding what women can actually rightfully demand to potentially increase their status in their community and in interactions with the local government when it comes to claiming different social benefits and schemes. The officers' interaction with them will often occur in the form of woman-to-woman conversations about what can be done to ensure the woman's empowerment both in the local society and in her ability to access state benefits. As another example, during training on issues such as land literacy, it is the rights of the women and how they can empower themselves through these that are in focus, not their potential to contribute to economic growth or increasing agricultural outputs. One reporting document from such a workshop explicitly mentioned that the training was focused on the capacity and ability of women to 'Defend their rights'.

The form of the different interpretations, especially at the level closest to implementation, also touches on an issue to which I have not devoted much attention thus far, namely that of project outcome requirements in the form of milestones and continuous reporting, mainly taking the shape of quantitative frameworks. 'Donors are looking for measurable change that can easily be presented and understood', as one staff member explained.[40] That is, across both professional groups and geographical space, the results have to be easily perceived and communicable, whether by gender experts or macroeconomists, and whether by people in Odisha or in the US. This reflects a concern not strange to any development project or programme. The orientation of results towards quantitative evidence has increasingly been adopted as a tool from the world of management for use in global development contexts. In the context of the present case, there is more than one reason why these ideational battles mainly take place in a hidden realm, avoiding symbolic, direct confrontation with formal authority. First, the complex nature of women's empowerment makes it exceedingly difficult to quantify and measure progress, as opposed to the number of secured land titles (a main reporting requirement imposed by the Gates Foundation), livestock or harvest results. Secondly, reporting requirements, largely established by the donor in question, do not provide much room to address qualitative issues that are not easily measurable or applicable in a logical framework. More importantly, a focus on outcomes that are not explicitly agreed in a contract or a grant with the implementing agency (such as an explicit focus on rights) can easily make the donor question the emphasis and efficiency of the implementer. The resource-determining relationship between donor and implementer means the latter is rarely willing to confront or resist donor requirements directly, at the risk of losing significant funding. This provides resistance with a distinctive form:

> All the more invisible changes, or those that at least appear so as we report on how well implementation proceeds, we choose to uphold as we can witness the progressive effects. We are proud of the social change produced by our work, and no matter the specifics of our projects, will we always preserve that.[41]

These are strong actions in which local staff essentially assume roles as project-makers, not just responding to policies and strategic directions from headquarters, but actively adjusting the project, producing new practices and discourses. What actors may do between different levels of development projects, then, is to resist the dominant interpretations of other actors and to construct alternative and contending interpretations. It is not so much a direct form of power (A getting B to do something, whether through persuasion or coercion) as an indirect form that does not necessarily entail direct or symbolic confrontations with actors further up the system, illustrative of how development projects are generally loosely coupled systems. Decisively, we see in action here the development as systems of negotiation and translation of meaning, with the notion of a 'system' implying how development projects are embedded in sets of nested organizations and organizational levels that are mutually dependent, and among whom translation and reinterpretation processes continue to shape the project. Most development projects function within a hierarchical form of governance in which a donor, somewhere, has the final say on financial and formal policy. However, this does not mean that there is no room for interpretation and ideational influence along the chain – quite the opposite. There is a natural difference in formal authority that sees more money and power concentrated in Seattle than with the local implementing agency in Odisha, but beyond material resources different forms of power flow in complex ways that potentially allow influence at all levels. What we witness, then, are fluid spheres of influence, often manifested in different forms of resistance, and certainly not less powerful at 'the bottom', near implementation, as this case underlines.

Final remarks

Development projects take place in organizational systems that almost resemble forms of multilevel governance, in which many organizations and organizational levels are interwoven and mutually contingent. Within these, different forms of power flow in many different directions, gaining strength and legitimacy from diverse sources, with meaning continuously negotiated and translated at the different levels and between them. Translation processes may help stabilize certain meanings across actors and organizational layers in development projects,[42] but beneath these surfaces of apparent stability we find substantial degrees of contestation, resistance and power at play. And though a project may on the outside be seen as 'stabilized', or be perceived as such by the funder, we often find that actual practices of implementation are radically different from those that were imagined. The case discussed here leads us to consider who has power and who has not, in the systems that are development interventions. Those in positions of more compulsory forms of power, frequently found at the 'top' of the organizational system, such as the Gates Foundation, often have at their disposal instruments of fundamental control over resource disbursements, project acceptance and continuous evaluation. Yet, they mostly have to exercise such control from afar, that is, remote from the project's implementation. Closer to implementation, organizational actors begin assuming a role of not just peacefully aligning or brokering agreed milestones and deliverables with the local implementation context, but resisting and reinterpreting these, remaking existing or adding new practices and discourses to the project at hand. Tangible indicators decided by the Gates Foundation are used to communicate successes back to it, but local development workers also incorporate several new elements of transformative change not envisioned by the foundation by using covert tactics, knowledge of which may never reach Seattle and the Gates Foundation. Instead of different degrees of strength or power, then, these actors employ profoundly different instruments to influence the project, some more compulsory or institutional, others more ideational. Reconceptualizations of the project by Landesa staff were not just ideational in nature or consisted of different interpretations of a fixed set of practices and ideas, but implied tangible consequences entailing the adoption of an additional set of goals, functions or purposes than those demanded by the Gates Foundation. Escaping institutional convention and defying existing hierarchies is what creates the distortions that pave the way for such changes in ideas and practices (and here, concretely, those manifested in development projects and programmes). Though the organizational actors who are closer to implementation will often have lesser forms of power over direct issues such as funding or agreed deliverables, they have the ability to resist both ideationally and practically, thus translating and changing the purposes and functions of the development work in which they are engaged. In the case of the Gates Foundation, this means that, for projects like the present one, the strong neoliberal and instrumentalizing logics rarely make it all the way to implementation, with the transformative changes that are palpably produced locally being far removed from what the foundation had imagined and its critics expected.

Notes

1 This chapter is adapted from Fejerskov, A. 2018. 'Development as resistance and translation: remaking norms and ideas of the Gates Foundation', *Progress in Development Studies* 18(2): 126–143. Copyright © Adam Moe Fejerskov. Reprinted by permission of SAGE Publications India Private Limited.
2 McGoey, L. 2015. *No Such Thing as a Free Gift: The Gates Foundation and the Price of Philanthropy*. London and New York, NY: Verso; Storeng, K. 2014. 'The GAVI Alliance and the 'Gates Approach' to health systems strengthening', *Global Public Health* 9(8): 865–879; Holt-Gimenez, E. 2008. 'Out of AGRA: the Green Revolution returns to Africa', *Development* 51(4): 464–471; Edwards M. 2009. *Just Another Emperor? The Myths and Realities of Philanthrocapitalism*. London: The Young Foundation and Demos; Thompson, C. 2012. 'Alliance for a Green Revolution in Africa (AGRA): advancing the theft of African genetic wealth', *Review of African Political Economy* 39(132): 345–350.
3 The project includes different components that are best grouped under the heading of 'Women and Land' for the sake of coherence.
4 Interview with Bill and Melinda Gates Foundation staff.
5 Interview with Bill and Melinda Gates Foundation staff.
6 Interview with Landesa staff in Seattle, WA.
7 Interview with Landesa staff in India.
8 See www.landesa.org/our-leadership/our-founder.
9 Haque, T. and Lair, J. L. 2014. 'Ensuring and protecting the land leasing right of poorer women in India', paper presented at the 2014 World Bank Conference on Land and Poverty, Washington, DC: The World Bank, 24–27 March.

10 Landesa. 2014. 'Women Support Centres increasing women's rights to land', project material from Landesa.
11 Interview with Bill and Melinda Gates Foundation Senior Programme Officer.
12 Interview with Bill and Melinda Gates Foundation Programme Officer.
13 Interview with Bill and Melinda Gates Foundation Programme Officer.
14 Interview with Bill and Melinda Gates Foundation Senior Programme Officer.
15 McGoey, 2015.
16 Chant, S. and Sweetman, C. 2012. 'Fixing women or fixing the world? "Smart economics", efficiency approaches, and gender equality in development', *Gender and Development* 20(3): 517–529.
17 Interview with Bill and Melinda Gates Foundation Senior Programme Officer.
18 Interview with Bill and Melinda Gates Foundation Programme Officer.
19 Interview with Bill and Melinda Gates Foundation Programme Officer.
20 Interview with Landesa Director in Seattle, WA.
21 Interview with Landesa Director in Seattle, WA.
22 Interview with Landesa staff in Seattle, WA.
23 Interview with Landesa staff in Seattle, WA.
24 Interview with Landesa staff in India.
25 Levitt, P. and Merry, S. 2009. 'Vernacularization on the ground: local uses of global women's rights in Peru, China, India and the United States', *Global Networks* 9(4): 441–461.
26 Interviews with Landesa staff in India.
27 Interview with Landesa staff in India.
28 Interview with Landesa staff in Odisha, India.
29 Interview with Landesa staff in Odisha, India.
30 Interview with Landesa staff in Odisha, India.
31 Interview with Landesa staff in Odisha, India.
32 Interview with Landesa staff in Odisha, India.
33 Interview with Landesa staff in Odisha, India.
34 Interview with Landesa staff in Odisha, India.
35 Interview with Landesa staff in Odisha, India.
36 Interview with Landesa staff in Odisha, India.
37 Barnett, M. and Finnemore, M. 1999. 'The politics, power, and pathologies of international organizations', *International Organization* 53(4): 699–732.
38 Streeck, W. and Thelen, K. 2005. 'Introduction: institutional change in advanced political economies', in *Beyond Continuity: Institutional Change in Advanced Political Economies*, edited by W. Streeck and K. Thelen, Oxford: Oxford University Press, 1–39.
39 Interview with Landesa staff in Odisha, India.
40 Interview with Landesa staff in Odisha, India.
41 Interview with Landesa staff in Odisha, India.
42 Mosse, D. 2004. 'Is good policy unimplementable? Reflections on the ethnography of aid policy and practice', *Development and Change* 35(4): 639–671.

8 Chameleon politics

In late January of 2017 The Bill and Melinda Gates Foundation was granted 'official relations' to the World Health Organization (WHO) despite existing criteria that private actors cannot be permitted such privileges. In elaborating on the decision the WHO Executive Board noted that the breadth of the collaboration between the two organizations would be 'Deepened, strengthened and expanded' in the foreseeable future and that the foundation will support WHO's governance reform.[1] Prior to the meeting a group of civil society organizations had issued an open letter in which they criticized WHO for including the foundation despite its own rules about conflict of interest safeguards and due diligence. Citing the foundation's billion-dollar investments in many of the food, alcohol and physical inactivity-related consumer products that cause 'The current crisis of preventable heart disease, stroke, cancer, and diabetes' as well as commercial pharmaceuticals, the group accused WHO of undermining its independence from commercial interests.[2] It made no difference in the end and the foundation now sits on the governing bodies of the WHO, including the Executive Board. The decision was hardly a surprise as the Gates Foundation is the largest private donor to the WHO, providing some $600 million out of the organization's $4.5 billion budget in 2016, and the foundation declared itself honoured that it had 'Been invited to establish a formal relationship with the World Health Organization'.

No matter the dubious nature of the decision, it was one in a series of culminations of a decade-long process in which the foundation has attempted to establish itself as a major power in the international system. As the foundation has ascended to power, it has moved from a state of resistance, dismissing the international institutions and dominant normative frameworks of international relations and global development, to one of gradual interaction, progressively relating to norms, practices and organizations that are considered legitimate by established international actors, and towards which it earlier stood in opposition. The decision was also a strong indication of the most apparent process of change occurring in the foundation as it has established itself internationally – its growing hybrid ability to shift between different organizational identities, including the adoption of state-like behaviour far beyond its private roots and self-conception as a distinct non-state actor. Traversing tools of power and influence traditionally associated with different actor-types, from states to multinational corporations

(MNC) to advocacy NGOs, the Gates Foundation increasingly practices a hybrid form of 'chameleon politics'. Just as the chameleon changes colour to convey a state of mind or body to other animals, the foundation is able to reinterpret and change its actorness to fit different situations and contexts in which it aims to attain influence. It practices tools of influence typically associated with non-state actors such as lobbying for its causes in international organizations, or uses the celebrity and plutocratic nature of the 'Gates' brand to ensure meetings with and political support from heads of states around the globe. But it also breaks with traditional non-profit behaviour by commercially investing its $40 billion endowment, employing a weighty corporate power, and by providing international grant-making in the size of $4 billion annually, swaying the priorities of global health and development. In addition, it breaks with traditional foundation behaviour when it aggressively funds core activities and reforms in international organizations like the World Health Organization (WHO) or seconds its employees to these to ensure its interests are represented.

The authority of the Gates Foundation is not only private in form then – it is fundamentally hybrid. This chapter explores how the Gates Foundation strategically practices its hybrid authority, while also asking what the consequences of this shape-shifting ability are for its capacity to influence political processes and for our understanding of contemporary actorness in international studies. Because exactly what kind of actor is the Gates Foundation becoming, and does it matter if we cannot exactly pinpoint this? The notion of hybrid organization is becoming a key avenue of organizational research,[3] as this field struggles with the gradual dissolution of idealized and widely practiced categorizations, and the consequences of increasingly observing organizations embedded in competing (social welfare and commercial) logics, often exemplified with the social enterprise.[4] Whilst an oft-used term, the explicit hybridity of specific organizations or actors has not been engaged to the same degree in international studies. It is pertinent here since the hybrid nature of the Gates Foundation not only shapes its intraorganizational life but also greatly defines and expands on the tools through which it exercises political influence.

Non-state influence on international politics

The last 50 years of academic attention and inattention to non-state actors in international life is a history well known and told. Work on transnational actors as a broad reference group largely emerged in the 1970s denoting 'Regular interactions across national boundaries when at least one actor is a non-state agent'.[5] Nye and Keohane's special issue from which this quote is taken constitutes early-1970s work on transnationalism that challenged state-dominated views on world politics, though primarily by focusing on MNCs and not the breadth of non-state actors studied today. The attention to non-state or transnational perspectives somewhat faded away through the 1980s, yet, as we approached the 1990s, fundamental changes to state sovereignty and governance beyond the state again redirected attention towards international relations as multi-layered and multi-dimensional, and this time with renewed strength that could confront state-centric theorization. New heterogeneous constellations of actors challenged Westphalian conceptions of power and influence, but also accountability as private authorities rose to influence with little democratic backing, an issue that naturally applies greatly to the Gates Foundation. The late 1990s and early 2000s then saw a (re)surgence in recognition of the influence of non-state actors besides IOs and corporations, in particular global civil society and transnational NGOs, networks and other organizational forms.[6] Still, the focus was on how these actor-types influence international and national policy-making, thus continually seeing them as a peripheral or exogenous source of impact onto something else.[7] Today, the interest is not in whether non-state actors are important or if they are able to influence nation states and international politics, but rather how they do so and through what means, i.e., through a recognition that they do not stand outside an interstate system and exercise influence but make up a core component of contemporary global governance.

Non-state actors have distinct ways of approaching influence that includes symbolic actions, agenda-setting,[8] pressure on states or efforts to secure the institutionalization of certain international norms or national policies (the compliance of which they then monitor[9]), and they are often seen as working through different means or institutional strategies than states.[10] These actors are still typically understood across fluid dimensions of internal structure (formal organizations or more or less loosely connected networks) and constitutive purposes (primarily driven by self-interest or by a notion of the 'common good'),[11] and we should of course consider their tools of political influence fluid as well, with no definite walls of demarcation between them. Still, there are limits to such fluidity and no one organization is commonly thought able to activate all forms of normative or material influence across the band of non-state actors. Reinalda and colleagues argue that we can witness three separate categories of non-state actors today: 1) public-interest-oriented non-governmental actors; 2) profit-oriented corporate actors; and 3) public inter-governmental organizations.[12] Others likewise conceive a line of separation along the purposive orientation of non-state actors that sees them pursue either profit or issues of public interest.[13] Next I will briefly discuss this array or spectrum of tools and approaches of political influence, before we return to how the Gates Foundation is potentially able to traverse this spectrum.

A well-articulated source of non-state actor influence comes from the diffusion of norms and knowledge, as well as authority through expertise.[14] As international politics has gone through increasing institutionalization and legalization, actors able to further global normative concerns, thus facilitating or shaping such processes, have grown in influence. Particularly the early stages of agenda-setting or norm emergence are seen to provide opportunities for non-state actors to exercise influence.[15] This type of non-state actor influence is naturally dependent upon a range of factors referring to the organization or actor itself (what are its capacities, material and ideational resources, or strategies), and to contextual conditions such as opportunity structures. Non-state actors may work hard to further certain norms, but if they do not find resonance among states that can facilitate their place in international organizations or agreements, they may wither away as quickly as they emerged.[16] This influence does not only limit itself to normative processes, and non-state actors are widely also credited for their role in international legal processes, working to influence processes of legalization through direct lobbying, organization of parallel non-state fora or involvement in compliance control.[17]

While corporate actors are certainly also thought to exercise this type of political influence, it is commonly associated with the most widely discussed non-state actor, the NGO. Not thought to be in the business of making profits, contrarily to MNCs, NGOs are often identified as having a public purpose because of their ambition to influence national and international policy making.[18] Some see NGOs as asserting an 'Imagined shared citizenship in an emerging global polity',[19] and they are sometimes perceived as providing a balance between pluralism and corporatism by embodying counterparts to private-sector actors' involvement in policy making. Still, this group is as internally incoherent as any actor group and comprises heterogeneous organizations with conflicting motives and objectives. They may be pressure groups that lobby or consult for their interests, they may try to influence politics by participating in the entire policy-making process, and they may be social movements who aim to induce social change and transformation through mobilization and persuasion.[20] Their roles and tools of influence in global governance are thus often conceived broadly. Most agree that NGOs and civil society are crucial in raising and expressing political opinion, disseminating information and as watchdogs and counterweights to states.[21] The first set of activities may be covert actions that go below the radar of public attention, attempting to persuade legislators, administrators or bureaucrats to take their viewpoints into consideration, or through expressive and vocal activities with as much publicity and attention as possible, attempting to build popular support for their causes and, through this, to influence policy making. The second extends beyond merely being channels of publicity and information by communicating to the public. These organizations connect interest groups and exchange between expertise and societal support, acting as producers of legitimacy and consensus building for states and international organizations. They may also take the shape of mass mobilization and social movements, driven by a political purpose of collective action, often around social change, forming a type of collective actor consisting of individuals who see themselves bound together by a common ambition to attain specific objectives.

They not only disseminate to the public, but also provide expert knowledge and information to governments and their representatives in IOs whose access to information and resources may be limited in some areas.[22] This close relationship to international organizations and states not least develops from their business as contractors or executing agencies of these, implementing public funds from donors and thus forming critical providers of international public services. They do not simply push an issue onto the agenda of IOs then and stand outside subsequent political processes, but also heavily shape these through all stages of decision-making, sometimes using their partnerships with government representatives to shape negotiation texts, having individuals sponsoring formulations that NGOs themselves are not allowed to present. They may influence staff from international organizations who indirectly shape negotiations, but in particular also national delegates who have formal and direct influence or other international organizations partaking in negotiations or decision making. Such multidirectional influence implies they may both seek to influence states that in turn influence international organizations, or they may seek to influence international organizations to influence states. Over time their pressure has gradually become formalized in certain international fora, with the use of 'consultative status' granting them a formal right to be heard (albeit with no voting rights), particularly in international organizations.

As a different yet also fundamentally political animal, recent decades have taught us how the shift from states to markets made political players of MNCs.[23] While Susan Strange's argument mainly was that these corporate actors functioned as political institutions themselves, with political relations, etc., and not that they influenced the foreign policies of states, this has also been the case for decades if not centuries. If not corporations directly, then at least their charitable offspring as the history of private foundations in the US well documents.[24] Some have especially pointed to globalization processes (including the increasing mobility of capital and MNCs) and the quest for foreign direct investments as key determinants in shifting the balance between state bargaining power vis-à-vis firms.[25] While sharing certain fundamental characteristics, they have many tools of influence available to them that NGOs critically do not, including the direct ability to transfer production and value from one place to another, shifting the trajectories of social and economic development while undermining national governments' abilities to control domestic economic forces. Some have argued that MNCs contribute to a regulatory 'race to the bottom' in their pursuit of ideal production sites,[26] while others maintain that the increasing sustainable-conscious consumer markets means MNCs are genuinely judged for their social and environmental impact.[27] As central organizers of economic activity in the world economy, MNCs are thus seen to have slowly turned from solely being committed to their shareholders to more widely refer to and assume forms of responsibility towards a broad array of stakeholders.[28] They are increasingly seen not only as regulatory problems requiring the attention of the international community to limit their actions, but rather as co-solvers of problems, in themselves contributing to the setting up of regulatory schemes and forms.

As with NGOs, we commonly see a focus on MNCs' inputs into international politics, whether as agenda setting, norm generation, etc., or on the output phase of norm implementation, policy evaluation and so forth.[29] As corporate actors, they are necessarily profit-oriented and sometimes narrowly instrumental in their pursuit of increased capital gains. Yet they also remain social actors whose meanings are constituted in and of social interaction. Relying solely on profit maximization to explain companies' modes of action is too rationalist and essentialized to account for the complex behaviour of these actors. They certainly have ambitions of influencing political processes as strong as any NGO, actively and directly lobbying and attempting to influence public international law, regulation, political agreements and norm engagement, also gaining indirect power through what has been described as the general societal acceptance of the corporation as a dominant and essentially beneficial institution in economic life.[30] This normative power of MNCs is shaped by the potential resonance of economic ideas, with some more likely than others to be supported, adopted or implemented by policy makers.[31]

Just as NGOs, MNCs are obviously highly diverse, and do not act as a cohesive group furthering a set of collectively agreed issues, but rather interests based on individual market positions, industry, etc. Some act as norm entrepreneurs,[32] some shape international regulation such as that on intellectual property rights[33] and set standards,[34] while others essentially supply public goods. Much like NGOs, they establish and maintain strong contacts in national delegations that partake in international negotiations, and through which they can further their own positions and interests, a widely exercised form of instrumental power. Any international negotiation will see an abundance of different nations engaged and several of these are bound to have convergence of opinion with MNCs on different issues, just as some national delegations are easier to influence than others. We would perhaps expect Least Developed Country (LDC) delegations to be most easily influenced seeing their willingness to attract FDI and the potential leverage from existing investments, but evidence has earlier showed this to not be the case.[35] Often viewed in a functionalist light as providing resources (financial, organizational capacity, personnel) and legitimacy to global governance that closes certain gaps and allows for more effective contributions to and implementation of governance goals,[36] MNCs, finally, are also centrally placed in decision making in public–private partnerships (a favoured modality of the Gates Foundation), or with representatives of industry granted consultative status in international organizations.

As the last major group of non-state actors, private or philanthropic foundations bring a different set of instruments to leverage political influence, as we have seen throughout this book. Instinctively considered private because their grant-making is dependent either on individual financial contributions (often from a single high-net-worth individual), or from corporations, just as they are essentially governed and controlled by these donors, many private foundations have long been engaged in public issues, supporting the delivery of public goods and being incited by governments to do so.[37] Some, in particular the smaller community foundations, often not only fund public services but actively partake in their delivery and implementation in close cooperation with local communities and citizens. Still, most of the largest foundations, including the Gates Foundation, act far removed from such local contexts and forms of intimate engagement. Despite application of some of the already mentioned tools of influence, private foundations are primarily considered financial intermediaries and known for the diverse material power of their dual weapons – grant-making and endowment investments. The first evidently revolves around the provision of financial grants to other organizations. Whereas traditional forms of grant-making have long emphasized 'responsive' and bottom-up approaches to philanthropy in which a board or group of selected individuals in the foundation would decide on incoming proposals, newer approaches value high engagement and directive forms of grant-making, driven by an emphasis on efficiency, effectiveness, and control over the manner and uses of funding. With this philanthrocapitalist turn has followed a diverse set of financing tools, such as social impact bonds, equity, debt, loans, but also non-financial forms of support through networking and mentoring. The second distinctive 'weapon' of foundations are their endowments, separating these from the many other types of non-state actors by making them free from external control, unaccountable to voters, shareholders and many other stakeholders. Aside from financial independence, the endowment provides for great financial leverage, and almost allows some of them to act as genuinely corporate actors, as we have seen for The Gates Foundation.

Embracing hybridity

Before we explore the chameleon nature of the Gates Foundation's contemporary political influence we have to appreciate how it initially practiced a very different set of narrow ambitions, far from any grand aspirations of global political power. During the foundation's prefatory period of organizational formation and expansion that we explored in depth in Chapter 4, from the mid-1990s to well into the 2000s, the foundation in fact largely followed a strategy of isolation that can be hard to comprehend given its contemporary reach. Pursuing action in only a few programmatic areas, and deliberately aiming for isolation in these, the initial idea for the foundation and its leadership was to find underfinanced areas in which it could apply its reasoning of technological progress and entrepreneurial solutions without too many interfaces with other actors. As a Senior Programme Officer put it, they 'Didn't care much for what the other guys were doing out there, and picking areas that few were interested in made sure that we could be in the driver's seat and not having to worry too much about what the other guys were doing'.[38] Reflecting on the belief that the foundation could change the state of its areas of global health by developing things that were desperately needed and distributing them on to others for implementation, thus maintaining limited contact with other organizations, then CEO Patty Stonesifer later explained how 'Bill, Melinda and I were a bunch of product-development people', and that they had 'Assumed others would focus on getting the products we developed to those who needed them'.[39] As it turned out, none really did. Another Senior Programme Officer explained how 'The foundation basically functioned as a candy shop for a group of medical scientists, who were interested in developing new vaccines and the like, not much more',[40] underlining the still open organizational form and work of the foundation, characteristic of many newly established organizations trying to find their footing. In this case, of course, the organization had its pockets full of resources as it did so.

The foundation was largely kept in the hands of the family during this time, without much external intervention. Combined with a hesitant approach to publicity, it intentionally favoured isolation all the way up until being the world's second largest foundation with assets of more than $17 billion at the start of the millennium. It conducted little if any consultation outside of the philanthropic milieu in the US,[41] and Melinda Gates herself acknowledged that when the foundation first opened its doors, a reluctance to work alongside other actors was dominant, maintaining that 'I don't think we had full appreciation for just how important it is to work in close partnership'.[42] 'Full appreciation' is quite an understatement as several people involved during the first years recalled how the attitude towards other organizations was one of fundamental scepticism about both their approaches and motivations, 'The general sense was that we didn't trust them. We may have been a new source of funding in their eyes, but they were mainly an obstacle in ours' as a former Senior Programme Officer explained it.[43]

The Millennium Development Goals, coming around during this time, is a good example of this attitude, as we have seen earlier. Recalling his own and Melinda's view on the MDGs at the beginning of the new millennium, Gates described in 2013 how they initially had strong reservations about the goals, explaining that the MDGs 'Were hardly the first time someone had declared that children shouldn't die' and that 'The UN had passed many resolutions calling for things that never came to pass'.[44] Gates later described himself and Melinda as having been 'cautious optimists'. This is an understatement as several involved during the early years of turning towards global development recall how foundation leadership perceived the MDGs as fundamentally constraining towards the organization's grant. As a former Senior Programme Officer framed it, 'People [in the foundation] thought of the MDGs as a set of constraining principles coming from a group of states that hadn't even been able to live up to their own promises for decades. Why should we respect their opinion?'[45] Displaying an inveterate scepticism of the established public donor organizations, it is no surprise that the foundation developed an immediate dislike of multilateral organizations such as the UN and OECD, as well as the WHO within global health. For a foundation that considers itself much like a non-profit for-good business, having such organizations impose rules upon them, constraining action and manoeuvrability, 'Was like having private firms being dictated how to sell their products and to whom'.[46] Over the course of a few years, however, this attitude would change.

Keeping a low profile was a guiding principle for the foundation during its first years then, but as it increasingly gained domestic and international traction as the world's largest private foundation, this began to change. 'In the beginning we let other voices be heard' Stonesifer explained in 2004, but 'now we intend to share our point of view'.[47] The Gates had now also become 'more comfortable using their status as celebrities to call attention to the foundation's work' and people in the US non-profit world were beginning to describe the foundation as the first 'superpower' of philanthropy, comparing it with the US government in terms of international political traction,[48] which was surely an exaggeration at that point in time. Becoming increasingly aware of its role vis-à-vis other organizations then, the foundation was now gradually more vocal about how its philanthropic efforts, in order to achieve lasting large-scale change, had to incorporate strategies to encourage effective public investment and leverage private sector potential, pursuing catalytic investments that augmented rather than supplanted government funding in the developing world. If the first period of organizational life for the Gates Foundation may be characterized by a strategy of isolation, though followed by increasing interest in shaping domestic policy on both national and international issues, the years that followed from the mid-2000s have surely been ones of increasing relations with other organizations in the field but also engaging with norm- and principle-setting institutions. And, most importantly, it now increasingly understands and utilizes its hybrid organizational form that allows it to sometimes project the organizational identity of an NGO, sometimes of an MNC, and sometimes almost even of a public actor. These organizational changes are strongly related to a strategy of expanding the foundation's reach into numerous domains and areas of interest. It may have been possible to maintain a strategy of isolation with a continued focus on domestic issues of education and a small share of foundation funds provided to global health and vaccine development. But with greatly increasing efforts in global development (animated by the $30 billion donation from Warren Buffett in 2006) the intake of different professional groups with experiences in other donor organizations, the apprehension that vaccine development should be accompanied by efforts in delivery (entailing a shift towards increasingly having to deal with political and social structural constraints to health, and necessitating the integration of short- and long-term action), and a growing role in national and international advocacy, the breadth of the foundation's form and functions were greatly increased but also acknowledged by key organizational actors inside the foundation. As one employee explained it, 'We're not just passive funders anymore, our advocacy and political work has grown huge as we've come to appreciate how much you can change by way of words and soft forms of power'.[49] Increasingly, then, the foundation has come to embrace an expansive repertoire of tools of influence, and today exercises an almost aggressive strategic use of its hybrid nature, being very conscious about the effects of such. As a Senior Advisor explains it, 'We do consider ourselves a multifaceted organization with many tools at our disposal. You could say we are like a chameleon. It would be silly of us to not use all of those tools'.[50]

Chameleon politics

It is with this context in mind that we now turn to the foundation's ability to negotiate its organizational identity, breaking with most actor typologies along the way. We will see both how it fits into and spans across several distinct actor categorizations, but also more broadly how it traverses the public–private divide in its approach to attaining political influence.

Non-state shape shifting

The Gates Foundation is first and formally a non-profit charity because it is registered as a 501(c)(3) organization in the United States, granting it status as exempt from federal tax. This in essence also defines its nature as a private foundation, and entails an obligation to distribute five per cent of its endowment for charitable purposes annually for it to remain tax-exempt. It is certainly non-governmental in form, and practices tools of influence associated with NGOs, such as lobbying or applying normative pressure on international organizations. Whilst the NGO brand is seldom used by the foundation, the notion of non-governmental frames it decisively and it remains particularly adept at utilizing the institutional frameworks created from decades of structured NGO–state relations in international politics. The case recalled in the introduction to this chapter is a case in point here. While several NGOs were vocal in their scepticism of the WHO formalizing a partnership with the foundation, the Gates Foundation itself skilfully utilized the institutional framework of structured NGO relations to the WHO, and were open about it. Following the formal decision in the WHO, Chris Elias, president of the Global Development division at the Gates Foundation, exclaimed that 'Formalizing our relationship with WHO under the framework that it has adopted for working with NGOs creates clear norms and guidelines for our ongoing support'.[51] The Gates Foundation has for years been pouring hundreds of millions of US dollars into the WHO (in justifying the move to official relations, WHO noted that the foundation's engagement with the IO 'has been of a funding nature, as well as providing support related to advocacy, communications, technical assistance, expertise and others'[52]), but moving from informal working relations to formal relations grants the organization a further set of options for exercising influence. Amongst many privileges, these include permission to: attend meetings of the governing bodies of the WHO, including the World Health Assembly (as a non-voting member), the Executive Board, and the six regional committees; participate in any other meeting organized with the purpose of exchanging views; and engage in technical collaboration with WHO on activities, e.g., concerning product development and capacity-building. Aside from the tangible opportunities to which it is granted access, the formal relationship also greatly legitimizes the foundation's presence in the WHO, recalibrating its engagement from being an external funder to a core part of the IO's work.

The status of having 'official relations' to the WHO was achieved by the foundation despite its commercial investments in food, drug and alcohol companies, in theory creating conflicts of interest with the global public health aims of the WHO. In the WHO register of non-state actors, where such information is to be disclosed, a basic set of statements merely read that the foundation has engagements with select members of the pharmaceutical industry, the food and beverage industry, and the health care field 'In pursuit of our public health goals'. This apparent disregard by the WHO of the foundation's commercial investments was not least achieved because of a key instrument facilitating the foundation's ability to negotiate its organizational identity: the two-entity structure of the foundation introduced in 2006 that saw the foundation's endowments move to a new organizational entity called the Bill and Melinda Gates Foundation Trust. Whilst it is difficult for outside observers to note any difference, the grant-making charity and commercial investments of its endowment were thus formally separated. Already the following year, as it saw a staunch criticism of its investment in particularly oil and mining companies, the foundation used this instrument to claim that, following the formal separation and new structure, it could not, nor would it be willing to, control in what the Trust was investing the endowments. The same instrument and response was brought to the front of discussions on its conflict of interests regarding WHO's stated aims, where the foundation has proclaimed that its charitable activities are removed from its investment activities, with no link between the two. Still, to the untrained or critical eye, it may be difficult to differentiate between the Bill and Melinda Gates Foundation and the Bill and Melinda Gates Foundation Trust.

Some draw a line of separation between non-state actors along their purposive orientation that sees them either pursue profit or issues of public interest (whatever the perceived state of such is),[53] i.e., that NGOs remains non-profit while MNCs pursue profit. Here, as well, the Gates Foundation falls in between two stools by following a much more fluid and interchangeable relationship between profit and 'public' interest. As Chapter 4 has detailed, the investment of its endowment has returned anything between a deficit of $8 billion during the height of the financial crisis in 2008 to a surplus of almost $6 billion in 2013, representing more than 150 per cent of its grant expenses, essentially providing annual net growth of its endowment. Whilst such funds are eventually provided to the foundation and not distributed to shareholders or the like, it surely represents a profit for the organization. Far from exercising a line between pursuing profit and public interest then, the foundation practices a modus operandi that sees the former facilitate the latter. Decisively, the investment of $40 billion is not merely employed as a neutral or passive way of increasing the funds available for charitable activities. Through the commercial investments, the foundation trust is able to wield a significant corporate power by establishing close connection to key private sector players in the foundation's areas of engagement, whether pharmaceuticals such as Merck, GlaxoSmithKline or Pfizer, or agricultural giants such as Archer Daniels Midland, Kraft or Unilever. These connections are crucial for its grant-making and the successful pursuit of its charitable objectives. The foundation has often enhanced these investments by providing charitable grants to the mentioned pharmaceutical companies, with GlaxoSmithKline alone granted approximately $50 million over the last seven years in direct charitable support.

Whilst resembling certain NGO traits, the foundation thus also remains fundamentally different from what we commonly associate with this actor type. To the points made can be added that whilst the majority of NGOs depend on external funding, and accordingly often assume a position of subcontracting to other organizations (whether state or non-state), the Gates Foundation is able to exercise a very high degree of self-determination through its endowment, which effectively provides it with complete financial independence. This greatly shapes its behaviour (just as it shapes notions of accountability and responsibility), providing it with a freedom of movement and action that NGOs do not experience.

Behaving like a state?

The General Assembly Hall is the largest room in the somewhat confusing complex that is the headquarters of the United Nations, by the banks of the East River in New York City. Without a doubt also the most imposing, the Hall is a symbol of modern international cooperation and co-existence, but also a site that caters well to the theatrics of hostility, such as Muammar Gaddafi's famous 96-minute rant against the UN Security Council. From the podium, below the golden UN symbol of the world, one has the oversight of all the individual desks, each given to a member state. In September 2015, as the Danish prime minister used his gavel to endorse the new SDGs that aim to drive global action against poverty, violence and inequality towards 2030, Bill and Melinda Gates stood up alongside the 193 UN member states on the floor of the General Assembly Hall and clapped, big smiles on their faces like everyone else in the crowd. For a couple (and representing an organization) that used to shrug off the UN as insignificant or even potentially harmful, this was a powerful manifestation.

As became clear earlier in this chapter, the Gates Foundation has progressed from a peripheral or even deliberately dissociated position, adopting a strategy of isolation in which it largely sought to work in confined areas of intervention and with limited partnerships or implementing agencies, to a state of global political ambitions and a portfolio of work that reaches into every corner of global development. As we have seen, non-state actors are thought to exercise influence on contemporary global politics because global governance today is multilayered, opening up multiple spaces of influence. This is certainly true for the Gates Foundation, yet over time its drive for political influence has led it towards forms of behaviour that go beyond what we would typically associate with non-state actors, just as it is accorded state-like status in many international policy domains.[54] That is not to say that we should conceive of the foundation as a new type of state, but rather that it conducts certain functionally equivalent actions to those of states, critically interesting for an organization that often defines itself most clearly as an opposition to all things 'state'. In particular, two sets of behaviour can be emphasized, where the foundation pursues influence through channels or forms we would habitually reserve for states: its interaction with international organizations and its direct state relations.

A deep IO engagement is a cornerstone of both state and non-state influence, and a discipline in which the Gates Foundation is adept. Its strategic approach to influencing political negotiations in IOs forms an all-out attack that sees it combining posting of senior technical staff with expertise to shape negotiation texts and engage with national delegations on equal terms away from the public's eye, staff that often have prior experience from representing such country delegations, with the high-level presence of either Bill or Melinda Gates who attract attention and exercise influence on this different level of political and public relations. Negotiation stances are often simultaneously furthered through 'scientific' means, as think tanks or other knowledge organizations are financed to produce reports that underline arguments furthered by the foundation. These reports are never published by the foundation itself but by institutions with high levels of scientific legitimacy, often only carrying a small note of how the foundation has sponsored the report but is not accountable for its findings. This construction of knowledge regimes, commonly presented by the foundation as 'best practice' or the result of 'systematic reviews' (*inter alia* by combining several randomized controlled trials, the positivist methodology par excellence of contemporary development economics), is thus used concurrently by foundation representatives, covert in the closed negotiations and publicly through the co-chairs. These efforts may again be supported by strategic media outlets or by high-profile social media campaigns. The former includes circumstances in which international media are paid to elucidate a specific theme or problematic related to the position of the foundation, formally with the editorial freedom to decide what and how, but in practice within narrowly conceived arrangements between the foundation and the media organizations. The latter may, for example, include the Gates Foundation's attempt at social mobilization, Global Citizen, in which 'People who want to learn about and take action on the world's biggest challenges'[55] come together. Members of this movement are often directly encouraged to tweet out standard messages delivered from the organization. When the Danish Government decided to cut back foreign aid to a minimum level of 0.7 per cent of GNI in 2015, thousands of tweets using the exact same formulations were delivered by Global Citizen members to popular Danish Twitter hashtags, meant to sway the opinion of the public and pressure policymakers.

Such tactics regard tangible negotiations that only occur every so often. Other forms of influencing IOs are put to use in the everyday life of these organizations, in this case denoting financial and human resource-related forms of support. Some private foundations have been important supporters of IOs, sometimes being crucial to their initiation (such as the Rockefeller Foundation's support to form the League of Nation's Health Organization, the predecessor to the WHO[56]) and at other times providing them with core funding such as through the UN Foundation set up by CNN media mogul Ted Turner in 2000 (though this approach is rarely used). Yet for the most part, such financial support is earmarked to specific problem areas or smaller UN organizations, allocated with a clear thematic scope or a delimited set of objectives such as the vaccination of 10,000 children against polio. This is certainly an approach practiced by the Gates Foundation, who *inter alia* have provided earmarked funds to UNICEF over the last decade, sometimes towards vaccine delivery or very specific programmes like $20 million for 'Improved iodine nutrition through universal salt iodization'.[57] But the Gates Foundation has increasingly taken steps towards providing financial resources for operational and core backing, often supporting organizational reforms such as the setting up of new offices or departments in IOs. This is an ideal way to further a specific priority of the foundation, ensuring that it is prominently featured in the relevant organization by having sufficient resources or by having it include management of a certain level or proximity to the secretary general. In addition to the close talks with management to which multi-million donations (if not hundreds of millions) grant the foundation access, another way for the Gates Foundation to shape organizational reforms in IOs is by contributing third-party consultants to draft policies, procedures or settle decision-making processes. The foundation is itself a pronounced purchaser of external consulting services for internal purposes, and by selecting consultants to IOs with prior work experience in the foundation (but who are formally removed from it) it is able to sustain a degree of influence as to where the organizational reforms or other processes land. This is a widespread practice by the foundation, particularly documented in the field of global health.[58]

In addition to the provision of financial resources, the foundation is increasingly moving into state territory by scaling up its secondment of foundation employees directly into the heart of IO bureaucracies. Seconding of national employees from IO member states into the bureaucratic halls of IOs is a well-versed approach to further national interests. In effect, it implies that individuals already employed by another organization or state bureaucracy are instated into an office or department in the IO for a fixed period of time, after which the secondee returns to her or his original organization. While the employee formally works for the IO and under rules of declarations of interests for staff (these, however, often only refer specifically to individual interests, not institutional ones), these types of employees are used strategically by states to further certain interests through the close connection upheld to their original organization or home country. In late 2015 the first ever review of the WHO's non-state secondments showed that the Gates Foundation was at the time involved in three top-level secondments to management.[59] That is, staff positioned in important leadership roles in the WHO are effectively sent from, and paid for by, the Gates Foundation and surely influenced by their original institutional affiliation. Altogether, while the UN certainly maintains a formalized system of rules governing its relations to NGOs, the Gates Foundation's engagement with it and other IOs seems to obviously extend far beyond it, into forms of collaboration or support we would mainly expect states to uphold. In addition to international governmental organizations, the Gates Foundation is notably well-positioned in other international partnerships, including public–private partnerships (PPPs). As we have seen, it holds membership of the board of directors in some of the largest PPPs of global development such as the Global Alliance for Vaccines or Gavi (which it was instrumental in setting up), and in the Global Fund to Fight Aids, Tuberculosis and Malaria. In both of these the foundation assumes state-like responsibilities by providing long-term funding of programmes and the buying up of vaccines and drugs from pharmaceutical MNCs to have these distributed in the Global South.

Other than its IO engagement, a different ballgame for the foundation has been the emphasis on developing direct state relations, leveraging political agendas through diplomatic means. Over time, the institution of diplomacy has largely grown out of its traditional form as an institution in a state-centric system to now increasingly reflect the contemporary configuration of international politics as multi-layered and encompassing a wide group of heterogeneous actors that each have certain but different forms of legitimacy.[60] Still, there remains a difference between the loosely defined field of political relations or networks between diverse state and non-state actors, and diplomacy as an institution of the state system. Much like in its IO engagement, the diplomatic measures of the Gates Foundation are two-tiered. The first level revolves around institutional relations between foundation staff and relevant national staff in partner countries and in the US. In the US, the Washington, DC, office of the foundation, established as the first office outside of Seattle in 2001, maintains a deep relationship with US policymakers, the national political environment (just as it does to the IOs present there, including the World Bank and the IMF) and relevant departments, including the Department of State, USAID and the Department of Agriculture. Furthermore, in 2010, it became the first US foundation to establish an office in Western Europe when it formed the London-based office responsible for its European relations. From here the foundation has easy access to European governments, partnerships with whom mainly revolve around funding collaboration or pressure from the foundation to sustain European donor support for aid and to the foundation's priorities. In addition to Washington, DC, and London, the foundation also has local offices in Beijing, China, New Delhi, India, Addis Ababa, Ethiopia, Johannesburg, South Africa, and Abuja, Nigeria. These local offices provide a point of entrance to diplomatic relations in relevant regions, and combine grantee relations with maintaining a structured dialogue with relevant governments and their bodies, including relevant ministries. Though these local offices for the most part do not partake in local donor coordination groups, as we would expect the bilateral donors to do, they nonetheless function as small embassies who organize, sustain and expand the political presence of the foundation in the country and the wider region, and are focused on nurturing relationships with local government and state departments.

The second tier builds on the celebrity implications of the foundation's co-chair being the richest man in the world and perhaps the most well-known technology innovator through the company he built with Paul Allen – Microsoft. Some research has conceptualized the role of 'celebrity diplomacy' as a matter of agenda-setting through public relations efforts,[61] with cases including U2 lead Singer Bono's or Hollywood actor George Clooney's media stunts or calls on, e.g., the conflict in South Sudan. While increasingly using the media to convey messages, the work of the Gates Foundation, through Bill and Melinda Gates, also holds a more traditional set of diplomatic relations that includes ceremonial state visits and heads of state talks. All the way back in 2000, when the foundation had just started operating, its then CEO, former Microsoft-executive Patty Stonesifer, visited Ghana on a 'low-key' trip with director of global health, Gordon Perkin, where they had decided to 'Not call upon the heads of government'. Still, as they were leaving Ghana for Gambia, about to board their plane, Ghanaian President Jerry Rawlings landed in a helicopter and greeted them with a 'Someone like you shouldn't arrive in Ghana without announcing your presence'.[62] When they landed in Gambia a few hours later, news of their visit had reached President Yahya Jammeh who wanted (and got) an audience as well. Today, Bill and Melinda Gates travel around the world to meet heads of state, in Africa, Asia, Europe and beyond. Whether in Dakar, Senegal, or in Paris, France, Gates is received ceremonially with high levels of performativity at play: national and international press is summoned, hands are shaken and pictures taken, before the world leaders continue their conversation in the presidential chambers. Only days after US President Donald Trump announced his 'America First' budget blueprint to cut international programmes by 28.5 per cent in March 2017, Bill Gates was granted an impromptu meeting with the President at which he laid out his concerns for cutbacks in foreign aid to development and global health. Asked about why and how Gates had asked for the meeting (not least seeing as the President largely appeared inaccessible at this time), a spokeswoman for the foundation explained that it 'Has a long history of working with officials on both sides of the aisle to pursue shared priorities like global health and development and domestic education' and that 'Bill will meet with members of the administration and congressional leaders to discuss the tremendous progress made to-date in these areas and the critical and indispensable role that the United States has played in achieving these gains'.[63] These visits are not merely courtesy calls in hopes of attracting Microsoft investments or fulfilling personal aims of meeting the world's richest man, and they are certainly not available to NGOs, MNCs or even private foundations. They are likely a testament to the international political influence that Bill Gates is increasingly seen to wield personally and through the foundation.

Hybrid authority

The hybrid nature of the Gates Foundation allows it to practice a flexible interpretation of its organizational form, projecting different organizational identities depending on the situation at hand, thus traversing common actor categorizations such as private foundation, NGO, MNC and even state actor. Engaging with private-sector actors, it may entice or sway these with its multi-billion investment schemes; aiming to utilize the institutional framework in IOs for engaging with NGOs, it may further its non-state nature, dismissing its commercial activities by proclaiming that its investments are formally removed from its charitable activities; aiming to influence heads of state, it may use its celebrity or plutocratic nature to have its co-chairs meet these under personal circumstances; confronted by claims to public accountability through reporting, transparency or public insight, it may refer to its status as a 'family foundation' and take cover behind the extremely lax legal requirements imposed on this actor type in the US. Former CEO of the Gates Foundation (and Microsoft Executive veteran) Jeff Raikes once proclaimed about the foundation he headed: 'We are not replacing the UN. But some people would say we're a new form of multilateral organization'.[64] Of all the attempts at delimiting the Gates Foundation's actorness, this is probably the one farthest from the truth. The Gates Foundation may be in the midst of challenging core multilateral organizations such as the WHO, but its modus operandi remains deeply unilateral. It does not represent an open room for opinions of numerous stakeholders, accountability or democratic principles. It rests confidently on the nature of plutocratic influence by reflecting the logics and ideologies of its founders and co-chairs.

In the organizational literature, categories of private, public and non-profit organizations are traditionally conceptualized in idealized terms with organizational forms taken to reflect an 'Archetypal configuration of structures and practices regarded as appropriate within an institutional context'.[65] To be identified as one such specific actor, organizations attempt to manifest those particular characteristics. Private organizations are largely seen as guided by market forces to maximise financial return, whilst public organizations are guided by principles of public benefit and collective choice, and, financially, non-profit organizations are seen as pursuing social or environmental goals.[66] Positioned fluidly between these three categories, a hybrid organizational form is taken to be 'Forms as structures and practices that allow the coexistence of values and artefacts from two or more categories' and draw 'On at least two different sectoral paradigms, logics and value systems'.[67] Hybridity then in essence means accommodating differing values and practices, and is often approached from the tensions arising from having to strike a balance between pursuing commercial and social or charitable objectives. Contrary to forming a response to a challenge posed by an external environment, when the Gates Foundation uses its hybrid organizational nature to make claims to membership in externally defined organizational types, it proactively employs a selective strategy of drawing forth and pushing into the background different organizational traits. Key here is the notion of organizational identity, and not least the projection of such by the foundation towards external audiences.

Organizational identity is commonly seen to reflect the organization's members' collective understanding of what the organization is and what is not. This identity is not durable and fixed but represents a potentially precarious and unstable notion. Identity may change over time and is frequently up for revision, redefinition and reinterpretation.[68] That it is not necessarily enduring does not mean it cannot be guided by continuity, with certain core values being interpreted differently over time and thus also projected in different forms. The Gates Foundation does not necessarily go through structural or functional change as it readily shifts from projecting an identity of an NGO to one of a private actor. It merely shifts the interpretation of its organization and reflects that interpretation outwards. This underscores the importance of projection or outward reflection, with narratives of organizational identity acting as forms of self-expression.[69] Seeing as organizational identity is a relational construct formed in the interaction with others through social experience and activity,[70] the projecting of organizational image to maintain or build organizational identity is crucially important. In such instances, as we have seen in the Gates Foundation, organizational members make explicit claims about the identity of the organization as a collective whole, what it is and what it is not. Foundation employees can use different strategies in their attempts to paint specific organizational images of its identity of both denying certain actor-group memberships (when, e.g., proclaiming that it certainly should not be subjected to the same demands for transparency as public actors), or constructing a sense of inclusion in others (when, e.g., exclaiming that 'we are a non-profit' and should thus be allowed to operate under the framework of NGO engagement in IOs, despite vast commercial investments).

Projected images of the organization do certainly not represent an objective or definite picture of what the organization is and what it is not. Such images are made by the organization to convey desirable impressions and may just as well conceal or misrepresent its actual workings and form. They are largely constructions made to appeal to different audiences. What matters in the way the Gates Foundation projects its organizational image is not so much whether it is a true representation of its organizational nature, but rather how such images are externally received by those who interpret them. Such concerns of resonance and dissonance have their own conceptual history in discussions over framing efforts.[71] Significant again is that external constituencies interpreting the images of organizational identity do not have to believe them to be *true* in any form, to instil resonance in them. These interrelationships of projection and interpretation are filled with strong elements of power. The WHO does not have to truly believe that the Gates Foundation have no conflicts of interests in global health to accept them as a formal partner. But they need to have a strong motive for including them in such a formalized relationship (in this case it is tempting to conclude this motive is found in the fact that the foundation is amongst the IO's greatest donors), seeing as they may also jeopardize their own legitimacy by doing so, and they need to be able to justify the decision to other strong constituencies.

Hybridity is often seen as a challenge – how can an organization, caught at the intersection of multiple competing logics, respond to the conflictive demands exerted by these and their audiences? Here, because of the nature of the Gates Foundation, hybridity is not so much a challenge of satisfying ambiguous demands as it is a set of opportunities shaping resources, mission objectives and strategies, and essentially granting the foundation a form of authority-through-hybridity. As a hybrid organization, the foundation has available to it a repertoire of practices and tools of influence borrowed from different organizational types that it can combine in new ways, providing it with an advantage if it manages to do so without wholly compromising its legitimacy. More so than just a natural (fluid) organizational form, hybridity becomes a guiding strategy in the foundation's pursuit of political influence, making the notion of pragmatism unavoidable here. The foundation appears exceedingly pragmatic as it readily shifts from projecting one organizational form to another, exercising a whole host of tools of influence across the main actor categorizations that we know. It pragmatically uses those tools available to it and attempts to claim shifting actor-group memberships through what appears to be an experimental process, responding to reactions as they arise. Others have referred to somewhat similar processes as 'strategic isomorphism',[72] but again from a perspective that assumes a need for organizations to comply with different institutional templates. The Gates Foundation practices a strategic hybridity, not because it feels a need to (symbolically) satisfy institutional demands about legitimacy from different sides, but as a purposive strategic selection in efforts to amplify its political influence.

In fact, legitimacy remains an open question. Common issues associated with hybrid organizing are mission drift (i.e., the unconscious shifting of organizational objectives in other directions than those instated in original mandates or aims) and problems with stakeholder legitimacy.[73] Mission drift is certainly relevant to accentuate for a foundation that is engaged in almost every corner of global health and development, that requires handling by an ever-growing bureaucracy. Stakeholder legitimacy is more difficult to pinpoint. As shown, the foundation repeatedly crosses lines of expected behaviour for the different actor groups of which it projects membership. Theory would suggest that deviation from these different forms of institutionally established expected behaviour would entail social or economic sanctioning,[74] i.e., a loss of legitimacy. Yet it is difficult to find instances of the foundation being 'punished' for its institution-defying behaviour. As in the case of the WHO relationship, certain NGOs may question the involvement of the foundation, or its claims to be included under the framework of NGO cooperation, but these calls have limited influence and are often advanced by smaller organizations or ones without economic ties to the foundation. At the same time, not all organizations would be able to act as the foundation does. Traditional NGOs would likely have their legitimacy questioned immediately if they crossed the expected behaviour of this non-state actor type, as would likely other actors. High-status hybrids like the Gates Foundation may have more room to deviate for different audiences without being sanctioned, but such room can also be possible because the fields within which the organization acts are themselves in flux.[75] This is certainly the case for global health and development, with the increasing heterogeneity of both actors involved and approaches employed.[76] Two related features of the foundation are worth including here as well, namely its position as a main private benefactor in global health and development that sees it embedded in financial relationships with the majority of principal actors there, but also its continued status as a newcomer and, more importantly, as an outsider to the established field. Both of these factors seem to sustain the foundation's legitimacy or to raise its threshold for loss of such. When confronted with questions about its behaviour and thus apprehensions for its legitimacy, the foundation is vocal about how it only needs to uphold the accountability and legitimacy expectations of a single actor type – the private foundation. Faced with questions over its investments in mining and oil companies, the foundation responded by proclaiming that it is a private foundation and that scoring investments for their social or environmental impact is 'A governmental role',[77] not something to be imposed on private foundations. Strategic hybridity, then, not only refers to the ability to expand the organizational form to include many different actor types. It just as well includes the ability to compress one's actorness to a single identity of choice if necessary, making it a continuous process of broadening and narrowing one's organizational form to fit the situation at hand.

Final remarks

This chapter has tried to scratch at the surface of the Gates Foundation's hybrid organizational nature and its ability to continually re-interpret its organizational identity and claim membership of diverse actor groups by way of projecting these shifting identities, with significant consequences for the international political influence it wields. The case of the foundation brings a different perspective to those that see hybridity mainly as a reactive challenge for organizations having to abide by different institutional worlds and forms of expected behaviour. The foundation in theory has to respond to multiple logics of appropriateness, but, rather than blindly following institutional prescriptions, it enacts many different types of responses, many of which fall outside expected forms of behaviour for different actor types. Hybrid organizations like the Gates Foundation thus present a challenge to (neo)institutional theory's core proposition that organizations have to follow specific institutional templates in order to be considered legitimate,[78] by combining and spanning different institutional logics and boundaries. Still, the room for manoeuvring and the exceptionally high threshold for legitimacy loss is likely only available to very few organizations engaged in international political concerns, making the Gates Foundation a case from which it may be hard to generalize. As argued, the foundation's strategic hybridity allows it to alternately expand and compress its organizational identity, sometimes assuming multiple organizational forms and, at other times (particularly when faced with questions of legitimacy), reducing itself back to its initial shape as a private foundation, with genuinely limited accountability obligations.

Is the Gates Foundation a novel institutional form that challenges traditional conceptions of organizing? Probably not. We have moved past the time of idealized organizational forms that manifest 'pure' generic structural features and characteristics, if one such has ever existed. The hybridity of the Gates Foundation perhaps represents traits that are becoming increasingly prevalent today; a fluid organizational form given further weight by the increasingly blurred boundaries between private, public and non-profit organizational forms. Related to this, does actorness matter then, we might ask, if the foundation can readily shift between projecting different forms of it? The answer to this must certainly be yes. Though few organizations likely rest firmly within a single actor type, these constructed categorizations that have been built over decades if not centuries of international political relations, legal institutionalization and also academic work serve as tangible instruments or tools themselves, each one in theory loaded with institutional and symbolic rules and expectations, but also opportunities to exploit. Hybrids like the Gates Foundation may be able to utilize these categorizations and their inherent institutional systems of expectation and meaning to negotiate their organizational identity and leverage influence beyond any one such category, whilst retracting back into its formal organizational shape if faced with too many institutional demands from its stakeholders and environments. In an increasingly institutionalized realm of international politics, hybridity is an effective strategy for the lucky few that may help grant access to decision-making fora, special rights and privileges but also the circumvention of certain demands, rules or obligations. The ability to seemingly project a shifting array of organizational identities across broader categories of public or non-state actors, but also more specific ones like NGO, MNC or private foundation, provides the Gates Foundation with an extensive repertoire of tools and approaches with which it can influence its areas of involvement.

Notes

1 WHO. 2017a. Executive Board 140th Session, EB 140/42.
2 'Open letter to the Executive Board of the World Health Organization' available at: http://healthscienceandlaw.ca/wp-content/uploads/2017/01/Public-Interest-Position. WHO_.FENSAGates.Jan2017.pdf.
3 Pache, A. C. and Santos, F. 2012. 'Inside the hybrid organization: selective coupling as a response to competing institutional logics', *Academy of Management Journal* 56(4): 972–1001.
4 Doherty, B., Haugh, H. and Lyon, F. 2014. 'Social enterprises as hybrid organizations: a review and research agenda', *International Journal of Management Reviews* 16(4): 417–436.
5 Nye, J. S. and Keohane, R. O. (1971). 'Transnational relations and world politics: an introduction', *International Organization* 25(3): 329–349.
6 Risse, T. 1996. 'Exploring the nature of the beast: international relations theory and comparative policy analysis meet the European Union', *Journal of Common Market Studies* 34(1): 53–80; Prakash, A. and Hart, J. A. 1999. *Globalization and Governance*. London: Routledge; Arts, B., Noortmann, M. and Reinalda, B. (eds) 2001. *Non-State Actors in International Relations*. Aldershot: Ashgate; Hall, R. B. and Biersteker, T. J. (eds) 2002. *The Emergence of Private Authority in Global Governance*. Cambridge: Cambridge University Press.
7 Risse, T. 2013. 'Transnational actors and world politics' in *Handbook of International Relations*, edited by W. Carlsnaes, T. Risse and B. A. Simmons, London: Sage, 258.
8 Betsill, M. M. and Corell, E. 2008. *NGO Diplomacy: The Influence of Nongovernmental Organizations in International Environmental Negotiations*. Cambridge, MA: MIT Press.
9 Keck, M. and Sikkink, K. 1998. *Activists Beyond Borders*. Ithaca, NY: Cornell University Press.
10 Joachim, J. 2003. 'Framing issues and seizing opportunities: the UN, NGOs, and women's rights', *International Studies Quarterly* 47(2): 247–274.
11 Risse, 2013.
12 Arts, et al. 2001.
13 Risse, 2013.
14 Hall and Biersteker, 2002.
15 Finnemore, M. and Sikkink, K. 1998. 'International norm dynamics and political change', *International Organization* 52(4): 887–917.
16 Checkel, J. T. 2001. 'Why comply? Social learning and European identity change', *International Organization* 55(3): 553–588; Cortell, A. P. and Davis, J. W. 2000. 'Understanding the domestic impact of norms: a research agenda', *International Studies Review* 2(1): 65–87.
17 Peters, A., Koechlin, L. and Förster, T. (eds) 2009. *Non-State Actors as Standard Setters*. Cambridge: Cambridge University Press.
18 Arts, et al. 2001.
19 Watkins, S. C., Swidler, A. and Hannan, T. 2012. 'Outsourcing social transformation: development NGOs as organizations', *Annual Review of Sociology* 38: 285–315.
20 Reinalda, B. 2001. 'Private in form, public in purpose: NGOs in international relations theory', in *Non-State Actors in International Relations*, edited by B. Arts, M. Noortmann and B. Reinalda, Aldershot: Ashgate, 11–41.
21 Lindblom, A. 2001. 'Non-governmental organizations and non-state actors in international law', in *Non-State Actors in International Relations*, edited by B. Arts, M. Noortmann and B. Reinalda, Aldershot: Ashgate, 147–160.
22 Keck and Sikkink, 1998.
23 Strange, S. 1996. *The Retreat of the State: The Diffusion of Power in the World Economy*. Cambridge: Cambridge University Press.

24 Arnove, R. 1982. 'Introduction' in *Philanthropy and Cultural Imperialism*, edited by R. Arnove, Bloomington, IN: Indiana University Press, 1–23; Parmar, I. 2012. *Foundations of the American Century*, New York, NY: Columbia University Press.

25 Rittberger, V., Nettesheim, M., Huckel, C. and Göbel, T. 2008. 'Introduction: changing patterns of authority', in *Authority in the Global Political Economy*, edited by V. Rittberger and M. Nettesheim, Basingstoke: Palgrave Macmillan, 1–9; Smythe, E. 2004. 'State authority and investment security: non-state actors and the negotiation of the Multilateral Agreement on Investment at the OECD', in *Non-State Authority in the Global System*, edited by R. Higgot, G. Underhill and A. Bieler, Abingdon: Routledge, 74–91.

26 See Risse, 2013.

27 Börzel, T. A. 2011. 'Networks: reified metaphor or governance panacea?', *Public Administration* 89(1): 49–63.

28 Zadek, S. 2007. *The Civil Corporation: The New Economy of Corporate Citizenship, 2nd Edition*. London: Earth Scan.

29 Brühl, T. and Hofferberth, M. 2013. 'Global companies as social actors. constructing private business in global governance', in *The Handbook of Global Companies*, edited by J. Mikler, Chichester: Wiley-Blackwell Publishers, 351–370.

30 Sell, S. 2004. 'Structures, agents and institutions: private corporate power and the globalization of intellectual property rights', in *Non-State Authority in the Global System*, edited by R. Higgot, G. Underhill and A. Bieler, Abingdon: Routledge, 91–107.

31 Sikkink, K. 1991. *Ideas and Institutions: Developmentalism in Argentina and Brazil*. Ithaca, NY: Cornell University Press.

32 Flohr, A., Rieth, L., Schwindenhammer, S. and Wolf, K. D. 2010. *The Role of Business in Global Governance: Corporations As Norm-Entrepreneurs*. Basingstoke: Palgrave Macmillan.

33 Sell, 2004.

34 Peters, et al. 2009.

35 Levy, D. and Egan, D. 2004. 'Corporate political action in the global polity', in *Non-State Authority in the Global System*, edited by R. Higgot, G. Underhill and A. Bieler, Abingdon: Routledge, 139–154.

36 Brühl, T. and Rittberger, V. 2001. 'From international to global governance: actors, collective decision-making, and the United Nations in the world of the twenty-first century' in *Global Governance and the United Nations System*, edited by V. Rittberger, Tokyo: United Nations University Press, 1–47.

37 Anheier, H. K. and Toepler, S. 1999. *Private Funds, Public Purpose: Philanthropic Foundations in International Perspective*. Berlin: Springer.

38 Interview with Bill and Melinda Gates Foundation Senior Programme Officer.

39 Wilhelm, I. 2004. 'A view inside the Gates', *Chronicle of Philanthropy* 11 November.

40 Interview with Bill and Melinda Gates Foundation Senior Programme Officer.

41 Eisenberg, P. 2000. 'New giving reflects old priorities', *Chronicle of Philanthropy*, 9 March.

42 Wilhelm, 2004.

43 Interview with former Bill and Melinda Gates Foundation Senior Advisor.

44 Gates Foundation. 2013. *Annual Report 2013*. Seattle, WA: Bill and Melinda Gates Foundation.

45 Interview with Bill and Melinda Gates Foundation Senior Advisor.

46 Interview with Bill and Melinda Gates Foundation Senior Programme Officer.

47 Wilhelm, 2004.

48 Ibid.

49 Interview with Bill and Melinda Gates Foundation Programme Officer.

50 Interview with Bill and Melinda Gates Foundation Senior Advisor.

51 Saez, C. 2017. 'Is Gates Foundation, WHO's biggest private funder, ineligible to join WHO?', *Intellectual Property Watch*, 29 January. Available at: www.ip-watch.org/2017/01/29/gates-foundation-whos-biggest-private-funder-ineligible-join.

52 WHO. 2017b. *Engagement with Non-State Actors, Non-State Actors in Official Relations with WHO*. EB140/42. Geneva: World Health Organization.

53 Reinalda, 2001.

54 Moran, M. and Stone, D. 2016. 'The new philanthropy: private power in international development policy?' in *The Palgrave Handbook of International Development*, edited by J. Grugel and D. Hammett, Basingstoke: Palgrave Macmillan, 297–315.

55 Global Citizen. 2017. Available at: www.globalcitizen.org/en.

56 See Parmar, 2012.

57 Gates Foundation. 2017. 'Awarded grants', available at: www.gatesfoundation.org/How-We-Work/Quick-Links/Grants-Database.

58 Storeng, K. 2014. 'The GAVI Alliance and the "Gates Approach" to health systems strengthening', *Global Public Health* 9(8): 865–879.

59 *IP Watch*. 2015. 'Outside sources: unease over seconded philanthropic foundation staff to top management at WHO', *Intellectual Property Watch* 15 December. Available at: www.ip-watch.org/2015/12/15/unease-over-seconded-philanthropic-foundation-staff-to-top-management-at-who.

60 For reflections on the new global diplomacy see Cutler, C., Haufler, V. and Porter, T. (eds) 1999. *Private Authority and International Affairs*. Albany, NY: State University of New York Press.

61 Buddabin, A. (forthcoming). 'Documentarian, witness, and organizer: exploring celebrity roles in human rights media advocacy', in *The Social Practice of Human Rights*, edited by Joel R. Pruce. New York, NY: Palgrave Macmillan.

62 Strouse, J. 2000. 'Bill Gates's money', *The New York Times* 16 April.

63 Sirtori-Cortina, D. 2017. 'Bill Gates, opponent of plan to cut foreign aid, meets with President Trump at The White House', *Forbes* 20 March. Available at: www.forbes.com/sites/danielasirtori/2017/03/20/bill-gates-opponent-of-plan-to-cut-foreign-aid-meets-with-president-trump-at-the-white-house/#f6811353f88f.

64 Beckett, A. 2010. 'Inside the Bill and Melinda Gates Foundation', the *Guardian* 12 July. Available at: www.theguardian.com/world/2010/jul/12/bill-and-melinda-gates-foundation.

65 Greenwood, R. and Suddaby, R. 2006. 'Institutional entrepreneurship in mature fields: the big five accountancy firms', *Academy of Management Journal* 49(1): 27–48.

66 Billis, D. 2010. 'Towards a theory of hybrid organizations', in *Hybrid Organizations and the Third Sector*, edited by D. Billis, Basingstoke: Palgrave Macmillan, 46–69.

67 Doherty, et al. 2014; see Jay, J. 2013. 'Navigating paradox as a mechanism of change and innovation in hybrid organizations', *Academy of Management Journal* 56(1): 137–159.

68 Gioia, D. A., Schultz, M. and Corley, K. G. 2000. 'Organizational identity, image, and adaptive instability', *Academy of Management Review* 25(1): 63–81.

69 Czarniawska, B. 1997. *Narrating the Organisation*. Chicago, IL: The University of Chicago Press.

70 Albert, S. and Whetten, D. A. 1985. 'Organizational identity', in *Research on Organizational Behavior*, edited by B. M. Staw and L. L. Cummings, Greenwich, CT: JAI Press, 7, 263–295.

71 Benford, R. D. and Snow, D. A. 2000. 'Framing processes and social movements: an overview and assessment', *Annual Review of Sociology* 26: 611–639.

72 Pache and Santos, 2012.

73 Doherty, et al. 2014.

74 Glynn, M. A. 2008. 'Beyond constraint: how institutions enable identities', in *The SAGE Handbook of Organizational Institutionalism*, edited by R. Greenwood, C. Oliver, K. Sahlin and R. Suddaby. London: Sage Publications Ltd, 413–431.

75 Battilana, J., Besharov, M. and Mitzinneck, B. 2017. 'On hybrid and hybrid organizing: a review and roadmap for future research', in *The SAGE Handbook of Organizational*

Institutionalism, edited by R. Greenwood, C. Olliver, T. B. Lawrence and R. Meyer, London: Sage Publications Ltd, 128–163.

76 Fejerskov, A. M., Lundsgaarde, E. and Cold-Ravnkilde, S. (2017) 'Recasting the "new actors in development" research agenda', *European Journal of Development Research* 29(5): 1070–1085.

77 Guo, J. 2010. 'In interview, Gates describes philanthropic journey', *The Tech* 23 April.

78 See Battilana, et al. 2017.

9 Conclusion
The Gates Foundation's rise to power

Out of the immense wealth creation and accumulation that has characterized the last decades, a novel group of predominantly American philanthropists and private foundations has emerged. Holding Silicon Valley as their ideological epicentre, these individuals have been characterized as hyper actors with immense expectations about their ability to change the world, driving what they see as a social revolution through technological innovation. Against an unquestionable backdrop of neoliberalism, the new foundations advance a hybrid set of logics that blend scientific progress with a belief in businesses and the market as intrinsically efficient, refocusing efforts towards corporate and private influence on, and delivery of, societal progress. Inspired by methodological individualism, they predominantly consider the social world a system of linear causality where levers and handles can be pulled to change different parts and achieve an anticipated outcome. In this realm of thought, quantification and systematic decision-making, perceived often as apolitical or value-neutral, forms the basis for purposive action, with scientific rationality in designing and executing interventions becoming a practice of domination.[1] As several Gates Foundation employees have longingly told me on different occasions: 'If only we had a model for that'.

The global political influence of private foundations has been significant, if fluctuating, since the beginning of the 20th century. Over the last decade, however, their activities in and financial support to global development have increased greatly, strengthening their apparent impact and political influence in all parts of the world. In this new époque since the turn of the millennium, private foundations have been hailed as saviours of global development by some, seemingly representing an alternative to bureaucratically heavy and ineffective state agencies,[2] driven as they are by fierce self-confidence and ambition on a bed of innovation, effectiveness and an orientation towards measurable results. Others again have called for caution and especially advised against the approaches of foundations led by this new generation of 'philanthrocapitalists', who apply logics and practices from the world of business in their attempts to fundamentally alter the practices and trajectories of development.[3] The re-emergence of foundations on to the scene of global development has been as evident in discursive changes as it has been traceable in practice, with the increasing attention given to them likely stemming as much from a fatigue of traditional donor agencies and state-led intervention in the developing world, the effectiveness of which remains an object of everlasting discussion, as it may be a result of their actual potential for contributing to global development.

Steering this train of thought and action is the Bill and Melinda Gates Foundation. An immense political and economic force, currently at full throttle towards shaping the trajectories of international policy-making, far beyond global development and health. More so than the foundation following a tendency of growing influence for foundations broadly, it has literally come to embody that trend, appearing vastly more powerful and greater in size than any other foundation in modern history. Some perceive the foundation as a coherent and unified, almost unbending, object, whose inherent values and beliefs have followed in a straightforward trajectory from its organizational genesis in the early 2000s up until today. Opposing this view, this book has shown how the foundation has gone through significant phases of organizational change over its short span of life. Beneath cursory readings of the foundation's discourses and actions we are able to identify fairly complex processes of organizational change inside it that have continuously challenged the dominant values and modes of operation of the foundation to this day. Gradually shifting attention towards issues of global development has entailed growing interaction with established organizations, ideas and norms, resulting in exposure to, and accordingly mounting expectations of relating to and perhaps even aligning with, these. The foundation appears to have progressed from a state of deliberate isolation in which it fully understood its position vis-à-vis other actors in the field, yet was unwilling to assume an equal role as a development organization, to a state of actively interacting with and increasingly aiming to shape norms and principles of the field, while still practicing a self-conception of difference from well-established donor organizations.

While the foundation is fundamentally built on a logic blending an almost blind faith in the strength of private or corporate thought and action with that of societal progress through technological innovation, other strong ideas have increasingly entered into the foundation and challenged organizational fundamentals. Since the beginning of a process of gradually entering into the field of global development, the political nature of efforts here has challenged perceived apolitical notions of a technological and market-based logic. This is not least illustrated by the rise of gender equality and women's empowerment as a key priority for the foundation, the story behind which I have told here. Melinda Gates has noted in the changing mind-set of Bill Gates about this priority that 'He admits that he thought women's issues, including contraceptives, were "soft" issues. Now, it's, like, a priority for him. It's a huge priority. Because he sees the data'.[4] Of course, Gates had to see the data to understand the dire necessity of addressing this social and political issue. It might not be a huge priority today, but it certainly has grown to form a substantial one. And probably not only because of the data, but also because of the foundation becoming exposed to the complexity of causality in trying to solve social issues, gradually acknowledging that isolated interventions rarely change the big picture. The significant exposure to different strong ideas in the field of global development, and the resulting change in foundation practice and discourse, makes us appreciate how no organization is an island. No organization operates in a vacuum devoid of interrelationships with other actors or isolated from expectations, norms and ideas emanating from dominant discourses and practices of the fields within which it is situated. As an organization increasingly engages in work or relationships with organizations embodying a specific field, it gradually becomes part of this field, willingly or unwillingly. The processes of change that arise from doing so may have significant organizational consequences. Only by diving beneath the surface of formal organizational discourse and action can we gain insight into these stories of (dis)continuous organizational change, diverging interests and influences, and struggles over the legitimacy of the ideas and practices that shape an organization's evolving relations to the field of which it increasingly forms a part, and thus the organization itself.

From conscious isolation to deep engagement in core issues of global development then, the foundation has been on an organizational journey characterized by an immense haste. Over the course of 15 years it has developed from a lean family foundation concerned mainly with global vaccines and national education in the US to a beasty bureaucracy that aggressively invests its resources in almost all corners of global development. 'Why don't you just give up your options and join the Peace Corps?' Bill Gates shouted to his Java team in 1997, offering them an insult that they might as well work for a non-profit with their apparently weak protection of the operating system Windows and of the Microsoft brand. It is unlikely that Gates would extend such an insult today, given the challenges his foundation has faced over time from the complexities of non-profit work as it has multiplied in size and engagement. Complementing the striking processes of change in the foundation's reach and breadth of activities has also been an organizational realization of its not just private but essentially hybrid form. For that reason, the foundation today employs a multi-faceted approach to attaining impact that combines deep-pocket funding of a concentrated set of issues with advocacy through political and diplomatic engagement, and extensive media use, shaping global public policy as much through its increasing ideational and normative power as through its material resources. The extensive repertoire of tools of political influence available to the foundation essentially originates from this hybrid nature that sees it able to sometimes appear as an NGO, sometimes as a multinational corporation, and sometimes even as a state actor. It can invest its $40 billion endowment commercially, sway the priorities of global health and development by providing charitable grants with a combined value of several billion dollars annually, or use its Gates brand to meet and influence heads of state or shape political negotiations in international organizations. In 1982, Robert Arnove wrote that the watchwords of foundations up until that point in time had been 'Efficiency, control, planning'.[5] Today, these words are strongly mirrored in the Gates Foundation's quest to influence and exercise control over its core areas of focus in global development and health, facilitated by its hybrid organizational form that lets it employ a vast repertoire of instruments of control and influence.

Organizational change and new actors in international political life

Complementing its focus on the Gates Foundation's rise to power, this book has attempted to broaden the scope to understand, theoretically, some of the processes organizations go through as they enter into new fields. Attention has particularly been given to the consequences of increasingly being exposed to new ideas and norms. Chapter 2 built an analytics of key processes of institutionalization, theorizing three main processes occurring as ideas and practices moved across and enter into new organizations: 1) emergence, concerning how ideas potentially find their way to organizations as much through field-level fashions as from actors interacting with the organization or already positioned inside it; 2) internal negotiation and consensus production, denoting how organizations are inherently political arenas in which struggles over power, information and resources are key to determining how ideas are localized into organizational practices and policies; and 3) extroversive appropriation and negotiation, underlining the processes of negotiation with the organization's environments, including partners and peer organizations, that take place as the idea is gradually translated and institutionalized. These three processes collectively accentuate how adoption and institutionalization of new ideas and practices requires constant negotiation within and balancing between internal and external processes. Running through both the theoretical approach and the empirical analysis of the book, then, is a line of thought arguing that the spread of ideas between, and institutionalization within, organizations in international life is not a mechanistic process of transferring or diffusion. As ideas move between different contexts they are reconfigured and renegotiated as their content is transformed, interpreted and localized.

From these insights on the entrance (and, over time, institutionalization) of new sets of ideas or norms into organizations, we moved on to the argument that different idea-sets or institutional logics are not always compatible and easily brought together in a hybrid form. Rather, in instances where radically different (as in holding fundamental contradictions) logics or ideas are to be blended, whether in policies, strategies or projects, a hierarchy emerges in which core characteristics of one or the other, or however many are involved, are lost. Concretely, we saw how logics of gender equality and impact effectiveness, because of their inherent and fundamental differences in perception of change, are not naturally compatible. Accordingly, the blending of these two logics will always result in a hierarchy in which one takes the upper hand, while the other loses core characteristics. In the Gates Foundation we come to understand how work on gender equality and women's empowerment cannot simultaneously be structural and functional, political and technical, context-sensitive and scalable, but that key choices are made as these logics meet, with one likely always dominating the other. This underlines the relative strength, both of new ideas and logics entering into the organization as it increasingly becomes part of the field of global development, but also of those inherent logics that the organization may have adopted from organizational genesis that have a path-dependent effect on the intake of new ideas.

By focusing on the everyday practices of bureaucratic life in the Gates Foundation, we have seen how these processes of translation and institutionalization are about sense-making, consensus production, and negotiation over frames or systems of interpretation. What happens as ideas find their way into development organizations and are institutionalized are not grand narratives or scripted translations, but rather messy processes of agency, coincidence and unintended consequences. This emphasizes the importance of not conceiving organizations broadly, but also more specifically private foundations or even the Gates Foundation, as coherent systems of thought but rather as political arenas in which the institutionalization of ideas and practices is shaped by struggles over interpretation, power, and material as well as immaterial resources, all facilitating or resisting institutional change. In Chapter 7 I extended these notions beyond the immediate context of the foundation's headquarters by studying the entire chain of struggles over the production of meaning and functions of development work, focusing on a specific project as it is transformed from the Gates Foundation's headquarters in Seattle to the local offices of the INGO Landesa in the Indian state of Odisha. We witnessed here how the same project is reconfigured between the different organizational layers that encompasses its design and implementation. In the Gates Foundation the project is widely presented and understood as an instrumentalizing of women to increase agricultural productive capacity and outcome of not just the particular Indian region but of India in general, producing a policy recipe that can be scaled up across contexts. In the implementing NGO's headquarters and in its country office in New Delhi, India, it appears as a legal–functional project with the purpose of securing gendered equality of access to land titling. Lastly, on the ground in Odisha, it is implemented through a transformation-driven approach to empower women and appears more as a political endeavour to challenge and eventually attempt to change the socio-economic culture and its inherent (mis)understanding of women. We come to understand how actors at different organizational levels have diverse opportunities and instruments at hand to break open and shape the question of how the project is pursued. Beyond incoherence or weakness of project design and execution, such reinterpretations are attempts to resist and localize ideas and practices, entailing changes that have not just ideational but very tangible material consequences on the ground. The influence of different organizational levels should not be understood as a hierarchy that sees an overload of power concentrated at the 'top', but rather that actors at different levels employ profoundly different instruments to influence the project, some more compulsory or institutional, and some more ideational, and that those available at the 'lower' levels may be just as influential as those higher in the system. Translation processes may stabilize certain meanings across actors and organizational layers in development projects,[6] but behind such surfaces of stability we find substantial degrees of contestation and resistance at play.

The interdisciplinary nature of how contemporary global development is studied, and especially the issue of new actors entering into this particular field, means those of us engaged in it are required to continuously look for novel inspiration as we attempt to strengthen its analytical capacity and extend its theoretical foundations. This entails a need to uphold theoretical pluralism (breaking down paradigmatic boundaries), combining various fundamental logics that govern the production of new knowledge, and blending theoretical constructs from different literatures to create new perspectives on the empirical phenomena of development cooperation we try to explain. The challenges that confront contemporary studies of development cooperation require an ever-growing conceptual toolbox. In this book I have brought one such element to the table by showing how organizational and institutionalist perspectives shed important light on such research avenues. Indisputably, institutional theory has had many more fundamental problems in explaining change than stability over its lifetime, while for decades it has followed methodological paradigms far from the grounded reality of studies of development. Over time, however, these theoretical directions have come to take a much more dynamic, empirically focused and methodologically diverse approach to understanding institutional and organizational change, providing a set of helpful conceptual and theoretical middle-ground frameworks or vocabularies for analytically exploring some of the core concerns preoccupying contemporary studies of global development. By coupling organizational institutionalist perspectives with the empirical rigour of the study of global development we are left with a great opportunity to produce new knowledge, striking a healthy balance between the empiricist purpose of exploring phenomena and that of building theory and more generalizable forms of knowledge from these.

As we have seen, much work on private foundations has drawn on a Gramscian tradition, providing critical accounts of foundation thought and practice by studying these as agents of capitalism, elite projects serving the interests of the founder, and by centring attention on their perceived spread of US intellectual hegemony and intentions to normatively promote core logics of the market. Such critical notions have not been cast aside in the book, but it has been the aim to argue for the importance of also studying private foundations in their own right, as organizations, to fully understand the effects these have on international life and on global development, and vice versa. Rarely are organizations driven by a complete unification of thought in which no contestation over discourses and practices take place deep inside the organizational machinery. That certainly applies to private foundations as well and is not least an important argument to make in the case of the Gates Foundation. Sweeping assertions are often made that the foundation furthers an aggressive form of neoliberal hegemony. There is truth to this claim, surely, but it also accentuates a dire need to look below the surface of mythical monstrosity. Reiterating a point from the introduction, the face of the Gates Foundation is known to most people, but we do not know much about what lies beneath its exterior. This, combined with difficulties of access to the foundation's inner halls (of course an issue attributable to the foundation itself), and its questionable accountability often leads to oversimplification of the ambitions and consequences of its mission and work, and a black boxing of the foundation. The foundation certainly exhibits more than a handful of very questionable characteristics and dispositions, but we should not assume it is a monster in which there is a complete unification of thought and action. Below the surface of what appears as immense cohesive ambition, we find individuals and groups of people coming together from different backgrounds and with different missions and purposes, who contest over ideas, meanings or material resources, engaging in intra-organizational processes that we need to understand to not take as a given that the foundation is a streamlined machine. Accordingly, it is imperative we lift the lid and try to recognize some of these, as only then can we come to understand this almost mythical beast and launch a profound critique. This is not a defence of the Gates Foundation; it is a defence of the proper study of organizations.

Ultimately, the book demonstrates how organizational life is amenable to qualitative analysis, with its micro-sociological approach reasonably allowing us to consider perspectives in, and of, action in organizations. Far too often the complexities, dynamics and contestation taking place among multiple constituencies inside organizations are neglected, and streamlined end results (as outcomes of such processes) in the shape of policies or other public material are taken as proxies of a unification of thought and beliefs, constructing stereotypes and oversimplifications. Despite its limitations, the approach followed here permits us to explore and examine nonlinear processes of change as ideas are translated and reinterpreted among multiple constituencies. Studying the interaction between organizations as systems of meaning and the 'world' outside of these, whether we conceptualize it as a field or something else (environment, network), then, is a central task in the organizational sociology of global development. That is, looking closely at where the work, beliefs and emotions of individuals meet structural constraints and opportunities, whether in the form of resources, formal structures, or of broader institutional relations. And, above all else, what a qualitative study of organizations is most adept at explaining are the dynamics of organizational change. It allows us to pursue questions such as what exactly constitutes change, how such change is driven from inside the organization or from its environment, and if we can see these processes materialize as long rhythmic waves of incremental change or as rapid and dramatic shifts. Without in-depth qualitative work, the complexities of organizational change and stability are difficult, if not impossible, to understand.

The power of plutocracy in global development

For many, the proclaimed potential of the early 21st century to become a second golden age of private foundations, mimicking the unprecedented global growth and policy influence of these a hundred years back, is a nightmarish vision for the prospects of democracy and progressive social change. As quasi-aristocratic institutions, foundations flourish in a climate of growing inequality that sees wealth concentrated in the hands of the few, appearing as the fruit of capitalist economic activity and accumulation. They may formally be established to pursue philanthropic and altruistic objectives for the benefit of the public, yet they are often organized in a manner that sees the public with little if any influence on, or insight into, their operations. We are continuously reminded that foundations may easily function as vehicles for those they serve, their organizational form and purposes so open for interpretation that their outcomes cannot be expected to fall in certain directions or have anticipatable productive effects. At worst, foundations are but tax shelters that serve a purpose of retaining fortunes within the figurative walls of the family, without providing much benefit to the public. Or they aggressively further conservative agendas opposing social change and development, something the history of foundations is replete with.[7] At their best, however, they can also drive progressive agendas by aiding the marginalized groups of society, demonstrated by the lighter side of their history, as they played a critical role in supporting the civil rights movement in the 1960s and opposing the apartheid regime in South Africa in the 1980s. As for their impact on 21st-century global development, the verdict is still out.

This book sets out to explain what I described in the introduction as the meeting in contemporary global development between simultaneous forces of increasing heterogeneity and homogenization. Embodied in the first is the entrance of novel actor types, from middle-income countries once recipients of aid now turned donors, to different private and non-state actors. The second denotes increasing attempts to construct normative frameworks for what is considered 'good development', both in the form of prioritized issues and in the more technical governing of modes of operation, from the Paris Declaration on Aid Effectiveness to the Sustainable Development Goals. The ambition thus became to explore what happens as a new actor increasingly enters into the field of global development and is faced with dominant normative frameworks, ideas and practices. The findings principally speak to the continuously growing literature on (re)emerging and new actors entering into global development. As we have seen, work in this vein has predominantly focused on the consequences for the field of development, centring on the perceived challenge new actors present to the legitimacy of established ideas, practices and actors.[8] I argue that this is only one side of a binary story that sees change to be as likely to happen in the entering organization itself as in the field. Rather than addressing field-level changes in global development, the book has explored the ideational and material–organizational changes that the Gates Foundation has been through over the course of almost two decades, as it has increasingly interacted with and entered into global development. I would definitely refrain from considering it a process of full-out socialization, as the foundation continues to practice a self-conception of difference from well-established donor organizations, and shows certain signs of difference in its continued operations, practices and values. But changes in the foundation bringing it closer to established organizations in the field of global development are certainly traceable over a period in time. The transformation evokes a strong sense of historicity and underlines how socialization to a field's norms is a dynamic process that takes place incrementally and is shaped by many different factors, from staff migration to pressure from peer organizations. Change resulting from the entrance of new actors, I argue, is multidirectional in its form, potentially entailing changes to the entering actors as much as field-level changes stemming from the new actor itself. This process of clearly becoming part of global development through increasing interaction with (and at some stage perhaps even adherence to) its collective norm and principle setting, I argue, is presumably not unique to the Gates Foundation.

As for engagement with the normative frameworks of global development, most private foundations never became major supporters of the UN's Millennium Development Goals, which they perceived as strictly a government agenda, alignment with which would only constrain their work. On the other hand, some of the major foundations did eventually accept the MDGs as an important agenda, and some, like the Gates Foundation, went further in completely embracing their ambitions, mainly with a view to their measurable, technical and fairly narrow or reduced understandings of development processes. Similarly, initial attitudes to the post-2015 process varied between outright opposition and gradual support. For some foundations, indifference changed into a more positive tone, while for others such as the Gates Foundation, the proposed SDG agenda, right from the time the Open Working Group suggested the initial 17 goals and 169 targets, was far too political and comprehensive. Just as not all public donors share all priorities in the SDGs, of course there will also be priorities that foundations do not share. One of these is governance issues, with fewer than three per cent of US foundations' donations seemingly being given to support elections, access to information, democracy or municipal reform.[9] Similarly, foundations still do not invest in fragile and conflict-ridden contexts[10] but are mainly involved in more stable contexts where the outlook for results is better. As poverty is gradually concentrated in these contexts, they will have to overcome this neglect in the coming years, and especially so if they would like to maintain their self-proclaimed risk-willing reputation. But this can never become an excuse for foundations not to engage in the financing regime for the SDG agenda, and there is a dire need to build up a feeling of ownership of these global agreements in the philanthropic environment. Regardless of their questionable attitudes to the UN conferences on both the SDGs and the Financing for Development tracks, foundations will have an important role to play in financing development over the next decades, and there are certainly valuable efforts that will not be made if foundations do not wish to pursue the SDG agenda or engage in collaborative endeavours. Just as public aid agencies cannot replace the work of the foundations, the latter should never be tasked with taking on some of the 'heavier' challenges that are often the target of international public financing. Complementary forms of partnership have always been the most effective when these two substantially different groups of actors are brought together, and especially concrete partnerships built around specific issue areas in which the relative strengths of both parties can be utilized to the fullest. We do not have to look very far to see why foundations ought to move away from too isolated and fragmented efforts in development; such work simply risks doing more harm than good and crucially undermines the core principles of today's private foundations, namely impact and effectiveness.

Still, it is an open secret that many foundations in global development value autonomy and independence of action above coordination and collaborative efforts. Regrettably, such attitudes reduce the impact and effectiveness of their programmes and projects. The aim of genuinely including private foundations in global efforts for development such as the SDGs is not to streamline them to adopt the approaches, cultures and practices of public aid agencies, but simply to increase the poverty-reducing effect of philanthropic grant-making. Private foundations need to acknowledge the importance of thorough coordination, even if this means limits to their autonomy and independence of action, just as public donors have to acknowledge the special modes of operation and logics of private foundations when they seek to include them. The Bill and Melinda Gates Foundation for one seems to be somewhat shifting from attitudes of isolationism or indifference towards a gradual willingness to interact and contribute. Though it naturally strengthens the influence of the foundation markedly, it is a constructive sign of engagement that replaces indifference with a deeper commitment. What form that commitment then takes on is for the rest of us to follow and critically observe. Questions of legitimacy must be expected when an organization crashes onto the scene as the Gates Foundation has, aggressively increasing its spending on global development over the course of only a few years. Private foundations are, by their very nature, different from official development agencies who at least in theory depend on democratic elections, scrutiny from elected parliamentarians, are forced to present and discuss strategies with the public, and have clearer lines of accountability. A board selected by the chairs of a foundation is not a strong line of accountability, and as Bill Gates himself has underlined about his own position: 'I'm not gonna get voted out of office'.[11] The legitimacy of foundations actively involved in global governance often *de facto* comes from their financial resources, whether we like it or not. Legitimacy here may not be what I or any other person considers legitimate, but rather a legitimacy affirmed by formal access to decision-making fora and processes. When the Gates Foundation is granted official relations to the WHO, it essentially becomes recognized by states as a legitimate governance actor,[12] also illustrative of shifts in the relationship between public and private authority. Ultimately, whilst it is of dire importance to question the ways of the Gates Foundation, it should not be with a different drive than that which we use to confront other new or existing donors, public or private, as they are engaged in global development. What is the legitimacy of Saudi Arabia to become involved in global development, we may ask? Does it represent values that are better aligned with those of the SDGs or other normative frameworks in global development than the Gates Foundation? Does it hold a legitimacy or accountability more democratic than the foundation? Probably not. Likewise, the foundation does likely not fare worse than many bilateral donors who claim to be investing in global development but spend the vast sums of their taxpayer-provided funds on issues pertaining to the domestic realm. Today, as an example, Denmark is the largest recipient of Danish ODA. It is hard to believe the hypocrisy can reach another level from here, and that even for one of the historical pioneers of global development. Traditional donor organizations may have administrators or ministers prone to losing their jobs in elections, and they may send new strategies to public consultations. But their policy- and decision-making often appears almost as clouded as that of the Gates Foundation. To say nothing of the world's largest multinational corporations who are now expected to carry forward global development, exercising equal influence to the largest foundations whilst being every bit as unaccountable and undemocratic.

As many are left worrying about the consequences for global development as private foundations, and the Gates Foundation in particular, grow in influence, it is appropriate to remember as well that foundations may in theory provide support for addressing shortfalls in development finance. Encouragingly, the Gates Foundation is increasingly emerging with a mind-set that sees foundations complement rather than supplant traditional sources and actors of development, not least reflected in the foundation being a firm advocate for maintaining a strong ODA regime. Moreover, we have to remember that not all foundations are like the Gates Foundation; extremely aggressive and visible, deploying so many tools of influence to simultaneously fund interventions, influence policy, and woo government leaders. Many smaller foundations work through established channels of development work, often multilateral ones, providing resources that may not otherwise have had an impact for the world's poorest.

Final remarks

The Gates Foundation sometimes seems to be making the fears of the early 20th-century foundation critics appear prescient.[13] Clearly utilizing the privileges of wealth, the foundation demonstrates well the almost inevitable relation between financial resources and political leverage. As elite views are privileged over popular participation, the costs for democracy seem self-evident. In this context of power and wealth resistance often seems futile, with any attempts at pushing back against the authority of private foundations like the Gates Foundation appearing almost as quixotic crusades. Not least as we may be witnessing a move from many small and varied grants to having larger-than-life foundations who concentrate all of their wealth and power on a few issues, becoming disproportionately influential. Foundations may be more agile, risk-willing and innovative than government, and they may very well serve niches that traditional donors miss. But there is no guarantee for such behaviour, nor that they can produce the fruitful impact often blindly assumed. By way of access to networks, knowledge, organizations or heads of state, the Gates Foundation today sustains and expands upon a system of institutional power that sees it able to influence any issue it sees fit. In 2016, 'The Bill and Melinda Institute for Population and Reproductive Health at the Johns Hopkins Bloomberg School of Public Health' launched The Challenge Initiative, a global urban reproductive health programme supported by the foundation. Never mind the grant, just consider the name of the grantee. Today, exponentially growing numbers of institutions are deeply embedded in foundation engagements and institutional arrangements, many even relying on such funding for their very existence. At the same time, others are blinded by their plutocratic shine. 'Bill and Melinda Gates are among the best things that have happened to Africa', *The New York Times* columnist and Gates Foundation darling Nicholas Kristof enthusiastically put it in 2008.[14] Despite the productive implications of their charity, this was certainly a pronounced exaggeration back then, just as it is today.

That is not to say the foundation does not contribute with substantial fruitful impacts in global development. When Gates speaks to the audiences where he traditionally has felt most at home, to computer scientists, software developers and ultra-rich billionaires, he certainly does something good. Already early on, 17 years ago, he confronted these audiences when, e.g., speaking to a Seattle conference on 'Creating Digital Dividends' and confronting the notion that what the poor need is access to better information technology:

> The mothers are going to walk up to that computer and say, my children are dying, what can you do? They're not going to sit there and like, browse Ebay or something. What they want is for their children to live. They don't want their children's growth to be stunted. Do you really have to put in computers to figure that out?[15]

Today, this point should serve as the answer to anyone who blindly advocates for the infinite need for new technology in the developing world, including Bill Gates himself. Before you bring in your technology and your innovations, take a deep breath, understand what you are trying to change and those who you are targeting and make no narrow-minded assumptions on what you believe they need.

It is the foundation's modus operandi, the core logics that govern its thoughts and ways of working, which might, and perhaps should, worry us. Social issues, particularly in the developing world, but equally in the well-off parts, are not easy or quick to fix, and there are significant limitations to what can be achieved through the celebrated ideologies of technology and innovation. The Gates Foundation takes extraordinary care to repeat messages of learning, gradual experience, and humility to the task. But these virtues are certainly not always reflected in its actual work. The motto of Facebook and its founder Mark Zuckerberg, hanging on the walls in the offices of the tech-giant, was for years 'Move fast and break things'. If not for its overtly aggressive connotations, such a motto might just as well have covered the glass-clad walls of the Gates Foundation's Seattle headquarters. The foundation sees as its prime guiding line of attack that of disruption, upsetting social systems and challenging the status quo to evoke radical change. And that within a view that sees such systems as fundamentally closed, allowing us to compose a plan of which levers to pull in order to produce certain foreseeable consequences. The problem often remains, however, that the social world is not a computer system that can easily be hacked. On the other hand, as we have seen throughout this book, there are signs that the foundation is moving towards a more holistic approach to reforms, not least acknowledging that social change is often incremental, complex, and that a long-term perspective is not always bad. These perceptions ought to be dead centre in all its endeavours, as principles of engagement. Much of this change has been prompted by hard lessons, simply by witnessing projects amounting to hundreds of millions of dollars, if not billions, failing to make substantial impact because of different sets of causal or contextual factors that were not properly understood or that could not be accounted for in project design.

At all times the Gates Foundation will walk a fine line between being seen as a benefit for, or a negative influence on, society. There is a reason why foundations are more or less exempt from tax, and thus will eventually distribute money that at some level belongs to all of us – they are expected to create real value for society. Real value in what form we might ask? Social change is not about reaching the pace or faith in technology of the 21st-century philanthrocapitalist euphoria, just as it is not about imagining an inherent effectiveness of business approaches to social and economic transformation. Serving society in its entirety means targeting the poorest communities, working to eliminate the vast discrepancies between those that have and those that do not. It means catalysing transformative social change by questioning dominant economic models, and the distribution of power and resources in our society, not shying away from its largest problems because of their inherently political nature. The issue here of course remains that foundations personify that very thing they should try to oppose, being, as they are, the ultimate testimony to the inequalities of contemporary society. By their very nature, then, we can never look at foundations without seeing charity and social justice in tension with each other, leading us to question whether foundations may have any ability whatsoever, or interest for that matter, in bringing change to a global economic system of which they themselves are a product. No matter the purposes or intentions of altruism, the fact that individuals may singlehandedly pour tens of billions of dollars into a foundation and still remain the richest man or woman on earth is disturbing. Perhaps that is exactly what foundations must work towards at home and across the world – eliminating the very reason for why they exist in the first place.

Notes

1 Paraphrasing Schroyer, T. 1973. *The Critique of Domination*. New York, NY: George Braziller.
2 Adelman, C. 2009. 'Global philanthropy and remittances: reinventing foreign aid', *The Brown Journal of World Affairs* 15(2): 23–33; Bishop, M. and Green, M. 2010. *Philanthrocapitalism: How Giving can Save the World*. London: A. & C. Black.
3 Desai, R. and Kharas, H. 2008. 'The California Consensus: can private aid end global poverty?', *Survival* 50(4): 155–168; Edwards, M. 2009. *Just Another Emperor? The Myths and Realities of Philanthrocapitalism*. London: The Young Foundation and Demos; McGoey, L. 2015. *No Such Thing as a Free Gift: The Gates Foundation and the Price of Philanthropy*. London and New York, NY: Verso.
4 *CBS News*. 2017. 'Melinda Gates on making a successful life', *CBS News*, 5 March, www.cbsnews.com/news/melinda-gates-on-making-a-successful-life.
5 Arnove, R. 1982. 'Introduction' in *Philanthropy and Cultural Imperialism*, edited by R. Arnove, Bloomington, IN: Indiana University Press, 1–23.
6 Mosse, D. 2004. 'Is good policy unimplementable? Reflections on the ethnography of aid policy and practice', *Development and Change* 35(4): 639–671.
7 Tompkins-Stange, M. 2017. *Policy Patrons*. Cambridge, MA: Harvard Education Press.
8 Richey, L. A. and Ponte, S. 2014. 'New actors and alliances in development', *Third World Quarterly* 35(1): 1–21; Gore, C. 2013. 'Introduction – the new development cooperation landscape: actors, approaches, architecture', *Journal of International*

Development 25(6): 769–786; Zimmermann, F. and Smith, K. 2011. 'More actors, more money, more ideas for development cooperation', *Journal of International Development* 23(5): 722–738.

9 OECD. 2014. *Development Cooperation Report 2014: Mobilising Resources for Sustainable Development*. Paris: OECD Publishing.

10 Ibid.

11 Moyers, B. 2003. 'Bill Moyers interviews Bill Gates', *PBS.org*, transcript available online at: www.pbs.org/now/printable/transcript_gates_print.html.

12 Williams, O. and Rushton, S. 2011. 'Private actors in global health governance' in *Partnerships and Foundations in Global Health Governance*, edited by S. Rushton and O. Williams, Basingstoke: Palgrave Macmillan, 123–143.

13 Katz, S. 2013. 'Curb mega-foundation', *Boston Review*, March/April.

14 Kristof, N. 2008. 'Bill Gates and Creative Capitalism', *The New York Times*, 27 June.

15 Verhovek, S. H. 2000. 'Bill Gates turns skeptical on digital solution's scope', *The New York Times* 3 November.

Index